D1648530

REFLECTIONS IN A SILVER EYE

This is all so peculiar. It's as though I'd just been born, full-grown and with all the proper instincts, but without the proper knowledge to correctly stimulate those instincts. Everything seems at first glance to be totally unfamiliar, yet at second glance it seems somehow reminiscent of something —of what, however, I'm reluctant to say. It appears coherent enough, yet the coherency is made up of the oddest parts, things together that have no business being together. For that, it's ludicrous. And, more, there are things I see that I should not be seeing among men, and things I think I should not be seeing at all. It's difficult to know where to begin to sort all this out.

STATUS QUOTIENT: THE CARRIER

RALPH A. SPERRY

AVON
PUBLISHERS OF BARD, CAMELOT, DISCUS AND FLARE BOOKS

STATUS QUOTIENT: THE CARRIER is an original publication of Avon Books. This work has never before appeared in book form.

AVON BOOKS
A division of
The Hearst Corporation
959 Eighth Avenue
New York, New York 10019

First Avon Printing, October, 1981

AVON TRADEMARK REG. U.S. PAT. OFF. AND IN OTHER COUNTRIES, MARCA REGISTRADA, HECHO EN U.S.A.

Printed in the U.S.A.

WFH 10 9 8 7 6 5 4 3 2 1

To John DeMatteis
and as always
for William Sternman

DAILY TEXTS

Winter, 9503

Having transferred down to the guesthouse as much as I can manage for now, I ought to catalogue my efforts and plan my days.

It's snowing heavily again today and, as pretty as that is, I have no desire to go out for other materials and get myself soaked. Not that it matters, I suppose. I did much of what I've accomplished so far in Fall's cold rain and I didn't get ill, though I stupidly expected I would. I imagine I hoped I would. It was always said a person gets ill from getting wet, and I did get uncomfortable, but that's all. I've never been ill, though I used to attribute that to being careful. I've always been apprehensive about contracting even the commonest particle infections. They always seemed so debilitating—the fever and chills that make the least effort so much extra labor, the general weariness Morin always complained about (and he got these infections more often than anyone; actors do, or so he professed), the difficulty breathing and swallowing, the headaches and nausea. It sounded to me like death itself.

But I can't be ill. The whole notion's irrelevant, which is the very reason I'd hoped to become ill, even just this once. Still, it's a nasty enough feeling to be encased in cold, sticky clothing. And, practically speaking, clothes get dirty faster when they're wet. I'd have to keep washing them, and too much washing would wear them out. Then what would I do, being perfectly healthy and stark naked?

I have to be practical. In the long run—the fact must be

faced—things will not last, so there's no purpose in hastening their ruin through carelessness. I've already broken a whole box of cooking glass because of my foolish fears and reckless haste. It's irreplaceable, not that I expect to be cooking conventionally forever. I have lower-grade substitutes that were here at the guesthouse, but they're metal—I must abandon the idea of rescuing my mother's quickoven—and they'll wear quickly. Quickly! In a hundred years they'll be nonexistent. Glass would have lasted longer. How odd to reckon things that way.

I suppose I'm lucky, having all this. I'd be lucky having a ten-tenth of it. In my mind, I suppose, I counted on it. The lodge and all I knew it contained—everything I was sure would still be here, despite all evidence to the contrary—these were the things that kept me going. Eighty days of escaping—and it really was not much more than that in time, I think—all premised on untouched abundance.

Well, it was untouched, though marauders were obviously here. The lodge is quite isolated. How did marauders know to come here? Was it by accident? The lodge is visible in any season from the mouth of the valley, but there's nothing in that vicinity that would have drawn them in the first place. The whole region is uncharted except for an enclave like this one here and there on the periphery. Why my father chose this site for his lodge was a wonder even to those who knew him well.

Perhaps marauders were drawn by the Broadcast tower across the valley, but it still stands. It's certain that it shouldn't. Perhaps they followed my father. Perhaps they found the location in the records at the Starship Complex.

Perhaps a lot of things. But they left no other evidence than the results of their shooting—a burned patch by the lodge's gardens. No flier stands in ruin. The lodge was left intact. In fact, the lodge was left as though I were expected: the power on, the lockers filled, the rooms in the kind of order my mother always kept them, even my father's study neatly arranged, for once—as though the place had just been opened for the season. At least for that I'm very lucky. What would I be if I had not found it so? What am I for having it all?

At first I thought everything had to be done at once. I mindlessly rushed through the lodge grabbing at this and that, spending hours and days piling things together and bringing them back here. I was so afraid to be seen, as though I were pillaging the middle of Athlan at Midday instead of doing what I assumed I had to do. But it was all so much stupidity. I wasn't calm enough to be doing it—or anything—right, in any case. I felt myself an intruder in my father's house—that more than usually. I felt myself a fugitive after getting here, the more fugitive for being here, when I should have felt the opposite. By that time, I reckon now, there was likely no one left to be fugitive from. I was running, I suppose now, from that burned spot by the gardens, something that had already happened, and is unlikely to happen again. Or so I assume. At least at present.

I didn't even have the common sense to use the roadways connecting the lodge with the guesthouse. No, I had to behave like a groundscurry, darting down the lodge's hill in the underbrush, skirting way around the clearing, scampering up this hill, making a dash for the cover of this house, all the while carrying boxes and bags of things and things, assortments of stuff I'm only now beginning to make some orderly sense of, three whole changes later. It must be the way of the One I didn't destroy more than I did, or maybe I did and just haven't discovered the destruction yet. I secured so much electronic equipment—I'm not entirely sure what, nor why I concentrated so much on that. I've only tried out a few of the pieces, the various carriers, and they operate, though to no apparent avail.

But once the rain started and continued—that awful, sickening rain—I couldn't be so rambunctious. I didn't want to go out in it, though I had to. I didn't want to be touched by it at all. But staying in this house made me so impatient I found myself pacing the winter lounge ceaselessly until I began to realize how ridiculous that was, how ridiculously I'd been acting.

Actually, it wasn't the pacing that made me reflect. It wasn't impatience. Ancil, be honest: You got cold. I'd forgotten to turn on the heat. That made me think how much worse things could be than they were. How much worse I might make them if I didn't start using some reason. What would I be without the things that I have here? What is a man without the evidence of his own sort? And what will I be when these things are finally gone?

9

But is there any danger still? I didn't know then, and I still don't. But judging by what I saw on the way here, in the unlikely event anyone is left, it's likely he won't survive Winter, for nothing was left standing, nothing at all. And no one who didn't have a gun or a blade or a flame or the physical power to overcome and drown someone else. I can imagine the final fury of the last few at finding no other victims than themselves. But I'd rather not.

Fortunate that my father was important enough to be able to have such a secluded, self-sustaining world up here. For the time being I have amenities: a solid house, electricity, water, food. There's time enough to learn how to maintain them for as long as things are maintainable. I've never had a mathematical mind, but a perusal of my father's books suggests that upkeep is possible without an absolutely intimate knowledge of technology. After all, didn't some workers do much this sort of thing, though they paid dearly for the ability? But how long does it take for things to wear out? Loren would certainly have known. Could I but have his set of mind. How long? How long must I wait? There's time enough. There's time enough.

My father's library surprised me. I would have expected my mother to want my books, but what would *he* do with them? The chronology and lectures, yes; they might interest him. We shared certain wild notions—though from opposite points of view, obviously. But the stories and songs? My impression was that he despised them: "Your writing is a pastime, not a profession. No, worse than a pastime because it's pointless—even a Second Son wouldn't bother! No one reads anything that doesn't teach. You lecture,"— which he made sound nearly as bad—"you should know this."

But what would he have wanted? He had my profile. It was done repeatedly—more, I think, than anyone else's. People who lectured nontechnical subjects—history in particular—endured such accountings, as though to make sure they weren't just being perverse or aberrant. The additional analyses, he requested. That I know, though I was never supposed to. And profile after profile recorded my inability to do anything else than what I was doing. My speech section was off-scale, which was undreamed of, though I must confess my private working knowledge of

10

Imitator was at fault in that. But what would he have wanted?

I asked if I should write for the Broadcasts. That was more respectable than being a lecturer, at least by some opinions. "You shouldn't write at all," he declared. "It's a disgrace." And, when I did write for Entertainment, he refused to see me for the remainder of Winter.

My nonteaching books were failures, which I expected. "They are the stories which are not to be written"—as it happens to have been written. Except the last one, which was widely read in Athlan. But I had no intention of writing an exemplary book. I'm no Allesis, much as I might want to write so powerfully. Yet with each failure my father denounced me the more, as though I were in fact succeeding. And always it was the same. Always he ended with the same statement that I'd heard from him from the first day words made sense to me, perhaps even before that: "I must deal every day with Darks, and I must deal with them amicably. I must have their respect. Whatever I believe in private, however much I disagree with their shortsightedness, you cannot, you shall not cause me public embarrassment by doing things nobody else would dream of, by producing things nobody has ever had any use for!"

To tell him some others had written was pointless. Not only would he deny it, but he'd go on to describe in detail every ugly repercussion such writers had suffered. His examples were all pre-Confederation, of course.

To ask him why a set of written characters even existed was to put him on the verge of a paroxysm: "To record information, not to make it up! To save the memory, not to bewilder it! Writing is a convenience. It's a tool. It's designed to save a person's energy. Like an Imitator, you'd use it to waste." On the whole, however, he was far kinder toward Imitators. It was difficult being the First Son of a man like that. Everything else in the world was permissible, but I.

He was so perturbed last year by *The Present Tense*, despite the fictitious names. I'd thought his dear friend, Heremis, was better disguised. Certainly the character came off better than I'd intended, though maybe it's just because characters do seem to take their lives into their own hands despite the will of the writer. Morin often remarked as much concerning acting, and I suppose my

11

sort of writing is a sort of acting. But I never knew another writer to ask him. I knew of only two other writers contemporaneous with me, neither in Athlan—one in Amaria on Great Ocean—both much more careful, appealing exclusively to unmarried women with domestic dreams and little hope of the reality. Dark writers.

The One! All writers I've ever heard of were Dark and, except for Allesis, wrote the sort of stuff that wasn't acceptable even for Afternoon Entertainment. How slow-witted I can be! It would do no good to go address the burned spot on the subject, though.

Nevertheless, my father seems to have read *The Present Tense* repeatedly. I can tell by his unfortunate habit of folding back page corners and ticking off lines in the margins. His other favorite was *Old Words in New Form*, also much marked and scarred, though how he ranted when that was first given out. "A slander! How dare you revise songs of the practices? What if somebody reads them?" Well, he needn't have worried; few did. Several of my songs became popular when set to music, though for the wrong reasons. But books that don't teach are failures. I've always been prepared to allow that. *The Present Tense* had its brief notoriety for all the wrong reasons. I was not prepared for that strange result.

When my songs appeared in performance, and I lamented their misuse, Morin, that useless Son, claimed it didn't matter: "Exposure is exposure, Ancil. You know how I think: I'll accept any kind of exposure." And he'd dismiss my argument that they were written songs, not meant as entertainment: "To compare: You're a First Son, and yet a second son. And you're an only child—which were *you* meant to be?" Dear Morin. As for *The Present Tense*, he claimed he knew for a fact it sold more copies than the 9502 revision of *The Handbook of Care for Natural Fabrics*—"itself a book of no slight depth. You may yet convince man to read, you know. And while reading may well be neither practical nor rewarding, once I'm dead, Entertainment will be worthless." He seems to have been right.

But I have all my books here, except two—three, really, including the manuscript that must have been destroyed in Athlan. I could always rewrite that one. But otherwise, I'm missing the juvenile book *Foolish Friends*, and that

12

stupid scenario that had been better not done in the first place.

I didn't like the scenario when I was writing it. Entertainment Broadcasts are by nature episodes of highly visual activity with just enough story to get the characters from one scene to the next plausibly. They're rather like the event summaries on Information, but with a plot. And I didn't like it when I watched it. I couldn't believe I'd produced something so banal. Morin said he liked it, but I wrote it at his insistence and for him: His was the chief role, and if there was any substance to the thing, he provided it. He'd have to have liked it. It was a good vehicle for him.

Theras liked it. But we'd been companions, if briefly and peculiarly, and he was Morin's best friend.

Loren liked it, but we'd been companions nearly two years and more deliberately. And after that ended—after the hiatus of several changes—he was suddenly amenable to everything about me, which, when we'd been together, had not been the case at all. I wonder why. I'll never know.

But Paras, his twin, liked it—I would hardly have thought this or any agreement between them was possible. And Salis, that little wretch, liked it, too. A pair of discreditable supporters.

Heller claimed to be very fond of it. I never knew Heller well enough to know if that was a valuable judgment. He always kept a distance from me that no one could explain. "He's secretly fond of you," Morin ventured, but that, at least, proved to be entirely wrong.

And Aren—Morin made great mention of it to him, so that I had to admit I'd written it. Aren said his family had watched and that his sister, Elenie, had liked it especially. But she would have. And for himself? "I'm not a Thinker," he said, "but it was all right." I took that to mean it had less than the expected quota of action to it, which was true in any event. But then he smiled and added what was his major principle in life: "If you spend a lot of time at something, you must be good at it or you wouldn't bother." An empty sentence, but it seemed a comfort then.

It snows so heavily that the skies must be bursting with moisture. I can't imagine why, since it rained almost all three changes of Fall, and such a dirty rain: water speckled with black that left a scum on every surface, bits of char, the ashes of the whole world. When I went out in it, even after a few tenths, I was sooty. As I made my furtive trips I couldn't help but think I was being deluged with my friends and all their possessions, incinerated every one. Snow is a relief.

So my books:

Old Words, Tales of the Forty-Five, One of Each, The Present Tense, and the little story *I Want.* Then my lectures: *The Fulfillment of Necessity,* which my father seems to have noted as the companion to *I Want,* though I can't imagine why he should have. And *When Families Unite, The Age Before Ath, The One,* of course. Those were the very first things I secured along with all the paper and writing materials. Fortunate that I thought to do so before the rain started to come steadily. And I never cried once.

I find I sleep too much, but there's little I can do just now. Things occur to me slowly, but, so far, in enough time to prevent serious problems. I estimate I have ample kernals and tubers to plant in Spring, and there's still enough food in the lockers at the lodge to avoid starvation until I can harvest. I can set their cold rooms to those various "optimum temperatures" for proper storage. My mother used just to freeze everything solid. Which, I wonder, is the better course?

But do I have to worry about spoilage and poisoning? I wish I knew more about this problem of mine. My father's library seemed to have only scant information on biology in general, at least at a glance. But I have found a brief reference in some notes in one of his desk drawers that suggests everything I want to know was in material in the Research Compound. How funny, that! I wonder how I would have written *The Present Tense* had I known more about that hapless building. But I'll have to make a more careful search of my father's library for more information on regeneration, and for other reasons.

I've arranged the kitchen here in a workable order, but there's so much stuff. Sometimes I wonder why I don't just live in the lodge. It's so much more spacious—it's so enormous, really. And, of course, it's so open. The guesthouse is much more to my liking and always has been, besides being relatively well hidden. It's of the sort of scale I'm used to, since I had the top floor of a third daughter's house in Athlan.

I never could abide large rooms or high ceilings, as Morin could. Anything less than the social floor of a First Son's house made him seem grotesquely large and overpowering. In my rooms he would sit as if tight-lipped and bound, as though the least of his gestures or the quietest of his declarations might reduce a partition to shambles or burst out a window. I, on the other hand, felt intimidated in his quarters. I would almost shout, for fear of not being noted across the space, and I had the sensation of being a pester in aimless flight alone above one of the vast Starship Project fields in The Land by Aren's. But, of course, now I don't know what to expect, if anything at all. I cannot help but fear everything, even opposites. So, scale aside, this house is preferable. It's not noticeable.

As it is, I've closed off the summer lounge here and the bedroom above it, not only because there's no heat in that end of the house, outside of a hearth on each floor, but also because I have no use for such space except for storage. I really need only a couple of rooms to use for myself. I suppose it's nice to have a bit more for variety, however. Mostly I live in the kitchen, the dining room, the downstairs bedroom, and the winter lounge, which is designated my library. The two bedrooms upstairs are my repositories for clothing, cleaning supplies, paper, odd furniture, draperies and bedclothes, assorted electronic equipment, uncategorizable odds and ends, and even firewood in case something happens to the house's solar plant. And in that case I would live exclusively in the winter lounge, since it's the only room in this section with a hearth. I don't want to leave anything useful undiscovered, even anything I might use only seldom. But there's so much still up at the lodge, and I've yet to fully take account of what I've already brought over here. I'm surrounded by boxes of things, under tables and behind chairs, and piles of things dumped in corners of every room so I can have the boxes free. I want to acquire everything, just in case, but I'm sure I don't have the space here for all of it. I don't know what to do.

I suppose I shouldn't leave the electricity on in the lodge itself. The heat alone would make it obvious to anyone that I'm around and about, since the snow on the roof would melt. But without electricity, how well protected would what's still in the lodge be over a long period of time? I wish I had more practical knowledge. But how futile to wish for Loren.

I recall, when I moved my things from my father's house, that Loren helped. It was a catastrophe he simply waded through—cursing, I'm sure, under his breath—his bright hair falling across his already blank eyes like loosened grass blinds. He had a knack for having his face become completely vacant whenever he found himself in a difficult situation. I could not bear his doing this. It made it impossible for me to gauge him on the moment, even though I knew from experience that he'd find his way through his straits by himself.

Of course, the worst withheld itself: My father was not at home the entire five hours that afternoon. The next-worst, however, is arguable. Either: I had failed, for the two or so changes since I'd met Loren, to inform him exactly who my father was. Or: I had failed to remember that in this particular section of Athlan resettling was an occurrence of equal frequency to the discovery of an active volcano.

For the first: I told Loren as we approached the house that I hoped he wouldn't feel embarrassed. My father, I admitted, is Thalis Mekthedden, Director of the Starship Project. I at once received a look of wrath. Loren was by then working on the Starship Project.

But, really, I had no other alternative. I had no intention of becoming his companion at that moment. I didn't want my background bruited about, particularly by second sons, when I was already having enough trouble—since the publication of *The One*. And I wouldn't have had him with me at all, but that he was so very solicitous about helping. I could have managed to hire a couple of workers, especially since I was resettling to an avenue near their section. I could have saved extra transit expenses and done it fairly cheaply. But he insisted.

Actually—I might as well admit it now—I saved that information for the very last moment on purpose. For whatever reason—I don't know now—I wanted to see how he'd react. I had no idea it would put him in shock.

Well, from that moment on, for a while, he was automatic. And he was marvelously efficient. It took me some time to decide what to take with me. It took him no time at all to load what I chose on the transport. It was for the most part books and sound ribbons, and the player and my broadcast carrier, things like that. My new quarters were furnished decently. The only item of furniture I took was a great leather reading chair and footrest I'd gotten as a boy, when it became apparent that few things might distract my eyes from a printed page. My father loathed that chair.

I had not, however, anticipated the crowd that would gather before my father's house. This was a section of well-established professionals and Owners who had had their facilities long enough to no longer be called "new," even by the most jealous. But there they were—many of them—gawking with their wives and as many children as were handy. And there was Loren halfway down the front walk, standing frozen, muttering quietly, "If I don't move, they won't notice me."

"But weren't they here before when you came out?"

"Before? No, they just appeared," he said flatly, after which his face went blank again.

I propelled him to the transport, and astonishingly he was able to navigate it through the crowd and off down the avenue, its blades whirring and the grass beneath us fanning out against the draft. He drove to my new quarters in his peculiar state just as well as he had driven to my father's house prior to his trauma. And he helped me unload and return the transport to City Services. We had a small meal and he spent the night. And only once, for a fifth or nearly, did he sit down and giggle uncontrollably, and he never once explained why.

But then, when I took things from my father's house to my new rooms, I was choosing chiefly nonessentials. Sound ribbons, my broadcast carrier, books that I kept with me for sentimental value and not because they were useful or, in some cases, even valid. For example, I always had Vessen's *Progression of the Imitators*, a book so incorrect that the School expression, "It must be in Vessen's," to deny a statement, had achieved a kind of tradition as School expressions go. But I chose these things to provide myself a sort of continuity between my past and my future.

Now, I find, I'm collecting the same assortment of things as then: sound ribbons, players, broadcast carriers, books—but, alas, no Vessen's and no great leather arm-chair. It's as though I'm gathering up what's left of the past to keep it from the future, the future it would surely have without me. A future these things will still have; I merely prolong it. And so little of it all is really worth protecting—didn't I just write that so many are nonessentials? Except that this is all there is of anything, so far as I know. That makes everything seem worth protecting.

But I even brought down all the clocks I could find, I suppose so I can tell how long I'll be watching after everything. That's all clocks are good for: to tell me how long things remain the same. If I were Dark, I'd say that's all they've ever been good for.

I find myself grateful to Darks for one thing—and how it would make their hair stand out in shock to know it. My father's paper supplies were of the kind made to last indefinitely, developed eagerly by a Dark Owner even though it was intended for use in the Starship. Their concept of enduring tradition must have been so overriding, not to mention that they were prone to compromise for currency. So, for as long as I have blank space to fill, I can write what I want and keep it. That's worse for a Dark to consider than even the Starship—I can be out-spoken forever, a Light with whom no one will ever argue. But isn't that the pettiest thought? At least I can write forever. No one will stop me or denigrate me. I wonder how long that is, ever and forever?

But I suppose I should be judicious about what I write so that I can maintain some blank space for filling. The paper supply is not infinite, though there's always the note page, front and back, in every book. I can write about what happened, though I should concentrate more on what is happening, even if I expect there won't be much of it. Just a line a day, over all the years I have yet to live, will be more communication than the total of every remark ever passed by anyone throughout all history. Communication!

It snows. I wonder if the weight of snow could pull down the wires connecting the house or the lodge with their solar plants. I can fix that, I think, but it'd be better that I didn't have to just yet. How long do wires last, and should I salvage things like that from the lodge? Now, if ever, do I truly need you, Loren.

18

It'll be a while before I go up to the lodge again. I must sort through what I have here first. Maybe winter weather will eradicate the burned spot, if not this Winter, then next. It'll grow up green. In how long? And why do I keep thinking of *him?*

For that matter, what was he doing here, of all places, at the last? I'd have thought my father would go directly to the Starship. That would be most logical. Perhaps it wasn't safe there either. And perhaps my father wasn't here at all. But if not he, then who?

I should go back to the lodge relatively soon, though. I have a good deal of time to do things properly, plenty of time, but things don't. There is that limit to my world, if not to me any longer. And that's another problem. Another problem? There are problems, and there always will be problems.

I'll sleep some now. I write this to tell myself so. Certainly not for any other reason. But I'll watch the snow for a while. It blocks out the valley and the surrounding mountains. I can't see past the garden.

I can scarcely see out the window.

Winter, Change 4: 6?, 9503

I've made the necessary trips to the lodge, or at least as many trips as I can determine are necessary for the moment. I really can't tell. I really can't plan.

I've tried to examine things in detail, foretell what I'll need, day to day, and then work backward defining prerequisites for those things. But there's such a welter of prerequisites—so much more to everything when a person is responsible for everything. And so many items apply to so many different things, while others have only a single application. I become confused. I have no sense of what things will be more important. Sometimes, it seems to me, I would be better to have started with nothing. But that would have been impossible: Having nothing, I would still remember everything, and I would have no means at all, and I would be most frustrated.

I must have an order. I must have some approach to things. I'm trying to.

I was so apprehensive about going back to the lodge. I'm sure I wasted two or three changes simply assuring myself there was no hurry. For me there is no hurry, of course. For my body, for my living itself, so long as I have food of some sort, which is the easiest thing to provide, there is no hurry. I'm a regenerative. But for my mind there is, there has to be. I can stagnate. I would have. I did for a while.

I didn't want to go back to the lodge, so I made the most obvious excuse for not doing so—myself. But that's foolishness. All these most honored clocks I've collected have shown me that: Events do go on. Activity and its necessities have not stopped simply because time no longer has any biological meaning to me.

And then, on the practical side, there was my reading lamp, which I knocked over and broke and could not repair or replace, except by going to the lodge to find another one. As it happened, there was one, my mother's, but only one. I am not without lamps, certainly, but none intense enough for reading. I am now using the last reading lamp on Ath, and it is fragile. Things are. I must keep reminding myself that there are no more facilities, there is no longer a Choice Program, life is not replaceable.

I've come across an "eternal calendar" set that was devised for use in the Starship. I should concentrate on it as an example, as a reminder that days do pass. How funny that it was intended as a timekeeping item, but that I would use it as a way of recognizing time lost. I've set it on the wall next to my desk, where I am most of the time when I'm in the house. Unfortunately, it will take a while for me to accurately determine what day it is. I think it's the sixth of the fourth of Winter. I know I'm not wrong by too many days. But I'll have to wait a while, until Midday in mid-Summer probably. Then there's supposed to be virtually no shadow. I'm fairly far north on the continent, but at least, the beginning of three-thirteen Summer will have the shortest shadow. I can measure when the time comes. But I can figure Midday now, so, if nothing else, I'll know when the day starts.

I have most things organized around and about me now. The piles and boxes have been sorted out. I have more than enough clothing to last me, at least for as long as their materials themselves endure. I also have my mother's sewing equipment arranged in the corner of the winter lounge—my library, my workroom, a place where things are thought about and planned and done. I absolutely ransacked my mother's rooms.

Nearly all her things seem to be the most useful, the least complicated, the most basic, the most practical. How much she did, how many things she was interested in! I never knew, or I suppose I did but didn't pay that much attention. She was always so quiet, so deferent to my father, as though he and not she had been of the higher family. She was so invisible. I never had any feelings for her one way or the other until now. It was always my father and his ways to accept or reject. My mother seemed to have nothing at all, except what he assigned her. She had no definition to me, except as he defined her. But she had a whole world of her own, as silent and as invisible as she, a world of making things, growing things, preserving things, doing and being what she wanted and was, within the confines of her rooms, up here at the edge of an unknown wilderness.

In Athlan it must have been quite different for her. I know I recall no such array of pastimes, nor space for any, in my father's house there. Those rows of houses, not set as blocks but like the rungs of ladders laid flat, were built more to look different than to have room, inside or out. And it seems now—though, to be honest, I paid scant attention, since I was at the School full years then—that she spent as much time up here as possible, most of Spring and Fall and virtually all Summer. That's eight or nine changes, fully half a year, at least. And I know they spent at least a change up here in Winter. A good deal of the early planning of the Starship took place up here. Perhaps, once I had my own rooms, she spent even more time up here. And, of course, that would explain why my father would have come here at the last.

I have all her things now, and it's they that strike me as having more immediate usefulness. And I have the source of all her interests and knowledge, or what can be assumed to be one of the sources—a wonderful book, a pre-Confederation one with a tattered binding and well-worn,

21

often-read pages: *The Practical Woman.* What a treasure it is, and in what an orderly way it approaches the world.

There's detailed information on carpentry, sewing, cleaning, growing and harvesting, paints and paint mixing, food preservation, conduct and courtesies, wild animals and plants, even making medicinals, which is irrelevant but fascinating. And perhaps it's not so irrelevant, as that section, I see, includes facts on poisons and poisonous plants and on antidotes. I know so little about regeneration, for suffering from it, that I must not assume anything I haven't already seen proof of or can't normally protect myself from.

I've also made a partial catalogue of the things still left in the lodge: tools and utensils for specific functions I presently am not concerned with; extra lamps and household equipment I have no need for now; carpeting and draperies and grass blinds which, except for the last, I consider convertible material rather than things I'm likely to use as such; some furniture, though not much of it—so much is too large to carry over or fit here, or too delicate or too frivolous, such as the garden chairs or anything from the lodge's summer lounge. I've never liked pierced-patterned screens, or bentwood furniture, or enamel-inlaid tables, or anything of a Great Ocean style. It's much too fussy. Theras adored it.

I have brought over all the light crystals and panels I could find, and that did afterward seem to present something of a problem. I wanted to shut off the electricity to the lodge itself, while maintaining power for the lockers, but since I'd already removed all the light crystals from the lockers and stored them here, I had no sure way of knowing at first whether I'd done the right thing. If only I could think to do things in a reasonable sequence!

Well, cold is cold, inside the cold rooms or out, at this season. But I traced the wires from the solar plant insofar as I was able, and it would seem I accomplished what I wanted. I checked the power with a vegetable refiner, the only gadget I could find readily to hand, and the blades spun. At least one thing is sure: Snow that falls on the roof of the lodge remains. The lodge appears abandoned. A person seeing it could assume it's no shelter. But of course that's a little ridiculous. This is a wilderness, and who would think to come here?

I've also looked more closely at my father's books, but they're all so enormously technical I don't think I could ever make use of them. I scarcely understood the titles of most of them. Books that teach, no doubt, but only for those capable of learning such information. They do represent a certain reserve of blank paper, though, and so there is a certain value in them for me, whether it's the proper value or not. I thought about those books for a moment when considering turning off the electricity, but the lodge itself is secure enough. All the windows and doors are shut tightly, and cold by itself won't damage paper.

I have all the electrical equipment here now except the large multiple carrier installed in my father's library and the accessory kitchen gadgets, which are pointless for me, as I don't plan a large gathering of discriminating eaters in the near or distant future. There are several portable carriers he used to use on outings and several household voice units that I took out of their mountings in the walls. As they are, as far as I'm concerned, they're useless, since there'll never be anybody in the kitchen to talk to while I'm in the winter lounge or in the garden or on the next hill over. But they represent potential parts, which a vegetable refiner or a worktable sauce blender doesn't. And there's also an old cylinder player and three more ribbon players and quite an extensive collection of cylinders and more sound ribbons. It's curious that my father would have a cylinder player. They were replaced with ribbon players before he was born. But I can entertain myself now. I can hear voices. And I've also a total of five Broadcast carriers, but with no Broadcasts they hardly matter.

I've tried the various carriers, but either they don't have enough range or there's nothing for them to receive, or they don't work. I'm not sure which. With the Broadcast tower across the valley I'd have thought, if there is anyone left, and if any of the systems still work, then I should pick up something. But I don't know enough about things like this to understand what, if anything, is wrong. One day I'll have to try to use my father's large carrier, since it incorporates everything. If there is any sort of activity through whatever medium, it will receive it.

There's a lot of other equipment I still don't understand,

even more than I first accumulated. One kind I know about —it's used to determine whether there's electricity passing through a wire. But I don't know how to use it. The rest is completely mysterious. Still, I have it all. For some reason I felt I ought to save it. When I don't have a definite purpose for something, and I still feel as though I ought to, I take it anyway. I see no harm in doing so.

But mainly my new rule comes from *The Practical Woman,* who says in the section on courtesies:

"When you have been invited to be in the company of another person, you do well to accept the invitation at your earliest possible convenience, for then you show your interest and that you have thoughtfully planned your time for the enjoyment of the occasion. To put such an invitation off with hesitancy, even for a brief moment, is rudeness. Here is the clear need for a dependable pattern in your life."

And so I shall develop a "dependable pattern." I think there is no alternative for my survival. Unless I keep myself active, next Winter will prove much worse. If I keep putting one or another thing off, however quickly I catch myself doing so, it will become a bad habit and, though I live on, I will surely live in a continually worse way.

And I'll devote a great deal of my attention to *The Practical Woman.* I think she will become a good friend.

Spring, Change 2: 20, 9504

The garden's planted and already growing, but I was surprised to discover that some of the tubers have produced flowers instead of vegetables, and others look like they will shortly. Apparently I have yellow clarions in with the weepers, and open-mouths with dayflower roots. Either I somehow managed to plant everything at exactly the right time, or else I chose an area that had been set apart for flowers, which could be the case, since I haven't been up here in several years and don't know how my mother arranged things. She was fond of variety: One thing I always associate with her was the way she'd annoy my father by rearranging the furniture in their rooms from time to time; another is her daily changing of the cut flowers in the main rooms and entry hall.

Aren would regard my project doubtfully. Or perhaps he'd be pleased at the amount of success I seem to be having. More likely he'd be dismayed I hadn't listened more carefully to him. It hardly seems worth considering which, though.

I was going to record planting dates and sproutings and harvests so I could keep the record as a way of checking, but it's not necessary. One of the best features of *The Practical Woman* is that it lists procedures by favorable weather conditions, not by fixed times of the year, and by regions and elevations, so I don't have to risk experiment.

It's a very personable book too, something like having a wise older woman with you who will scold genially when necessary, but who congratulates you on good work:

"Remember that frost in the mountains is an odd occurrence, happening sometimes as late as the beginning of Summer and often sporadically, in one place but not the next. Is your garden open and on a slight incline for good drainage? Then make sure the terracing is reinforced after dreadful, heaving Winter, and plant only after a very soggy ground has dried out some. Never, never plant if you can still squeeze moisture from the earth, for the year is not far enough along yet. Otherwise, if your garden is sheltered and in a small depression, no matter how good the drainage you should wait at least half a change more until the dirt actually begins to powder, for killing frosts often come unexpectedly in these hidden places, even while land just a tenth's walk away remains warm.

"How often have I known a cool night in Spring in the mountains when ground is soft all about the house, yet just over the rise it becomes cold and hard, deadly to green things and sometimes even with a faint sparkle of killing crystal! Yes, always know your land and always wait if you have any doubts. Plants grow remarkably quickly, their produce will ripen in time; never be motivated by a fear of fall frosts, for apprehension of the future can bring ruin as surely as present eagerness."

The guesthouse is on open, sloping land but well hidden by the lower border of trees, now that the leaves are coming out. In fact, I can't even look over and see the lodge

25

any longer, unless I go far back up the hill behind this house. From that vantage the lodge sits on the neighboring crest quite plainly in view of the valley, a place I am glad I am not. I remember my initial relief last Fall on spotting it from just around the mouth of the valley, but I think I should not care to be in a position of giving such relief to someone else with unknown intentions. I should really go over to the lodge, turn on the electricity, and use my father's multiple carrier to find out if any sort of Broadcast, visual or just voice, is being sent out from anywhere. That device is quite powerful. It could even send to and receive from the Starship.

At least I know the tower on the far mountain no longer operates, though I don't know why. It was fully automatic, I believe, with its own solar plant, like mine. I recall my father saying once, in some context I can't remember, that even if no Broadcast was on, a facility like that would have an audible hiss at its operating frequencies. I can't imagine why he'd say something like that to me. But I can't find any frequency hiss on any of the portable carriers or the Broadcast carriers. I've tried the whole range and I can't find any signs of life, though I'm probably not technical enough to know what to look for or even to be using the equipment properly. It always seemed so simple, but I may be doing something wrong.

I suppose I should take a few days to go visit the tower and see what the situation is. Perhaps there are things I could use, such as replacement solar units, extra wire, whatnot.

I remember now the circumstance of that explanation: My father was discussing the detection of life through evidence of basic technology with Osir Heremis, and I'd happened to be there, over at the lodge, in fact. Heremis! That man. I wonder what happened to him, and to the Starship. It must be still by Pleistar. It wasn't finished, wasn't supposed to be for another year. Heremis would likely have been able to get to it. It was habitable, if not navigable. I could use my father's carrier to contact it. Would I? Or did they have disturbances, too?

I am so very dependent upon the equipment I have here, I would seriously consider going to the tower, so far afield, to maintain it. It's odd because, objectively, things will only last as long as they will last. If I get wire for replacement, won't it have worn out by the time the wire I have has worn out? The solar units? Anything else? I don't know, and that puts me in a very ambivalent mood.

I'm actually frightened to leave surroundings that have become so familiar to me, even to go to the lodge. And that's odd, since I've traveled. While second sons did anyway, almost habitually—and, for that matter, Second Sons always did as a rule—and both traveled, in large part, because it was an obvious outlet for some of their income, I traveled more than that. Particularly when I was young, I traveled a great deal with my father. I wasn't sent to the Pre-School because my yearly examinations were always satisfactory. I'm glad because what I heard afterward about the Pre-School would certainly not have encouraged me to continue. But I went almost everywhere.

Second sons went only to the Great Islands, the Lesser Islands, and Amaria on Great Ocean; Second Sons never went to either islands, but to Lesser Ocean and to Port South and Lakeside on Great Ocean, all three cities offering routine outdoor activities that only heterosexuals could be amused by. For homosexuals the Lesser Islands had wagering; the Great Islands had shorelines, with sand on them almost exclusively, that were said to be very pleasant to walk on. I found it awkward.

But I've been on both Centrals. Only Morin was on either one, in Port Athel to play a part in a Family Broadcast piece. And while he was there he went to see New Athel, but anyone who goes to South Central does. It's nearly obligatory to take a look at the reconstruction.

But on that continent I've been in Akaria, Barenel and the city of South Central, all of them hot, humid, and depressing, both physically and mentally. The cities of North Central aren't much better, except that they're generally cooler or cold. They have the same sort of weather we do.

And the cities of Great Ocean are like the ones on South Central, but somewhat more interesting. I don't like the style of their buildings or furnishings, though they're certainly more practical for the weather, but at least Great Ocean isn't so Dark. The One! You can't move in a Dark city without feeling you've done something terribly wrong. They are all so formal and with a kind of surface amiability you cannot believe, it seems so understanding as to be condescending.

27

But I've traveled, and rather a lot, and yet I don't believe I've been out of sight of this house so far this Spring. In fact, I haven't been. How could I expect myself to cross the valley?

I'm busy, of course. It's not that I'm just putting it off. There is the planting and the tilling and the weeding and all. But I haven't even been up to the lodge to check the storage lockers since the next-to-last change of Winter. That's over seventy-five days! I should go soon, as I'm down to the last bits of meat in the freezers here. When I go I can try the multiple carrier.

The One! But I'm a victim of my own fortunate, elaborate circumstances, and what will I do when the time comes to give it all up, as the time must someday come? House, I will outlast you! How inconceivable. How horrible.

More than that, I'm a victim of my own memory. I remember all those cities, and they no longer exist. That much I am sure of. And I remember Athlan, and my mind is stymied by it and what it was, all that it was beyond what any city had ever been. And I recall my friends and the way they were, and Aren—ah, Chaos!

And Heremis and the way my father considered him. I wonder if my father saw anything of himself anywhere in *The Present Tense*. And then there's myself and the way my father considered me, when he had to.

And I remember the disturbances, and the start of the final one, and all that I saw, and what I know and don't want to know, and still hope is true, for safety's sake.

I simply can't dwell on things like these. Not yet, anyway.

So at least the garden is in and growing. I can always learn to trap animals when the time comes for that necessity. That's in *The Practical Woman* too. What a practical woman she must have been. What wouldn't she have been capable of, if she were I?

My fears are really irrelevant, and my hopes, for what they're worth, too. There can't be anyone left, given the rate at which they were killing each other last year. And I've known no evidence to the contrary so far, although this is hardly the most public spot in the world. It was always lonely and I always felt myself the intruder.

I remember once, when I was younger, my father had guests up here—his immediate subordinates on the Starship Project—and as daring as they were as thinkers, they all seemed to congregate together, never going anywhere alone or in groups too small.

But probably that was due as much to my father's tales of Imitators hiding in the bushes. How silly that an obvious fabrication, patently a joke from the style of his recitation alone, should be given such credence by such intelligent people simply because it was Thalis Mekthedden telling them.

"You never know," he'd say in a strange voice. "There are large parts of this planet we've never fully investigated. The wastelands, for example, and mountain ranges like this one and the one on North Central. Even though we're about to go out from our planetary system.

"But you'll say: 'Why should we have?' And up to now you'd be right. Soon enough we'll have to, since there will have to be more cities. Forty-five is not enough, even with outliers. Look at Athlan, the best example. But a new city will require new resources, which are, no doubt, in these areas. And then we'll find the truth of the matter.

"But do you know that at this very moment there is no adequate survey of the terrain just one day north of here? Who knows that Imitators haven't a whole city up there? Not we. We've never looked. We've never done any but the crudest of orbital photographing, and most of that for public show and the Broadcasts. You don't see cities in photographs like that. Not even Athlan. We know the other planets much, much better. We mine them as we need to. We've noted virtually every pebble on them, for each pebble—as such exist—contains usable elements.

"On Ath? We aren't interested in knowing about where we haven't been. But the hydroelectric potential in areas like this one will get us interested soon enough, I'm sure. Then, perhaps, we'll discover we have to share electricity with En-Narath-i-Something-or-other. Imitators had electricity, it's said. And wasn't it less than a century ago that reports of Imitators came from the city of Far North?"

Yes, he was right about the reports, but there'd always been such reports. There hadn't been any verifiable facts, however, since there haven't been Imitators on the face of Ath since our First Fathers. They had seen to that, unhappily. "Imitator" is a word of fear, a common curse, though one with emotional substance; not a beast, however

29

sentient; never, I suspect, the threat it was said to be; certainly not an agent of Chaos, now that the underlying principles of Chaos and the One are understood, if not admitted to by Darks. By all the evidence I ever saw, Imitators were actually very docile, their only even vaguely aggressive activity being their "dance," as they called it.

The reports probably were of brown or white manlikes, formidable beasts but simply animals. And reports from other far places, like Iceport and Far Westland on this continent and the interior of North Central, could even be attributed to manners or childers or even to chatterers—creatures that do look vaguely like human beings, but prefer to live in treetops or in dense forests. Those live primarily toward the south on South Central, but it wouldn't be too unlikely for one or another of them to get up even this far on their own continents. And they've been known to drift on pieces of timber to the Great Islands, on to the Lesser Islands, and even to Seternia southwest of here.

But anyone can bring himself to believe anything, given the proper "authority" to rely upon. I'm far more of an authority now on Imitators than my father ever was. I'm probably the greatest authority on Ath—or I was when there were others to be compared to—though practically no one knew it. It wasn't a proper subject for investigation, except to satisfy simple curiosity for those who knew no facts at all. That was the trouble with *The Age Before Ath*, not to mention *The One*, though I restrained myself a great deal there. But even then, when my father used to frighten his friends with lurking terrors, I knew better. The Imitators have all been dead for thousands of years. We killed them. But my father, as head of the Starship Project, connected to so many lines of research, could pose as an authority on virtually anything. He wasn't the authority he wanted to pretend to be, however.

Aren, the farmer, knew more about some things close to my father than my father ever did or ever could have. And I suspect my mother did too. Strange that I should find that out only now, after everything, when there's absolutely no cause for me to think about any of it, ever.

Summer, Change 3: 15, 9504

I set up a stake and measured its shadow. Since two days ago it's started getting longer again at Midday, so that was the thirteenth, and I'm back on the right days. I was only four behind. That's really not bad, considering I could only judge by the weather, and only by weather with which I'm most familiar, Athlan's. It was always more moderate here in Summer, but Athlan was in the midst of the south-eastern plain, which always had higher humidity in heat. Also I'm now close to exactly the right time, now that I know when Midday is so precisely. The clocks were wrong by almost a fifth. It's good that I'm so concerned.

Looking back on the earlier entries to see if I could recall why I'd assumed the dates I had for them, I find I've not written nearly as much as I'd thought. I was so sure there was more from Spring and certainly something earlier this Summer. I've been so often reminded of things, of Loren, of Aren, of others. I suppose that's it: I assumed I'd written about them as though to dismiss them. "Other stories are less honored and may be written," as *The Precepts of a Father to His First Son* has it, "but only so that the minds of men are not cluttered with lesser things. For all things are passing on the way to the Last Forming." Well, past though things are, I seem not to have uncluttered my mind of them. And I don't know that I can by writing about them. What is there to write of these people I regularly associated with, whether I liked them or not?

Each was unusual in a certain way. But their peculiarities—like Loren's obnoxious habit of foisting a blank face on a bewildering world—were so only partly what they were as people, that it would be unfair to every one of them to reduce or elevate one peculiarity as compared to another, or to their otherwise ordinary facets. They'd lose their reality. Theras, for example: What would I write about him? What, indeed, could I write to allow me to forget him?

31

How we met? Hardly. It was, I believe, on the Transit Avenue. I was on my way from Maronnen's, where I had purchased an overshirt and a light jacket. It was early in Summer. I was twenty-one years then, I think. The clothing was in anticipation of free days up here, where it's still cool evenings at that time of year. It's rather cool, evenings, at this time now. I can possibly recall the details of those garments. I may well still have the jacket around and about me somewhere. And, in fact, I do, I'm sure. I'd bought it for here and left it to always be here. A woven cloth jacket with pile lining, even in the hood, would be too warm or not warm enough for all but a very few days in Athlan.

I have so perverse a memory that the finest details of inconsequence stay clearly, while the blackest figures of necessity fade almost at once. It has always been so.

That day I was on to the rail stop on the Second Avenue. That I recall. And we met, Theras and I—there was a reason given, but I forget what. He fabricated it, or I did —I forget who. What else there was, however, escapes me.

He gave me his listing? Probably. Under the circumstances, that would be dependable. I saw him some days later in a place. I saw him repeatedly, I think, before we even spoke again. He was usually with people—Morin, as it turned out, always among them. I think, in the years, I seldom saw Theras to be alone. Then I always was alone. I still lived in my father's house and was attending the School full-year to qualify quickly as a lecturer. What time I had I stole, and a person never has a regular group of associates when engaged in such haphazard theft.

But soon enough I came to be recognized by him and his friends, especially by Morin, who took a kindly but not importuning view of me. And I seemed to see them often enough, and Theras often enough. Eventually he and I fell in together. Morin claimed to have connived, but the whole circumstance was much too strange even for Morin to have devised any part of it.

For some reason, Theras decided I had to see much more than I was interested in, and had to participate, at least by attendance, in more events than I cared for in either quantity or quality. Whenever I had a free day, Theras found some sort of gathering for us to attend. No matter when my free day was, however unexpected, there was always some small gathering to be located. Second sons are more congregational than new Owners, if that's possible. And we went to every sort of assemblage of them. I'll say Theras taught me Athlan as I'd never known it before. And I was born in Athlan. Theras came from Stes.

Much later he helped me find my rooms. Where I was on Thirteenth South was, as Loren put it, isolated, but only if you liked the places Loren liked to go to. I preferred another sort. Theras by that time knew it, and so he found the perfect location for me. I'd meet Lin on occasion in a place nearby. And after I knew Aren, of course, I proved to live in a very convenient spot, if, for that time, briefly.

But what else is there to say about Theras? He was most fond of anything in Great Ocean style, including the look of the Family Larien in people, though he had the blondish hair of the Family Menes. I do also, but that's due to quite something else that I'm rather sure never touched Theras. In Summer his appearance was of Amaria in clothes and in personal style, as much as anyone born in that city. Stes, his original city, I suppose had elements of that, as it was just across the channel from Great Ocean Continent and, with Westland, had been one of the link ports with the old Dark State. And in Winter he grumbled that, if Athlan weren't the only place for a designer, since Athlan was the center for the Choice Program, he'd as soon be even in Port Ocean or Sarane. Morin would remind him that he hated the sight, smell, and taste of fish, and Theras would respond only with a self-confirming silence.

And, yes, Theras was responsible for my knowing Salis. He was responsible for our all having to endure Salis. You meet people whom it is better not to know, and perhaps things get far enough, before you come back to your senses, that such people meet one or two of your friends. It happens to everyone. But Salis clung to those of us he met like the ocean's great bloodsucker. Father of us all! It took a great to-do to be rid of him, and I'm not sure now even that would have been efficient, had other things happened otherwise.

I met Salis in Summer one year, near my birthday, as I recall—the second year Loren and I were companions. Loren was scheduled to work that evening and night, and

Theras, always trying to engage me when Loren worked that schedule, had to show me his latest "fond friend." So he had me over to Salis's rooms high in one of the New Style buildings at the edge of the new City Center. I had wanted to take a look at the interiors of those buildings. They were no longer so new, but I still had never met a person who lived in one, and it was obviously quite difficult to imagine rooms in them without the direct experience. What sort of furnishings could a person choose? How did you maneuver through the arrangement of rooms? Photographs and layouts were of no help whatever. Also, I was curious to see the young man Theras was at that time simply raving over, though his interest was plainly determined to dissipate. Salis aside, Theras had no use for a companion.

That evening, Entertainment had scheduled one of the few worthwhile pieces that existed and, moreover, Morin was in it. Theras assured me Salis himself wanted to watch the piece, that the major part of the evening would be devoted to the Broadcast carrier. Instead, Salis, on learning that I wrote, proceeded to dredge up every manuscript he'd ever thought to scribble out and to harass me for opinions on them all! I certainly couldn't have done it on the spot, in any event. And Salis wrote by hand. Apparently, to afford rooms in a New Style building, he couldn't afford a mechanical writer such as this one. His hand was horrible. And I didn't care to do it at that particular moment, and I absolutely didn't want to after I'd congenially read just one page.

He made watching absolutely impossible. When we could get him to stop on the subject of his writing for a moment, he would turn to the carrier and begin to make running comments on the lines being spoken, the lighting used, the camera angles, the costumes, all with a superficial kind of expertise I found perfectly revolting, as much for his pretension to it as for the fatuousness of it. Theras was distraught. I was furious.

The attraction of Salis for Theras was obvious. Salis was as perfect a Larien type as if he'd been a model for the Family features. He had absolutely black hair, and the paler skin that made Larien always seem the subordinate copy of the Family Galien. He was slight of build and shorter than usual, even for Larien. He looked as if he

34

needed to be consoled and cheered, and who better than Theras to do that? In brief, he was off-color as though he were ill, and he was whiney. Soon after, Theras realized what had been made quite plain to me that evening.

But Salis apparently was interested in Theras because Theras was Morin's closest friend. Salis saw the situation as a means for getting to write for the Broadcast. And having met enough of us by the time Theras lost interest in him, Salis always joined us, invited or not, whenever he found us. He must have spent a lot of time keeping track of us, though we made regular enough rounds, I suppose. But he never, but once, made a transgression so great as to be dismissable. He was more a pester, and, while he never had the income for a writing machine until nearly the last, he generally bought us rounds of drinks or a small meal. I suppose it recompensed somewhat for his annoyance.

Morin, perverse as he is, however repulsed he was by Salis's real motives, finally gave the fellow the chance he wanted, assuming Salis would make a fool of himself. And he more or less did, by creating the most perfectly dreadful piece the Broadcast ever showed. Unfortunately, however, Salis wasn't completely enough the fool. In the course of production he latched onto one of the men working for the Household Broadcast and ended up writing for that regularly, which we all thought more than appropriate, but which convinced Salis he was now one of our colleagues.

Salis's most noticeable trait was that he dropped every final consonant in the hope, I supposed, of approximating the elegance of the very foremost Galien of South Central, if not of being mistaken for one of them. Unhappily, though, what he produced sounded more like a toss of prepositions and women's names than coherent words of any sort. It was sometimes difficult to know what he would chatter about, especially if he'd had too many drinks. He was the kind of person who could make me understand somewhat why Second Sons had come to take such umbrage at us. And, curiously, we found out that he wasn't truly of Larien. His mother was, of a tertiary family, but his father was of Menes and had married up, much as my father had, though the gap between Salis's parents wasn't nearly so great as between mine. Still, I never pretended to be anything but of the Family Paren, even if my mother

35

was of Galien. And I spoke as people of Athlan spoke, not with a so-much-feigned-as-to-be-habitual dilettantism.

The last time we endured Salis was in Spring, I think. Yes, of last year. We were on our way to a place, as usual, one that Morin liked on the Embankment by the Avenue of Places, though it didn't especially cater to second sons. It had good singers. And Salis accosted us on the Embankment. Morin always said he supposed that Salis lurked in that area of the Embankment every moment he got free, since sooner or later we'd inevitably come by.

At once Salis wanted to speak to me about writing. Thank the way of the One that the rest of us had previously agreed not ever to let Salis know who my father was. "I'm writing a new story for the Broadcast," he said offhandedly, smiling demurely.

"Oh," I answered, as noncommittally as possible. I couldn't have been less interested.

"I thought that, since you've written for it—"

"Salis," Morin said warningly.

"But I only thought—" the little fellow oozed at me.

"You did?" asked Morin. "You do?" He put his hand to his chest in breathless astonishment. "You mean, your creative urges are unfulfilled by the Household?"

"It's such banal work," Salis sighed. "Light Owners continually want me to write that their things improve living in some way, and Dark Owners that theirs are more efficient by tradition and more durable. And a Light item last year is a Dark item this year, so I always end up with the same thing twice. And how many ways can you say a person will look or feel or be better than before, and how many ways after that can you say 'efficient' and 'durable'?"

Morin sighed in apparent sympathy. "How many ways can you arrange your hair?"

Salis was temporarily dumbfounded at that. He never got a joke, much less a barbed one. "But that's just the point," he remarked at last.

"Oh, Salis," Theras muttered sweetly, "do keep still."

But Salis didn't, at least not to me. And in no time at all he was expounding all the worthless wisdom of youth. At twenty-three the world seems so much more soft-edged and malleable to a person's desires. The obstacles you walk into do deep damage, but it's the plasticity of the age and

36

not the obstacle that makes the damage seem so slight. And at last I told him as much.

"Well, how old do you think I am?" he asked sharply.

When I replied, "Twenty-three," he looked totally vanquished and quite resentful. "People always tell me I look older." He should have known I'd know his age, though he was never a person for the obvious.

"People have their devious reasons, I'm sure," Morin observed.

"Whatever your virtues," I replied, "your thinking is that age. I can recognize it. I was twenty-three myself once."

If the Embankment had not been crowded, the rest would have likely been rather inconsequential. But it was the first hour of the Spring evening. The weather was perfect, and the plantings for the New Year had not yet gone by so much that they weren't still delightful to pass. People were around and about, a great many of them. And Salis retorted to me and in the company of Morin and Theras—all of us blonds: "And what are you now, a regenerative?"

People near us actually stopped. Ultimately, I suppose, our safety—if there was any danger in the first place—was that no one but we could tell who it was who'd said that. But people looked, and they looked apprehensive. And Morin most quietly banished Salis from our presence with a glance and a brief gesture of the hand. Salis was just intelligent enough to get the point and leave unobtrusively, though in parting he had to say in a sharp whisper, "I thought it was just something new to say, just a nasty word."

Of course it was. And it is.

I've known Theras for eight years! And I can think of more to write about Salis!

But after all that time, how could I possibly write out enough about Theras, for just one example—enough to forget about him? He's not a character I've constructed so as to dole him out piece by piece until the book is done and I'm done with him.

I knew him seven years.

Summer, Change 3: 19, 9504

The weather has become much warmer and more humid. Mornings are oppressive, and Midday is virtually unbearable. Evenings it does not grow cooler, or if it does, only slightly. Nights I cannot sleep more than one hour, if that much.

I'm disoriented and constantly dry of mouth. It is not unlike the unpleasant results of that weed extract second sons now and then indulge in. I've drunk it several times myself. But the heat does not provide the pleasures the extract also generates. And I wake, when I do sleep, as though I'd spent twenty-five hours drinking alcohol, and wishing only that I could have!

I'm sweating profusely. I can't remember when I've ever sweated this much. Or when I've ever been so uncomfortably warm. Akaria, Barenel—those cities must have been as warm as this, but I don't recall the grade of heat, only that it was hot. But all the buildings there had controlled temperatures. I don't. That's it.

This has only been going on since the seventeenth, yet it seems to have lasted a change, at least. I never knew it to get so hot here. But perhaps I always just missed it.

I've rinsed myself repeatedly. It does no good unless I'm prepared to stay under the shower of water. I haven't shaved, and the face in my mirror now appears somehow disreputable. My hair needs trimming. The One! I can't describe how I look—I cannot find a particular word for it, or a phrase. I've never seen anybody look as I do now. I'd just become accustomed to it, since it happened so gradually. What a strange-looking being I am!

My skin is quite dark from my waist up. I've been in the sun in the garden without even a collarless pullover. My nose is the color of a well-used stewpot. My eyes even seem a darker brown. Are eyes affected that way? What shade were Aren's? He worked in the sun a great deal. But he never grew so dark as this. I've never seen anyone, except possibly workers, be so dark.

My hair is just below my shoulders now. It's the color of the Dark State metal currency they made from the alloy "the color of the sun," or what they took, in metal, to be that color. It also has lighter streaks in it. It has no shape. It seems to fall evenly to each side from the center of my skull. I wonder when I decided to let it do that? I suppose, from the hair, I somewhat resemble a street musician, though their hair would be much better-kept. Or the pilot of a flier, or the attendant on a rail car, or a seller at Maronnen's, or anyone who performed a job like those. Those sorts of people often wore their hair long. Mine was never so long as this. I wear it rather short as a rule.

The hair on my face! Well, I don't know. I rather like the look of it, or the way it seems it will be as it grows out more. Just now I look . . . dishonorable. But, practically speaking, I'll have to get used to it sooner or later. Perhaps I won't shave any longer. I'll trim the hair with shears periodically. And the hair on my head, too.

I'll look a fool or worse.

Well, who is there to know that I am or not?

I'll know.

Ah, Chaos! How am I going to do this?

Summer, Change 3: 21, 9504

It's cooled since last evening, and what a relief. It's very nearly cold in comparison, but I still feel physically un-settled, exhausted, even though I slept until just an hour or so ago. I don't feel able to undertake any activity, but I don't want to sleep again so soon, either. I'll do this a while until it tires me enough.

What I wanted to make note of was that, morning be-fore last, when I was so lamenting my looks, I was, for once, just like Loren. I don't suppose I ever grasped this insecurity of his so much, though certainly I understood its reasons well enough. All I understood, however, is not the same as actually experiencing what I understood. I knew his old point of view, but never before appreciated it. I wish I had, though what difference that would have made I cannot tell.

I don't think I ever took my appearance as seriously as he. People are more appealing or less appealing—attractive or not—but that has so little to do with a person's looks, unless, like Theras, a person sets his mind on a certain configuration of features. But there were relatively few people like Theras in that. The range of specific characteristics among us, as I think of it, was not all that great.

The types: The First Family Galien—and Larien, for that matter—typically had black hair, relatively fine features, and were on the whole slighter of build, generally a bit short. The difference between Galien and Larien, though it was of little matter, was that those of the Second Family had paler complexions than those of the First Family. Salis was "of Larien" for that.

The Third Family Menes were generally blond and rather less delicate looking, though "delicate" really describes the presence of those of the First Family and not particularly their appearance. Those of Menes tended to be wiry or, if overweight, solid-looking rather than simply fat. As the years went on, Theras, who always remarked on Morin's fluctuations of weight, himself tended to become so solid-looking from time to time, especially in Winters.

Those of the Fourth Family Paren were redheads on the whole. We were slightly taller than most—the length being chiefly in the legs—and broader of shoulder.

There's hardly enough merit in those few differences to make those such as Theras rely so much on them. And after the Confederation, though the traditional conceptions of Family characteristics were kept in mind, the combinations of features broadened, since increasingly the old ways were breached. People like my father—and Salis's—marrying up out of order; Second Sons marrying at last. Redheads were born "of Menes," even "of Galien." Appearance as such became even less important.

It was the way a person carried himself that made him more or less attractive. And the way he thought, and what his interests were, and how he bespoke himself. At least, that's the way most people approached the matter. Loren, however, was almost painfully concerned with his looks, with his facial features, with his physical appearance. I shouldn't have wanted to be a twin, in that case.

He never left his rooms for an evening out without spending at least an hour readying himself. In fact, he never left his rooms on any occasion without devoting the last fifth before his departure to analyzing the style of his hair—its length, its luster, its arrangement—and the coordination of his clothing and the state of his fingernails and the condition of his complexion. And then, on the way to anywhere, along the radials he continually examined himself in shop windows. He worried the most about his hair, which was luxuriantly blond but fine enough that it rarely stayed as he wished it. On avenues he would become fidgety, since the windows of houses were too high for him to see his reflection. He was immensely critical of what he saw whenever he saw himself, but he wasn't vain as Galien, though there was a certain vanity in his concern. Rather Loren was motivated chiefly by a strong dislike for his appearance, because it was the same as Paras's. Loren had a strong dislike for Paras.

Loren desperately wanted to look "good," and he did look good. He was unquestionably one of the handsomest men I knew. But his handsomeness was most pronounced, unfortunately, only when he was away from a reflective surface for a long enough time. Get him near any sort of mirror and he became uncertain of himself and rather dour to others, because, when he glanced at himself, what he really saw was his brother. For as long as I knew him, Loren spent a great deal of time and extravagant energy trying to keep away from his brother.

Paras was, of course, identical. He had the same oval face with its somewhat blunted but still well-proportioned nose, with large deep brown eyes framed by fine golden lashes and hooded by heavy golden brows, with a pleasant and expressive mouth, with a well-rounded chin, cleft just enough for definition, but not so much as the chins of the Family Ranoas. Still, Paras was different-looking from Loren. Paras's expressions were arrogant; Loren's were either very somber or filled with a kind of joyful innocence. It was no problem once you knew them both—or I had no problem once I did—telling them apart accurately. The bearing of each was so different from the other that they couldn't, as twins are said to be able to do, imitate one

41

another to the deliberate confusion of everyone. Not that I suppose Loren wanted to, but Paras certainly did, though he had success only once as far as I was concerned, and that only because I was still ignorant that they were twins.

I know Paras felt *he* was the less attractive of the two. In fact, because of the way he expressed himself, he was, but only because of that. It was because of Paras's conduct that Loren disliked his own looks. It was because of Loren's greater success with people, which Paras attributed to Loren's looks, that Paras was intensely jealous of Loren.

Loren found Paras reprehensible first because of what Paras continually did to him. If Loren knew someone, even vaguely, Paras went after the person with a vengeance. Every person Loren had sexual contact with, Paras had to have sexual contact with. I was such a victim myself, and I was as personally affronted when I found out the truth as Loren was, though my reaction was nowhere nearly so strong as Loren's—his was intensified by the repetitiveness of the deception. Generally Loren avoided any further involvement with anyone whom his brother had so enticed—I was the single exception, as far as I know, though I don't know why. And Loren avoided anyone who he knew had already had relations with his brother. He did not want himself to imitate Paras in any way.

Then, anyone whom Loren knew who did not fall into Paras's trap was inevitably subject to Paras's rancorous remarks. Most often these were provided only to Loren, although Paras was not above denigrating such people to their face in Loren's presence by the sly device of denigrating Loren's taste and perception. In my case, since I stayed on with Loren even after Paras's intrusion, I was always faced with a general nastiness from Paras. Everything he said to me, even the most casual things, was given an unpleasant point by the tone of his voice and the expression he assumed. And I was told that Loren's previous companion, who had always remained aloof from Paras's intentions, finally dissolved the relationship because he could no longer bear Paras's remarks. That sort of thing may have been partially to blame for the end of Loren and me— certainly I was relieved when I no longer had to constantly accommodate it—but there were other factors of more importance, and I shouldn't care to give Paras any due, however negatively.

But, what Paras did to Loren aside, there were a large number of things about Paras which were dislikable just by themselves. The people he knew outside of his work were all second sons; I think, next to Loren, Paras despised women. And he treated the people he knew as conveniences, means to getting a drink or a small meal without having to pay for them. He had no friends. No one who knew him well cared for him. People who met him quickly found him deceptive. He was constantly advancing his superiority of knowledge and experience and with precious little solid evidence of either, but by a great many words that tended to obfuscate his essential inadequacies. He was a sham and a predator, and anyone who pointed that out to him was sure to receive vituperation as thanks for the gesture.

With the people at his work, however, he was demure and self-deprecating. He was humble beyond the bounds of reason. He appeared to work very hard on his projects —and he may have, outside of the reason I personally knew him to do so. He always made himself available for extra projects, even or especially when there was no reason for it. I don't think anyone at the Starship Compound had the idea he had ulterior motives. Certainly Loren always complained that their colleagues made the mistaken assumption that Paras was dedicated to his work. But he was doing it all, as he did so much else, to achieve a noticeable superiority to Loren. At work, as well as outside work, Paras's goal was to be considered the firstborn twin. He was a fifth of an hour or so younger than Loren.

There is, of course, a certain honor in being the firstborn twin, an honor too tainted for Loren to enjoy. Although both twins are considered the same Son, if, as in the case of Loren and Paras, they're First Sons, then the advantage is obvious. Paras's intention at his work was to appear as though he deserved to be considered the firstborn, whether he really was or not. Paras's overall aim was to seem to be what Loren actually was; Loren's only desire was to be himself by himself. Short of Paras's death, that would have remained impossible. I suppose now it's even more so.

I became involved in the professional end of this tension between them at the moment that Paras finally learned who my father was. Whereas before that Paras had been merely unpleasant to me, afterward he treated me as though I were an insult to his dignity, and he treated Loren as though Loren were thoroughly guilty of the designs that were purely his own. "I can see," he more than once remarked to me, "that my brother has secured his future. And you've married up. How nice for all concerned." My only response was that, if he'd been interested in such rewards for himself, he'd have been better being more sexually customary in private. It was an invidious thing to say, certainly not the sort of remark I would dream of making to anyone else ever, but at least it was well enough known among many that Paras would have men act as women with him. When I said what I did, the remark got more than just catlike grins, and Paras left us. It was effective for that.

But, though I knew all the reasons behind Loren's discomfort—if it wasn't really an apprehension—of his looks, it was only the other day, as I considered myself in the mirror, changed as I am now by a year's worth of living here, that I realized how awesomely Loren must have taken his physical appearance. I thought to myself: If I am the last of my kind, how poor a representation of my people I now am. I no longer look Aten. It no longer matters that I do or don't, I suppose, but should there be someone to see me, would he recognize me? It occurred to me briefly that I should keep myself up to standard. I found I touched my hair and my face, just as Loren always did, as if to prove I saw myself and not someone else, as Loren always secretly feared he might. In my case, the impression was some*thing* else—not a duplicate, not a twin, but another sort of creature entirely. But the impact was the same: I was uncertain of the validity of my appearance because for a moment I wasn't sure I could claim the appearance as mine.

Loren had a natural vanity, too. I remember, when my association with Lin became a matter of concern to him, that Loren immediately questioned whether I found Lin more physically appealing. Well, in a way I did—I can say this now—though I heatedly denied I did, and in a sense I was being quite truthful. Lin was of the Family Ranoas. For that he was exotic. Some people—though not Theras —found the Great Ocean style appealing because it was exotic. In the ancient story, Arie most likely found Saris appealing chiefly because he was a Second Son and, thus,

44

an exotic mate. In honesty, though, Lin was striking, so striking that it was difficult to take him as being of Ranoas.

He had deep red-highlighted brown hair, the color of the russet breathswift—or the hue of an Imitator's pelt, so they say. And in sunlight his hair glowed as an ember glows, from within, as though the sun had nothing to do with the phenomenon. His face was unimaginably strong, his features as perfectly formed and proportioned as though they'd been rendered by the most flattering of sculptors, and his head itself was large—he was large without being tall—and formidable, forceful, making his features seem determined, his attitude unshakable. His eyes were more golden than brown, and deep set. A glance from him was a stare by the standards of another. An expression conveyed an unswerving judgment.

How astonished I was to discover, when we first spoke, that he was as mild as a sleeping woman, and completely without attitudes. The best Lin had to offer were opinions, though he had undergone Ranoas's "process," as his sister referred to it, and that was probably responsible for the lack of emotional firmness.

His physique was astonishing. I know I never saw anyone whose body even approximated Lin's. Every muscle he had was developed. His torso resembled a range of hills neatly graduated—the world was never so neatly and symmetrically arranged as he was—and his back seemed capable of bearing a weight that might fell two other men. His legs seemed ready to take him anywhere without effort, and his arms to lay the foundation of a city. And he had a grace of movement—Nata, his sister, had the same kind of grace—that made him seem perfection itself. "Handsome" is not an appropriate enough word for Lin. He compared to no one.

I recall making an effort to look more closely at workers I encountered after meeting Lin, to see whether his appearance could be considered common among them. And I found that, indeed, the resemblances were there in every aspect, but that somehow no worker possessed whatever unnameable quality it was that made Lin seem more intense than a man. In fact, I never saw any of Ranoas that appeared intense enough just to be men. They all seemed detached from the world around them, or from our world. I have no idea what they were like in their own section of

45

the city. A person wouldn't go there, as a rule, and if he did, he would see no one and no activity. Ranoas kept their lives completely away from our scrutiny, and if one of us entered their section, they would retire indoors and shutter their windows. Heremis told me that, and I'm willing to believe it.

But Loren became increasingly upset about Lin, even though he had no real reason to. My interest in Lin was an interest of writing—and when Loren read *The Present Tense* he finally realized this. Behind the appearance there was nothing to Lin. He was childlike. Nata said he'd be oriented to our ways after a while—she had become so —but that it would take quite a while, and she said that she doubted I'd appreciate Lin once he was readjusted. No doubt she was right. I know what I didn't care for about her, and certainly, the way he was going, Lin would hardly have turned out differently. Still, Loren displayed a natural vanity when it came to Lin. He wanted to know that he was as good-looking, at least. There was no comparison, and I told him so. But Loren didn't believe me, and eventually that was that.

Once we'd gone our own ways, Loren's attitude changed. Much of me that he'd complained about I found abruptly that he accepted. In essence, he'd always been annoyed at my writing: that I'd become so distant sometimes, particularly if I was working on a book; that I'd try to put myself in unusual circumstances in order to add depth of experience to what I was trying to say; that I couldn't always schedule my writing time as neatly as his hours at work were scheduled; that often I preferred to be alone and that, in apparent but not actual contradiction, I felt most satisfactorily alone in a crowd of strangers. I attributed his complaints to his being a practical mathematician in electronics. Such a field eschews abstract imagination more than most. I don't know to what I can attribute the change in him. I'd like to think it was regret.

I recall one funny scene with Loren, quite a while after we'd gone our ways. One afternoon Morin, in the company of Loren and Theras, snared me as I was leaving the School. I'd intended to go back to my rooms and work on my book, but Morin argued persuasively enough that, in order to relate life, I had to first experience it. I was weak-willed that day. And shortly we almost literally fell into a

46

place along the Embankment. Actually, Morin swooned in response to Theras's jibes about his then-increasing weight, calling out as he did so: "I expire from the wrath of ingrates and the needs of the flesh!" We dragged him into the place just to get ourselves out of public view. Morin had been there before, but the rest of us hadn't.

The place was dark, with deep red crystals glowing onto maroon walls, almost all their reflected light seeming to be immediately dampened by the black ceiling. My first thought was that the place catered to cats. The early afternoon sun had been so bright that my eyes couldn't adjust quickly. I had to follow the direction of Loren's voice as he remarked, "Being with you, Morin, is more fun than being electrocuted, but not by much." And when we'd assembled at the counter, I still couldn't see well enough to distinguish denominations of my jewel notes—Morin had decided I would pay the first round, since they had rescued me from an afternoon of drudgery. Thus, I got less than a clear look then at the second son who came up to us, but I did see his form lean over to kiss Loren, and I saw Loren back away.

"Well, I thought," the fellow said archly, "it would be good to see you again. But apparently you use your performance even with people you know." He sounded disgusted.

"Know?" I heard Loren say. "I think you must be mistaken in the darkness."

"You're going to try this?" the fellow accused. "Pretend you're someone else and wait to see what other chances you've got, and then get drunk and pretend you admired me all along?"

Loren began to protest, but the fellow went on to Morin and Theras: "He always says he's his twin brother. Twin brother! Can you imagine?"

Morin giggled. "He *is* his twin brother."

"Don't you!" the fellow warned. "I haven't met real twins since the last time I met an Imitator."

"But it's true," Theras said helpfully.

"And," Morin announced in a sweet voice, "if he's not who you think he is, he must be his twin."

"Morin, don't help," Theras said.

"It's only logical," Morin replied.

"My name is Loren," Loren informed the fellow. "My twin's name is Paras."

"The last time you told me just the opposite name. Do you change by the change? Does that make you twins?"

"I don't come here," Loren added.

"You're going to stand here and tell me that?"

"If you'll excuse me," I told the group, "I think I've heard this before."

I walked part way around the central counter, trying to find a spot in which I felt comfortable, but that seemed impossible. I still couldn't get an idea of the surroundings, it all seemed so bare of decoration that angles of walls and corners were hard to define. Moreover, everybody seemed to be moving about, rather in the way that people walked shorelines in the Islands in evening, not as though they were in a place. But there were practically no tables. It occurred to me that the place was unfinished, but that made no sense. Even those of Athlan would complete something before trying to make it over. We weren't that hasty.

Finally, out of self-consciousness, I took up a position against a wall and stood uncomfortably, watching others drift around me. They were all individual. I saw none that looked like companions together, nor groups of friends. This was that sort of place. For that, I thought, it was almost as good as being in my rooms writing, so I looked for a likely victim for my imagination to exercise itself on, and I came upon a fellow standing by the counter exchanging words with one of the servers.

He was of slightly less than medium height, but not small so much as compact. When he moved, he moved easily, slowly, resituating himself and his limbs most exactly, as though he were a runner or a Herald, but without the athletic sense that his body was his chief reason for being, to be shown and admired and at the same time protected on all occasions, except at the Games. He didn't pose. Instead, in a practical, assured way, he was simply making himself comfortable as he stood. And he did that with an attitude suggesting that he was completely familiar with the place and to the place. He didn't glance around as others were doing, nor did he seem to notice that others were glancing at him. It occurred to me he might not be a second son at all.

He had the look of Menes, his hair short cut and blondish, his face cleanly angular without being severe. His complexion seemed weathered—he appeared to be of a sailing family, himself perhaps a sailor. He was in strong contrast to everyone else, the common Paren and Larien types as well as those he might have a more direct kinship with. I thought he might just be in the city on a pastime or on some business, though I had to dismiss that, since he was obviously too well known by the server.

I spent quite a bit of time gazing at him, trying to analyze who and what he might be by his appearance. I had finally decided he must be a Herald. Nothing else resolved the majority of his physical details and the fact, as I had by now determined, that he must be a second son, despite that he gave not the least indication he was. Then my friends appeared, and I looked away from the fellow. Behind Loren came the second son who had thought he was Paras, still accosting him.

"Well, there you are!" Morin exclaimed. "Hiding again, or do you have your eyes on something?"

"Absolutely nothing," I replied. "I'm just surveying the cast as usual."

"You're supposed to be relaxing."

"That's how he relaxes," Loren said, obviously trying to do anything but continue being bothered by his follower.

"But I still don't understand," the second son remarked almost pleadingly.

"This should fascinate you, Ancil," Theras whispered in my ear.

"Why don't you find me attractive? Your brother does, and you're just like him."

Loren turned on the fellow coldly. " 'I am like my father,' " he announced, quoting the Credo. "And that's all. I do not share my brother's tastes, or his techniques, or his trysts. If you want Paras, take him. If you want me, take dreamweed and imagine!"

The fellow looked searchingly at me and I just shook my head and looked elsewhere. He wandered off, despondent.

Theras explained to me: "It seems he finds Paras most desirable. He likes what Paras has to offer."

"Poor, deluded chum," Morin added without the least trace of sympathy. "But, speaking of such, do you mind if we stay here a bit longer, Ancil? There is a fellow I've spotted whom Theras should meet. You'll get in no trouble, unhappily, and Loren has been made miserable, so I feel bound to cheer someone up."

"Oh, who've you picked out for Theras?" I asked in great curiosity.

"The little tyke over there." He pointed delicately toward a corner of the place. "The pale waif with the dejected look. You know how Theras lusts for that sort of challenge."

"Who is he?" I asked.

"No matter," Morin announced, taking Theras's elbow with one hand and Loren's with the other. "We'll find out when we get to him." He marched our two friends off briskly.

I glanced back at the counter, but the fellow I'd been watching was gone. I leaned back against the wall, feeling a bit dejected myself.

"You know him well," a deep but soft voice said non-committally from beside me. There was the object of my examination himself. "Morin," he added.

"Oh, yes, I do."

"He's a funny boy," the fellow allowed. "I don't know him well, but I've seen him perform."

"On the Broadcast?" I was surprised because Morin, for all his quipping, didn't normally do humorous roles.

"In here. But is he an actor?" He nodded to himself. "I guess I recall seeing him now. And are you?"

"No," I mumbled. For a moment I couldn't think what to say I was. Up close, the fellow was suddenly quite different looking, more attractive than I'd thought, to be sure, but really as though he were suddenly somebody else. I peered at him. "Are you red-haired?"

He chuckled. "Paren," he allowed. "Did you take me for Menes, too? It's the lighting in here, the red makes my hair look blond. Does that make a difference?"

I shook my head dumbly. I was too busy now trying to determine how old he was, as he somehow looked both very old and younger than I.

"But are you an actor?" he asked again.

"A lecturer," I decided. "History."

"Oh." He thought about that for a moment. "I guess your lectures are too large," he finally concluded.

"Not very. Forty people each one. Why?"

50

"That's still a good many, but do you know a girl named Elenie, Elenie Orris?"

I did. I couldn't help but know her, as she seemed to have an abiding interest in me that was not at all historical. But I replied guardedly, "Yes, I recall her."

"She's a pest, isn't she?"

I laughed uncomfortably. "Well, she's . . ." I paused to find a way of agreeing without doing so.

He nodded again. "So you're Ancil Mekthedden. I've heard about you." He smiled most warmly.

There was nothing I could say. I didn't know whether to ask him what exactly he'd heard, or to pretend I already knew whatever comments one of my students might make about me. I was also wondering if he'd been one of my students. There were enough that I could seldom recall anyone unless he was outstandingly interested or outstandingly bored or, like Elenie, outstandingly inquisitive about me.

"Elenie's my sister," he went on. "She likes you." He grinned. "She's young and sometimes bothersome, and she's often foolish. But sometimes she's not so foolish."

"I shouldn't," I ventured, "want her to be too disappointed."

"She'll endure," he replied. "I just hope she doesn't become jealous of me. Are you hungry?"

"Well, I . . ." I motioned in the direction of my friends. Morin, I could see, was energetically pairing Theras and the pale young man, while Loren stood watching intently, as though it were all some sort of technical experiment.

"Were you to have a meal with them?"

I'd never been approached like this before, so bluntly that there wasn't a single formality involved. "Nothing definite," I said.

"Good. They'll never miss you in here, anyway. I enjoy a meal when I come into the city, but I hate eating alone."

"You're not from Athlan?" I asked in surprise.

"South, The Land. I'm a farmer. Where shall we go? Do you know The Market by the Ranoas section?"

"I have rooms near there." But I didn't intend to suggest anything.

"That's convenient." He nodded toward the door of the place. "You probably know the place I'm thinking of." He

started walking toward the front, and I simply fell in beside him. "Oh," he added, "I'm Aren." We touched hands.

*   *   *

I've spent half a day, almost, on this. According to my
clocks it's N/1/1/5/4 . . . /5 . . . /6 . . . each ten-tenth as
fast as I can set down the previous one.

There's nothing much to do at mid-Summer. Just as at
mid-Winter. Except notice the time.

I should not spend time like this, for all the time I have.

Fall, Change 2: 12, 9504

Just about everything I wasn't prepared for seems to have
happened. My only success is the garden, which yielded a
good crop of preservable vegetables, despite my ineptness.
But I almost let them go to waste, too.

Everything in the lockers at the lodge was spoiled, so
much so that I couldn't bear to open the doors for the
stench. The wires to them had been broken by some
agency, probably the last ice storm of last year, as I suspected would be the case. If only I'd gone up before the
last change of Summer. I should have gone up early in
Spring. But it's all inconsequential now. I'll have to make
do.

The wires to the lodge itself were intact, though, and I
finally dared restore power to try my father's carrier. But I
wasn't entirely sure how it worked: There are so many
different frequencies and so many different power levels,
so many switches, gauges, and slides that, for all I know, I
may have been sending a message to Pleistar with only
enough energy to reach as far as this house, or trying to
scan North Continent on a Starship frequency. In any
event, there was nothing noticeable, no response, no Broadcast of any sort, nothing that I might recognize.

A window in the lodge's reception hall was broken—I
don't know how or when—and the draperies and some of
the carpet were ruined. Part of the flooring was warped.

And one table also was destroyed—apparently water dissolved the glue. I found it as a heap of pieces before the window and at first I suspected an intruder. But the parts themselves were intact. The table seems to have just fallen apart, just so, all at once.

I thought to nail a board over the window, but that would have given me away. Better to let the lodge look a little ruined. I simply moved everything undamaged out into the neighboring rooms and shut the connecting doors. I'll have to keep trying to preserve whatever I can. I'm losing too much.

There was little else of immediate interest: some more paper in a desk I hadn't investigated before because I'd always thought it was just decorative; a few preserved goods to augment my supply—foods I had left behind previously because I don't like them, but which I've taken now because I can't have the luxury of preference; some odd tools I thought I ought to have, though I may never need to do the jobs they're designed for; several more boxes of soap and a half-used jar of tooth cleanser.

Then, at the end of the last change of Summer, just as I was beginning to harvest my vegetables, the water pump in my house broke down. I didn't think I could take the time at that moment to make repairs. I didn't know how to—I didn't know how long it might take me. It was a mistake.

I got all the vegetables in and learned immediately afterward from *The Practical Woman* that water is an essential element in preserving. The moving parts of the pump moved stickily when I pushed them around by hand—the pump is self-lubricating, it says on the side, but only when running—so I couldn't work it to draw water manually. It refused to work more easily no matter how much effort I applied. I had likely waited too long to try to fix it, however I might have tried to. But the vegetables wouldn't wait long. I had to do something and quickly, and the only supply of open water is a very small stream far down in the center of the valley.

I made a hasty search through my father's library at the lodge, but I only turned up one volume on the subject, and the drawings in it led me to believe the water pumps described had more to do with the Starship Project than with anything on Ath. Besides, the book is premised on knowledge I don't have. But then it occurred to me that it would be a simple matter to extract the pump from the lodge and install it in place of the useless one. That proved, however, impossible at first. Not only had it not been used for so long that its parts didn't seem to move at all, but when I did get it over to this house anyway, it was too big. Obviously, I realized, it was intended to service quarters much bigger than mine.

The situation was growing very difficult for me. It was no longer merely worry over losing my crops, nor was it just the inconvenience of lacking indoor bathroom facilities: I needed to be cleaned badly. My fingernails had long been black from the gardening and all my pointless fooling around with the water pumps. My armpits and the joints in my groin and legs were both sore and itchy, and in a couple of places had broken into a rash, from accumulated sweat and dirt. I was beginning to sense just what it would be like one day, soon, when no repairs or replacements would be possible for anything, when I would be left with nothing but eternal squalor. You can go without the trappings of man—I have already a year—without contact with people, without the ways of life, without places and pastimes. But it isn't possible to continue as a man without keeping clean. I avoided the mirror for days.

I went back up to the lodge to my father's library and stared blankly at the books until, at last, I took one out at random and began to struggle through the complex, scientific pages. Technologists often don't even write whole sentences; *Comparative Mechanics and Mechanical Conversion* by Telen Asarin is not *The Practical Woman*, by any means. I still have no idea what I was reading, but somehow, perhaps by virtue of my reading something, anything, the idea came to me that the lodge's pump, while it didn't fit the original housing, could still be used, provided it worked at all, if a different housing were constructed especially for it.

The Owner who originally produced the device could never have dreamed of the creaking wooden frame and odd array of piping I created to finally attach everything together. Nor would he have approved of my method of renewing the lubrication, which was merely to pour machine oil into every conspicuous opening. Yet, when the power was turned on, the oversized pump moaned once

54

and began to function as it was intended, now audibly drawing water up from the well beneath the house and pushing it through the plumbing.

I might have had a second catastrophe on the spot if I hadn't managed to get to a faucet to turn it on before the new water arrived. On the instant the pump began to work I realized that its size would increase the volume of water and the pressure, which would rupture my pipes if there were no immediate outlet. I can't really recall now what made me think that. I can't believe I picked it out of Asarin's verbiage. But at that last ten-tenth, as I got the faucet open, I heard all the pipes in the house give a rattling shudder. The faucet hissed and spat like a cat in high season, and water shot out into the kitchen sink like an over-earnest cataract.

Unfortunately I can't—or I don't think I can—shut all the faucets off entirely any longer. I know I can't afford to try the experiment. Either it's the kitchen or the bathroom water that must be left on, though I find that both are not necessary. I'll have to learn to live with the constant sound of running water day after day. In the silence around and about up here—though it has been broken—that may seem most strange. But it's only a small annoyance, and the One knows the pump makes a racket, too, though I seem already to have gotten used to it. I did just now have to think a moment before realizing that that piece of machinery breaks the silence also.

The first thing I did was take a very long time cleaning myself. Then, at last, I got to preserving my vegetables. Remarkably, I only lost a very few. But the whole episode took ten days.

I have attempted Asarin's book since, but I'm unable to get even as far as I did before. I think, however, I had better learn how to read and understand material such as this. The new pump, for just one example, will itself break down eventually, and then I have not even the most extreme alternative but to fix it. Or forgo its value.

Another problem was caused by the rainstorm in the middle of the last change, which hurled one of the lower limbs of the stonewood tree by the house through the roof of the closed-off bedroom above the summer lounge. I can repair it, certainly, but not now that the weather's turning cold, wet, and blustery. By next Spring that section of the house will be ruined, but there's not much I can do until then. A whole section of the roof will have to be cut out and rebuilt, covered, and caulked. I'll have to get my materials, as I did the extra piping for the water pump, by judiciously dismantling the lodge. That necessitates abandoning another room there, moving everything out of that room beforehand, taking a great deal of time just to prepare for the work. But there have already been numerous frosts. Everything will freeze solid shortly, sooner than I can get prepared.

In any event, I've managed to remove the limb and provide what little covering for the hole I can: an old rug backed by odd boards nailed up to the beams. It's makeshift, and the roof still leaks, but not quite as much. The damage will be done when the leaking water freezes. It can't be helped.

I would be more worried but that the stairwell between that end and mine protects me. I used to think it was stupid to have two stairwells in a house this size. Originally, only the main part of the house existed with its interior stairs up from the winter lounge, and with an outdoor balcony and steps from that down to the ground at the other end. But the more people my father had visit from Athlan, the more room here he needed, so he chose—I thought foolishly—to simply add on the summer lounge and the bedroom above it as though the balcony weren't in the way. It became a landing, and its steps a staircase, and the space all that took up a second entry hall—what struck me as wasted space. But now I'm glad he did it that way, for if the summer-lounge end of the house is damaged beyond repair, it won't affect the rest, being so separated from it.

But even so, I know this house wasn't built to withstand everything forever. If the tree limb had broken through the roof of this part, I don't know what I would have done about it.

The most recent of my adverse events happened at the beginning of this change and had me in complete terror, hiding in a closet for half a night. A group of manlikes emerged from the woods and spent several raucous hours around and about the house, growling and grunting and doing whatever it is they do. I'd begun to notice an increase in the wildlife, chiefly the smaller vermin, but also bounders, and even a few breathswift, but I hadn't expected these gigantic beasts and truly thought them the marauders I'd all but forgotten. I was sure I'd be dragged out and burned. I was in tears.

In the morning, when it was quiet, I peered out to see the last of the manlikes through the thinning trees, lumbering far down the slope into the valley. It took me a while to calm down, even knowing now I'd been safe, or safer than I'd thought. Later I concluded that the manlikes, and many of the other animals I'd noticed, were being attracted by the rotting food in the lodge's lockers and had come over here to find out if there was anything else to forage. And it was silly, perhaps, but I realized I have nothing to use to protect myself—no hard-light or air guns, not even a blade of any size. I don't imagine myself wielding a kitchen knife while facing a manlike. Or worse.

So I think it's better that I stay close to home. There's obviously a good deal of danger around and about me. And although I am regenerative, and I see that every time I cut myself, I do not relish the thought of having to heal a serious injury. I'd rather not see how it's done.

And I do not think now that I'm prepared yet for very much else, either. I have a great deal to learn and, thankfully, the means to learn it. And, as with the last preserved goods and the tools I've brought over here, I cannot afford the luxury of inclination, nor the excuse of inability. Otherwise, I might as well learn to live as a manlike, or let them forage on me.

Winter, Change 2: 7, 9504

It's so difficult and frustrating to try to piece together a whole education out of disconnected books on incomprehensible subjects that I must take a few moments away from it all to do something more familiar: to write about it.

I've brought over every volume I could find in the lodge, no matter what it deals with, no matter that I can't even understand many of the titles. I even brought over all three hundred and ten volumes of *Starship Planning*. I simply have no idea what I ought to know. But my winter lounge is now nothing but books, on shelves from floor to ceiling, shelves on all the walls. I even had to make standing shelves, there are so many.

My father's library is completely barren, except for the odd piece of useless furniture and his desk, and the multiple carrier, and the portraits of him and of my mother and of their parents. I don't need the portraits; I'd rather not have them. I'd taken only a couple of the other paintings in the lodge, but now those are upstairs, swapped for the books I had stored up there. There's no space for the portraits to be hung where I might see them.

It seems to me that I'll be able at some time in the future to make some sense out of all these pages, at least enough sense to determine how much of what's available to me is pertinent. I must, however, sort these books initially somehow. I must try to arrange them by subject, and within each subject in an order from the least to the most difficult. But if I can't understand many of the titles—never mind that I can't understand much of the texts—then how can I do this? Where do I even begin?

Well, I've begun anyway, with electricity and electronics. That's the most basic science, the oldest and most omnipresent, and the only one whose terms I'm even vaguely familiar with. Loren saw to that. He used to describe his daily work to me, assuming, I suppose, that I was in a better position than most to follow at least the general lines of his conversation, being who I was, whether I really could follow or not. In any event, I never discouraged him, and I'm glad now I didn't. Though I've never before seen the words in print, most of them, when sounded out, sound like things he said.

But what a task! If I weren't who I am, I might never have read my own books. I had no idea reading could be so difficult. And not one of these volumes provides a thoroughgoing explanation. I have to search through them all to get any kind of continuity on any specific subject.

Parthis Bellenis's *The Beginnings of Crystal Technology* details many of the forerunners of the things I have here, but it's premised on an understanding of crystal structure, electricity, and batteries, none of which I understand. It's a well-written history, though. And his *Developments in Electricity Storage* presupposes a good knowledge of chemistry and metallurgy, not to mention electricity again, which I see now I've always assumed was just a matter of its being on or off. But *Developments* does detail the structure of the batteries connected to the solar plant, though what good that does me at present I don't know.

The collection, *Electron Flow in Conductors and Semiconductors,* appeared at first to be the most basic book, even though it is by seventeen different people, most of whom know less about speech than an eight-year-old. But much of it turns out to be founded on material in *Principles of Electronics;* and that book relies upon *Electrical Generation,* which in turn requires *The Practical Mathematics of Electricity,* which necessarily—and it even says so!—depends upon *The Beginnings of Crystal Technology.*

I'm reading as many as eight books at once, going from sections in one to explanatory sections in another, only to encounter obstacles requiring a third and fourth and so on. I hadn't intended to start studying the subject yet, only to organize it for study. It seems to me the only way a true student of electricity, someone like Loren, could possibly have made sense out of all this would be to have the benefit of explanatory lectures prior to assigned readings. How different from my profession!

With history, any books were complementary to the lectures: You didn't have to have a knowledge of the one to comprehend the other. For that, books were really only reference. You read a section of some daily text or some summary so that, when you heard the lecture on it, you could concentrate better on the flow of facts. Or it could be done the other way around. It was actually proper to both read and listen, but still it wasn't crucial. But with technology it apparently was, since these books I'm reading now all imply that lectures must have filled the gaps I encounter. What an effort! No wonder Loren was always so serious about his work.

However, besides the scattering of information among these volumes and the lack of basic facts in them, everything they present is primarily abstract. Descriptions of actual devices and systems are given in terms of their general principles. Of course, these books were never intended to instruct a person in the building of, say, a solar plant. But I'd appreciate them more if their writers had taken the time to be so realistic. I could unravel instructions, however abstruse, more easily than a technological thinking, however simply set forth. Loren would be laughing, I know. I've got to make the practical link myself somehow.

Even so, *The Beginnings of Crystal Technology* is fascinating reading, outside of its technical passages, I must admit. I could have used such a source for reference in some of my own research into our earliest days, and I would have been able to had I known about it before, since it was given out in 9495, two years before *The One* was first accepted by the School. Yet it's sad in a way, this book. Bellenis wrote it for I don't know who. People like my father, I suppose. But as a historian I can appreciate it, as a reader I can enjoy it, whether or not it makes sense to me completely. And I am the only person who will read it now, who will pass judgment on it. If Bellenis only knew.

If he'd only known how necessary his book would become, and how ridiculous the necessity to his point of view. Something like my *Tales of the Forty-Five* is no such book as this. If I were someone else in my position reading the *Tales,* it would only be a pastime. Scenes of life in the various Son-States will not help a person survive. The *Tales* were not intended for that purpose; neither was Bellenis's book, but it's much better suited.

I suppose I have to build a whole new world for myself out of all these volumes, a world I was never adept at before, but which I now need to know of, which I will need to know.

It's so different from what I am, from what my profiles, at least, indicated I am. I find it difficult to situate myself in all this technology, now that I must supervise it all. It was easier when it was somebody else's responsibility.

But I am so dependent on it.

On the other hand, it's all dependent on me. Nothing exists now but what I do, and nothing continues its existence without my efforts. Nothing of man, that is. Lower life goes on and on, the face of Ath changes slowly as it has always changed slowly, but none of this activity has any point to it without men. The One may have proven to be only a valid concept of universal balance, instead of a thinking so absolute as to be a conviction, but what other agency than man could make the intelligent adjustments toward that balance? And can I, single-handedly?

No doubt I'll find out one day. I have no choice. I carry all there is of man with me.

For now, however, I must return to my studies. I have much to learn, just about learning itself.

Winter, Change 4: 21, 9504

My father knew I was regenerative. He's always known.

In the back of *The Properties of Light*—how incredibly appropriate, that title—were several pages of notes from Osir Heremis on the subject of regeneration and on me. I can tell by some of the things Heremis refers to that he must have set these things down when I was two or three. How long ago that was! How much I've misunderstood some things and now don't understand others.

My father appears to have been even less of a Light than I'd assumed, and that puts a good many of his attitudes in a much better perspective. All his life, it would seem—or all of mine, anyway—he forced himself to assume a position he wouldn't normally have agreed with because it was more pragmatic or more advantageous. All because of me. It was easier to explain me if he was Light. It was easier to shrug off my personally embarrassing profiles.

And it's the very reason I never attended the Pre-School. It's the very reason I traveled so much with him—but what a potentially dangerous traveling companion!

The traveling I did might be one of the very reasons I write. I've thought about that on occasion. Certainly I always kept notes when we traveled, though I don't recall I ever did anything with them. But by his keeping me so close to him, like a sick child—in fact, I was just the opposite—my father might very well have encouraged the things he hated most about me. How funny.

But it's also the reason there were no more children than I. My father was afraid to produce another like myself, though it's not clear to me from these notes that he ought to have worried about that.

"Regeneration," Heremis points out, "is not a linear

genetic development. You cannot help now but be aware it occurs randomly and without direct hereditary cause. You are no more a regenerative than my father was, and you and my father are no more related than I am to a cat. Whatever is the source of the aberration, regeneration appears to have its origin concurrent with conception, but not specifically in the process so far as we can tell.

"Of course a regenerative will subsequently sire regeneratives, and his daughters, as far as can be determined, will also unfailingly bear them as the result of intercourse even with nonregeneratives. But that it becomes hereditary has nothing to do with the apparent fact that initially it is not inherited, but spontaneously generated. I say 'apparent' only because nothing is spontaneously generated, as you must also by now be aware."

And later Heremis petitions my father in my behalf, of all things: "You have been aware for a number of years that I am a regenerative. You have never reacted against me. As a matter of fact, you have found it quite useful, even advantageous to yourself. Your sudden feelings of disgust come as a shock to me. That you would want to destroy your son can only suggest your attitudes toward me were a sham.

"Of course, I can understand a very personal initial reaction, but not one which is sustained over so much time, especially from someone as experienced as you. I would think, however you might at first have felt as you saw Ancil's foreskin growing back intact, that you would soon have realized the great benefits of the situation, as far as you're concerned. You have been quite fortunate to have access to someone as intelligent, as trained, and as experienced in biology as I. Even now we know of few of us with the capability to learn or with experience in scientific matters. Regeneration respects no Family and guarantees nothing beyond blond hair and the ability to remain twenty-eight years old forever under normal circumstances.

"But you have a son who, by the indications even now, is intelligent and who has a good chance of being very much like his father in many essential ways. He might be capable of carrying on your work infinitely longer than you could dream. To destroy him, which you could do if you took extreme measures, would be one of the most foolhardy actions imaginable, and one which would require me to quite promptly sever all connections with you and your plans. As you are well aware, the Starship Project would immediately come to a halt, never to be revived in your lifetime, possibly, and certainly never under your supervision.

"I am not reluctant to make such a threat, or to carry it out. I would prefer not to consider you such a selfish man, but if I cannot appeal, as I seem not to have been able to before, to your sense of sympathy, then I will appeal, and as strongly as possible, to whatever base motive I can find in whatever small quantity in you. Your own sense of self, at least at this moment, seems most likely. You would, in a word, be ruined. I would see to that, I promise you.

"I have, however, provided you with as many of the facts of the matter as we presently know, in the hope that your reason proves the best point of assault. It should be clear from the information that killing Ancil would be no easy matter, unless you were prepared to sink to the bloodthirsty level of an animal. And I am quite willing to accept your present attitude as merely a prolonged but still momentary departure from what has seemed to be your normal way. I would dismiss the matter as such with a change of your mind.

"As you must know, things affect me differently at my age, and I cannot always be sure that a nonregenerative's emotions aren't entirely proper, given the circumstance of a fixed lifetime. But murder is not an emotion. It is the act of an aberrant. That I can assure you, from a far broader experience than yours."

I can scarcely believe it.

And though he seems to have let me live, the result was the same as if I had died. Which of us, then, is the more pathetic? I here and now finally trying to learn what I've always most hated, but would have truly made me my father's son? Or he who all but named Heremis his own First Son, a man no different than I in reality, and who discarded his real son to the position of Second, and in fact second?

But it's neither here nor there to consider.

The notes themselves are of immense value to me. Now, at last, I know my limits.

I cannot succumb to any sort of particle infection, though

63

I am liable to animalcules. I need never have been apprehensive of Morin's maladies, nor was he in danger from my "disease," as it was called, since a person cannot contract regeneration. Most poisons will make me ill to a greater or lesser degree, and for those which linger in the body an antidote must be taken, to fully recover. Certain poisons will paralyze me, leaving me alive but totally immobile. What a horrible thought! A very few can kill me, but none I think I have to worry about here. I can starve to death, or drown, or be burned, or die by having my spinal cord severed at the base of my skull. But I knew those last. I've seen those methods work quite effectively.

My teeth can wear down, leaving me with no way to chew food. That's a rather ghastly prospect. Before, it seems, regeneratives connected with the Starship Project would have a whole new set implanted as necessary. I haven't that option. But otherwise, my body stays exactly the way it is, growing new appendages if I lose them, repairing cuts and bruises swiftly and scarlessly, maintaining my weight and build, provided I eat properly—never gaining weight or growing taller, keeping my appearance that of a twenty-eight-year-old, simply never changing.

I cannot help but wonder.

Morin and Theras, they couldn't have been regeneratives. They could gain and lose weight, and anyway, Theras was clipped. Dark parents.

The twins, they could have been. But their parents were Light. After the Confederation it became common for the sons of Light parents not to suffer their foreskins to be removed. That's why I never thought anything of mine, though if I'd really known my father, I'd have had a second thought. And he did have me clipped, anyway, for all the good it did.

Why wasn't I ever told? I'd have had to have been sooner or later. And I'd think I would have been watched. What if I'd married? I'm sure my father never knew I was a second son. But I still carry the attitudes of the rumors of the Disease. Would that it were only a disease.

What about Aren? He was a redhead and absolutely no regenerative. That I know. But it would seem the only sure way of telling a regenerative is by looking at his penis. What a ridiculous solution! Short of carrying a knife.

Lin wasn't, certainly. But among these notes Heremis

64

remarks: "Peculiarly, regeneration, as far as we can determine, has never occurred among the Family Ranoas. Of course, there are no intermarriages with the other four Families, so it's virtually impossible to determine if a woman of Ranoas can bear a regenerative of a regenerative father." And, certainly, those like Lin and his sister, Nata, whatever else was done to them, were sterile, though I don't suppose Heremis knew anything about that until *The Present Tense* was given out. I don't suppose anyone did.

But what about others, everyone I knew, my students? What about the mysterious Heller, who often went around with us and whom I often caught staring at me, but who was always so distant? He was blond. For the rest, I don't know. People's faces appear one after another in my mind, and I'm trying to recall who had blond hair and who didn't. It's pointless.

At least I needn't consider any of the women I knew. According to Heremis: "For reasons which aren't at all clear, it would seem that the woman carries regeneration but is not affected by it. Women have a different body chemistry, and it may be that very difference which counters the condition in them. We do know that in a matter such as dental surgery, the female hormone must be introduced in order to lower the rate of healing sufficiently that the work can be done. This hormone is also helpful in dealing efficiently with severe multiple fractures. But it has been speculated that, quite simply, by the ability to give birth women avoid regeneration. Bearing children is their form of the matter. And certainly, for that, we would do well to ensure the condition of women. Their presence and perspective would be vital in a world of regenerative men."

But that my father knew, and would have killed me for it. How much I must have disappointed him. But how could I have done otherwise?

"I am like my father," so the Credo has it, "for we are all from one beginning." The first is not at all true for me. It never was.

Winter, Change 5: 2, 9504

I've tried not to consider any of it.

It has no bearing on me now. It only provides the reason that I'm here, and I should be more interested in the reasons that I continue here. It's history, and history has stopped.

But I'm a historian. And I can't seem to avoid thinking. My studies have fallen off—they've ceased over the last seven days. And now I do nothing but speculate, and speculation brings to mind too many things.

History should concern itself with the record of past events, not with the people who participated in those events: What happens takes place because of other things that happen, making, as it were, a chain in which as usual the links themselves are more important than those who forged the links. But I find that cannot be true. The last disturbance happened without, as far as I can determine, any preceding occurrence to instigate it. It just began. Yes, there were other disturbances before it, but the participants were all of Ranoas, unless a passerby was unfortunate enough to be in the wrong place. Everyone else was frightened by the disturbances until the last. People even began to be apprehensive of unexpected crowds, just as Loren was when he came out to find the crowd around the transport. It was only during the final disturbance that everyone became involved, everyone in Athlan and everyone in every city. But it seems hard to believe that everyone would accept the aberrance of Ranoas as a course of conduct.

People don't do what they're frightened of seeing done. Yet history would most likely look back at a year or more of disturbances, in Athlan and elsewhere, and decide that the final disturbance was inevitable. If things were indeed so mechanical, however, then we would have been able to infer the final disturbance in advance and prevent it. But we couldn't. And didn't.

The other disturbances had unknown causes. Who could tell why a group of apparently docile workers would suddenly decide to throw one of their own kind off the top of the Research Compound? One speculation was that they didn't like the architecture—Theras suggested that. He wasn't perfectly serious, but he wasn't entirely facetious, either. The Research Compound was in New Style, and Ranoas was known to abhor anything that wouldn't have pleased our First Fathers ninety-five hundred years ago. But the Research Compound had nothing to do with them, outside of its construction being employment. Those of Ranoas never availed themselves of medical facilities. And for thousands of years Ranoas had been employed at tasks which had to do with matters they didn't approve of. They never once before reacted. But it's hard to speculate on Ranoas. We really knew very little of them.

Obviously, though, at the last it wasn't just Ranoas. In fact, it mightn't have been Ranoas at all. I don't know, because, by the time we saw on the carrier what was happening in Athlan, it was already well under way. If it began with Ranoas, they were soon overwhelmed. But there are other reasons that make me think it didn't begin with Ranoas.

For one thing, the disturbance spread across the face of Ath too quickly. It was as though a signal had been given, at which everyone lost his reason. While the carrier still functioned we saw similar scenes, apparently long in progress, from other cities on North, or those that still had facilities operable to transmit such scenes. And the reader —someone Elenie knew, I believe—told us that the other cities on the other continents were also in flames or were being put in flames. Such simultaneity would have been beyond Ranoas's capacity to effect. They didn't believe in carriers, or in any electrical device save the most basic light crystals and the most rudimentary of voice units, and the latter they had because, in order to be called up to work, they had to have some means of contact satisfactory to the other four Families. You didn't send a Herald to assemble workers. Even so, Nata told me she recalled there being no more than one voice unit for every family block in the Ranoas section. She said there was no need for more than one, though she could not recall why. But if the disturbance spread from Athlan—as the reader on the

Information Broadcast suggested—or if it all happened everywhere at once, which was the implication from the visuals, it couldn't have been caused by Ranoas. They didn't have the means to manage it.

For another thing, those involved in the disturbance, the marauders and others like them, were unquestionably intent on eradicating regeneratives. They slaughtered individuals and crowds with equal intensity, men and women alike, proclaiming that they were removing those with the Disease because they deviated from the way of the One. The marauders and the aggressive throngs in the cities also accused their victims of a number of other perceived transgressions, citing a spurious variety of elements of the thinking of the One. People were killed for being Imitators, and for being second sons, and for being Light Owners, and for being just generally deviant, however their killers meant that when they claimed it. People were destroyed as agents of Chaos. People were burned in the name of the Last Forming. People were shot to death and their bodies mutilated under the charge that they violated the cycle of life. I never encountered anyone being murdered because he read a book or wrote one, but it wouldn't have struck me as absurd if I had. The other accusations make no more sense objectively.

But these would not have been considerations of Ranoas. It's perfectly possible many of the phrases I heard being used as justification would have made no sense to Ranoas. They lived a life that was thousands of years behind ours in every way, and they intended to. They did not wish to mix with us any more than many of us wished them to. They had always lived apart, or at least they had from the moment they were noticed historically. During the period of the Two States, when Paren elevated Ranoas, as seemed only logical, nearly half of them immediately removed themselves to the Dark State, where they became naughts. Those of Ranoas on the Centrals would have nothing to do with them. And the ones who remained on North Continent entrenched themselves even further into their sections and limited their contact with the other Families even more. I'm sure they had no idea what current life or thinking amounted to. It was certainly not they who did the most destruction.

But I can see, just thinking on these things, that history

was never an analysis even as crude as I've made. The human whys of an event were not put at issue, the reasons outside of the sequence itself were never sought. History was viewed as a fixed and inevitable progression of happenings. It was the way of the One. It was absurd.

History makes a pattern, perhaps, but it is not already a pattern being followed. Yet I lectured it that way myself, and if history is not what I've always understood it was, how can I tell what it ought to have been? Do I have the perspective, or the temerity?

I've also thought on the matter of my father. What, exactly, was he?

He was an anomaly, first and foremost. There was never before a man like him. No one, not even the First Father of ancient Athel, controlled so much, dominated so many people, directed so many transactions, managed the production of such a quantity of materials, had at his disposal so much power—power to make decisions that affected so many. But, of course, there was never a project so monumental as the Starship, and whoever directed that would have amounted to the man my father was. That would have been inevitable.

At least, to his credit, he never assumed a title. I recall that people often mistook him and called him "Owner" Mekthedden. He always corrected them at once. He never acted as though he had the position he did. And, although he could influence Ath Council as nobody else could, he rarely did, at least as far as I know. He was persuasive, and he was always rational—at least when it came to a matter of the Starship Project—and those qualities had their effects. I never heard of him forcing a decision favorable to his efforts. I never heard of him failing to get what he wanted either.

Historically, if such a consideration still mattered, he would have been one of the few ever to be known for his achievements by his own name. To be sure, daily texts were often veritable lists of names, but the clerical summaries of those texts were cataloguings of unattributed actions. "The Owner of thus-and-such a facility devised . . ." a volume of history might read; never "Owner Crissen devised . . ." Who the Owner was was inconsequential.

Further, those who were cited by name in history were always those who had deviated from the contemporary thinking. They were named to be remembered as bad examples. Allesis is one such. The Marinils were others. My father would have been the first man to have his name recalled in a positive context. Or I suppose he would have been. It's hard to imagine the Starship Project being put in a negative perspective.

The Starship was as much a solution as a venture. The other planets in our system are uninhabitable, unless a person could want to live always in an enclosure. And even then, most planets prohibited that. Their gravities were too great, or their atmospheric conditions too impossible. Only Pleistar, really, is in any way habitable, though enclosures were still crucial: The atmosphere was unbreathable. But Pleistar had life of a sort, and the conditions which allowed that allowed us our limited use of the planet's surface.

We needed the Starship. Our population had enlarged so much. It was obvious we would soon need more cities on Ath, and that was an awful thought to many. Some were concerned at there being more than forty-five. That was the traditional number—so traditional that Athlan was unimaginable until after the destruction of old Athel, and even then there was a long wait before the building of Athlan could even be proposed. With the Confederation, of course, Athlan simply had to come into existence. But forty-five was the limit, in the opinion of many. And they would have rather had more outliers, at whatever the cost to the quality of life, than the simpler solution. Outliers were like outposts on a distant planet, however close they were to the cities.

Another argument against more cities was that the face of Ath would soon become crowded with them. I doubt that would have happened. There is plenty enough land on this planet for twice the number of cities we had, even if, for a change, a city had to be built away from a body of water. If not—if Dark thinking demanded each new city still be built on a river or on one of the oceans—there would still have been room for at least several more on each continent, and the diversity of manufacture was certainly enough by my time to assure that two cities close to one another wouldn't be in competition. But many people thought otherwise.

In any event, as the old ways were altered after the

Confederation, the population began to double. At the last, Athlan had over half a million residents, and that was just the city itself, not including the outliers, and, of course, not reckoning Ranoas. The workers' section in Athlan took up something between a fifth and a fourth of the city. Who knows how many of Ranoas were in it? They, however, still practiced the old ways, so I'd guess there were far fewer of Ranoas than most people thought. The old ways did control the birth rate, whatever else they might also have accomplished.

The Starship was the answer. It was the means for finding another Ath and establishing a settlement on whatever distant body in the far sky proved suitable. The Starship Project was the prototype. It was the original exploratory vehicle on which other, later craft would be modeled. It had an advanced propulsion system—it was speedier at its peak rate than the interplanetary craft in use—but there were, I was told once, alternative propulsion systems being devised and tested. The goal was to locate another habitable planet in another system, by which time we would have devised faster ways of getting more people to it. The thinking went that if all the various activities were concerted, everything desired for the project would come to pass as soon as it was necessary. There was, it was thought, time enough. And my father oversaw everything.

But what was he? He must have been a Dark, despite all appearance. It would have been unusual for a man of Paren, but not impossible. Paren had its reactionaries. Yet as a Dark he couldn't have considered directing the Starship Project. Galien was set against it, even as the Owners of that Family profited by it. And many of Larien were against it also—those on the Centrals—though those on North thought it a good idea, and as usual those on Great Ocean and the Islands had no opinion to speak of.

My father must have been a Dark in order to marry my mother. She was of Galien, and the arrangement would never have been sanctioned unless her parents had found something worthy of themselves in my father. Yet I never recall her being Dark, what little of her I can actually recall. And our personal family practices were Light, while we still had them. My father stopped them when I entered the School, and he stopped them as easily as if they were irrelevant. I don't know what to think. I know we rarely

71

attended major Family practices—though always of Paren —but that was in deference to my mother, who would not have appreciated them. At least, that's what I always thought. We never attended any of Galien, that I know, but those weren't too common in Athlan.

But my father would have killed me, as he would not have killed Heremis. There seems to me to have been little difference essentially between myself and Heremis, though I never thought that before now. But there was a difference to my father—there always was for as long as I can remember. Heremis was a presence in my life, as much as if he'd been a family member. He often treated me like a little brother, which always annoyed me, and later, when I attended the School, he often had a paternal attitude, which annoyed me even more.

I don't know why I never liked him. He grated on me. His peculiar attitude irritated me as much as the touch of a blister vine. But of course, I see now, he was so much older, so very much older. Why, from his notes I see he was even older than the Confederation itself by thirty-five years. Had I known. But would it really have made an impression on me and thus a difference? I was jealous of him, purely and simply. And I find I still am.

But I notice just now the phrase in his notes: ". . . a world of regenerative men." That cannot mean what I think it does, or, if it does, then I cannot absorb the meaning. Is that the way we were going? It's an idea that would terrify even me, and I'm one of them.

But that would make life on Ath impossible. Without the Starship.

But the Starship Project would be the perfect way to begin a procedure by which such a circumstance could be dealt with. And Heremis was a regenerative. And there were others like him on the project, or so I infer from his notes. And my father knew about that. I don't know what to assume.

What I can't understand is the reason that no one—not my father, not Heremis, no one—made any effort to correct the rumors at the last, or even to counter them. The matter of the Disease unsettled everyone, even people like Morin for whom otherwise nothing was so disquieting that it couldn't be made subject to his wit. He joked about the disturbances at the Research Compound, even after he

72

nearly fell prey to one while he was recording exteriors for an Entertainment piece: "They're brutes, but such lovely brutes! If I hadn't been so sure they'd have done me damage, however accidentally, I'd have let them have my way with me."

Those remarkable pamphlets, when they suddenly appeared—no one did anything about them. My father collected several of them. I came across them on his desk in his study in Athlan, and he grew angry that I'd looked at them when I mentioned them. He refused to discuss them.

I can't tell what I might have said, had the conversation continued then instead of being abruptly stopped. But in reasoned retrospect I know what I could have said then, just on my experience then: "These things are dangerous." I don't know if he thought that. I would suspect he didn't. I would suspect he would have taken a dim view of them, but that he would have believed them ineffectual in their obvious goal. He would have claimed: "No one reads anything that doesn't teach." And he would have been right, and still so very wrong.

The pamphlets, and the single printed sheets that appeared before them, were all badly phrased and badly spelled. They were, to someone like myself, laughably illegible. But to someone less used to reading, those probably wouldn't have been considerations. A great many things that were ordinarily printed were badly phrased and badly spelled.

The annual catalogue for the Choice Program, to cite the most visible instance, was often, in its errors, a source of great amusement to Morin, Theras, and me. I recall one year they offered a variety of women's sheaths in a lightweight artificial fiber. The sheaths were attractive as they were pictured, but they were never produced for sale because no one seemed to be interested. The reason, I suspect, that no one was interested was that, instead of "sheath" the word was the verb "throw over." Morin managed to make some sense out of it, but only at the expense of our dignity. Even the printed rail schedules had egregious misspellings on them, and they had very few words to deal with. Most people were far more used to reading things that looked like the pamphlets.

And the pamphlets did teach. That was just the point of them. What they conveyed, I know now, was absolutely

73

wrong. Regeneration is not a "Disease," whatever it actually is. It was not the result of medical research gone awry, nor was it an example of the incursion of Chaos, nor was it an affliction given to us because we were violating the way of the One, nor was it the inevitable result of becoming a second son. But the pamphlets taught that all this was so, and people did read them and they did believe them. They took them as though the pamphlets taught, and no one stopped people from doing so.

I suppose it's easy in retrospect to say: This ought to have been done and not that. But it's not really a retrospective problem. As it happened, my experience with *The Present Tense* ought to have given my father some insight into the danger of those pamphlets. My book was given out in Summer, 9502, and almost immediately caused some commotion. The pamphlets began appearing much later that Summer, if not early in Fall. The similarity between the two is obvious, if unfortunate. And if he'd thought, my father would have seen that similarity. I could have, for once, been some help to him, even if by bad example.

Of course, I had no idea people would take my book seriously. It seemed to me, given the number of different associations and the misguided suspicions of the characters, that no one would think for an instant that everything in the book could plausibly happen to such an essentially small group of people. For that, I considered *The Present Tense* rather lightweight entertainment. Certainly, it didn't strike me as being as dense and serious as *One of Each*, a very much more historical book and one that I would have thought to arouse more concern than it did.

But quite the opposite—some people took *The Present Tense* as speaking out against the way things had become, while others imagined I was encouraging what I was merely describing, and others even got rather upset that I didn't describe more aberrations and describe better the ones that I did. What would they have wanted? I couldn't imagine. But the final indignity came when I learned that *The Present Tense* was being used as a piece of corroborating information in a matter before Athlan Council involving a Second Son who wished to separate from his wife. The wife's legalist had presented Council with a copy of my book as a demonstration of plausibility of motive for the wife's countercomplaint. Council wisely rejected the book

74

as having nothing to do with the matter. But the incident was reported, to my embarrassment, on Information. My book had been misconstrued as instructive.

On that basis alone—if it had been my concern—I would have immediately acted against the pamphlets. I don't know how. I don't know what the details of the whole situation were. But there surely must have been some way to squelch the effects of those pamphlets.

Unless, of course, as I could infer from Heremis's notes, the circumstance of regeneration had already progressed too far clandestinely to be brought into the public view with any certainty of making it seem less important than it was.

But once again I'm brought up short. What good does it do me to consider all these things? Still, I don't seem to be able to stop myself. I seem to think there is something among all this I can discover, when there actually isn't. What can I know about all that happened? I was in The Land, at Aren's father's house, when the final disturbance began. I was always on the periphery of things. And I doubt that, among the material I have here now, there's anything that will explain the past further. And yet I cannot cease speculating.

Well, but I must, because if I don't now and be done with it, I will speculate forever until the end of the very universe itself. The One! I cannot comprehend that, and it is an unquestionable fact in my life. But how could I pretend to comprehend things long past which now are simply irrelevant?

These things *are* long past. It may be but a year and a half or so, but it's all as long ago for the now I live in as if the measure of time were as great as I have yet to endure. And I must know this to be so, not merely think it and write well-balanced phrases expressing it. I must reconcile myself. But how, when I don't even yet know the length of a normal lifetime?

But perhaps, when I've lived as long as Heremis did, I'll appreciate it all much better. Perhaps I'll even appreciate *him,* though at the moment that seems unlikely.

The weather hasn't changed. It's still producing whatever combinations of precipitation it sees fit.

And I haven't changed.

I find myself thinking of Heller. How odd that I should. He was of such little consequence to me.

Or perhaps it's not odd. Perhaps I dwell on him because I'm looking for something new to dwell on. The One knows I've by now overreviewed all my closer friends, my family, and some others. If it's come to Heller, then I must desist.

But Winter is such an idle time!

This coming year I work, I no longer merely sit and write about my plans to work. I must do things—there are things to be done. I must find things to do. I must have projects of my own.

It's fruitless to write and write and write the way I have been. I read it all over and find little sense to it. I'll likely not read it again. And no one else will ever read all this. So why do I bother?

And why do I still think so much? What will it accomplish, and who is there to tell, should I come up with a solution to some historical curiosity, such as the true cause of the destruction of the forty-five, or of the destruction of the Imitators?

Simply answered: I'll write it out here. And the writing will provoke me into digressions and lingering memories and worse. This writing is a trap, my mind the captive of it.

I must this year find things to do to keep me busy, Winters.

I am better keeping silent.

I have a cat.

I have a cat!

A kitten, really—brown-black, the color of earth at sunrise, with four white-tipped paws, a long white streak from the throat down the belly, a black face with white whiskers, golden eyes that have a tinge of green. It, he—I think it's a male, but he's too young to tell, or at least I'm not sure —he's found his place already on the couch in the winter lounge, asleep in front of me now, curled up, a small handful of fur rising and falling slowly.

Alive.

I call him Carath, "question."

I've never thought why cats are always given Imitator names, or rather named with Imitator words. They just always are. I automatically thought to name him with one. Perhaps it's because cats were originally the pets of the Imitators, brought to man by the Imitators. "Cat" itself is actually an Imitator word, as is also "murder" and "book," among a few others.

That suddenly seems so strange to me. But I suppose I'm as much a victim of the old stories as anyone, despite all my pretensions. I suppose I, too, unconsciously consider that Imitators were "animals," even though consciously I'm quite sure they were not. After all, as *The Generation of Athel* says:

"The Imitators are not like men.

"Their bodies are covered with dark-red hair, both the males and the females, and they pride themselves on their coats, like any animal. The Imitators are not like men. Their heads are long and narrow, their eyes small and close together, their noses blunt, their mouths large and with large, flat teeth. The Imitators are not like men. They wear only what covers their most delicate parts. Otherwise, they have much jewelry, trinkets and baubles of polished metals, and crystal in many colors. The Imitators are not like men. Their speech is rough and simple, unlike the smooth flowing sound of a man's voice, and they say they talk among themselves without a sound, which is to say they gesture with their bodies like animals, except that none have ever seen this. When they are together they either dance or stand mute as grazing animals."

They were not like men, perhaps, but they were also not like any other animal on Ath. Their "dance," for example, seems to have been a storytelling device, not just a mating ritual. And *The Generation* also says: "They have already turned the noblest animal to their own purposes and hearths, and they would with us likewise."

Animals don't have pets.

Well, it doesn't matter.

But Carath scared the breath out of me.

Some days ago I was tending to the first seedlings, when I heard a rustle from the underbrush upslope by the house. I froze, just as Loren did before my father's house. There have been manlikes around and about this Spring, awakening from the Winter hungry and likely remembering the spoiled food in the lodge's lockers of several years back, though the lockers have long since been cleaned out to the last scrap by every kind of scavenger. Before, I'd only heard the manlikes at night; but could they, now disappointed and hungry, be out in daylight and possibly interested in me? I didn't dare even look. If I don't move, I thought, they won't notice me.

But then this tiny whining started, and out from under a low stayalive rolled Carath, headfirst, squalling, mewing, hissing. I couldn't believe it. I can't imagine where he came from.

He saw me and reacted, coming to an abrupt stop upright, legs out, body flat, one ear up, one back. We must have stayed that way for a fifth, each scrutinizing the other without a motion. Then I went over to pick him up. He shook once in fear, howled once angrily, purred slightly as if he'd never done so before, then curled up in my arm and went to sleep, absently nursing on a fold of my shirt sleeve.

I don't know what to feed him. I get meat only sporadically when I manage to trap a bounder. Can a kitten eat meat like that? I eat primarily vegetables, whether I like them or not. Last Summer I discovered some wild droplet trees nearby, and though the fruit is extremely bitter raw, it's edible if carefully prepared. I'm learning, with good fortune and the help of *The Practical Woman*, how to find and cook nonpoisonous marshpillars. I've even eaten a groundscurry. That's hardly a diet for a hungry kitten, but there's certainly no mother to supply him.

Still, he eats what I eat and seems to enjoy it. He hasn't starved yet, but in the long term I don't know if it's good for him. Morin used to feed his cat with the remains of meals. "I always withhold myself from a certain portion," he'd say, thumping his stomach, "as a precaution, and that goes to Penakh. It's certainly cheaper than spending facets on packaged scraps from a shop the way most people do." And Penakh looked more than just well fed.

I cannot imagine where Carath came from.

He's absolutely fascinated with the water pump. It rumbles and creaks on its makeshift housing, and he darts out and back at it, hiding behind a cabinet when it makes too much noise. He follows me about, making small squeaking noises, and I find myself talking to him, explaining what I'm doing, showing him how things work, describing plants, planting, the process of growing. The other evening I caught myself reading him a passage from *Channeling Energy from Heat Exchangers*, a book that has interest for me just because it exists to be read and I have the time to read it.

I'm speaking: Even now, as I write, I pronounce sentences out loud in his direction, trying them out, rewording them, repeating them after I write them out. He lifts his head to stare sleepily at me, yawns, and curls up tighter. I shouldn't disturb him. I suppose it's a good thing I can't use the mechanical writer, though I was greatly annoyed earlier this evening when I found the ink system had dried up completely. But I've been silent for over a year. I suppose I should have expected something like that.

It feels odd to speak. I can't remember the last time I did. I think it occurred when I tried my father's carrier, quite a while ago. I was even hoarse yesterday from talking so much. And he squeaks back as though he understood.

Naturally, I've got to increase the number of traps and catch more small animals. The bounder population has grown remarkably. Last Summer it was all I could do to keep the leafy plants from being eaten down to the ground by them, and already this Spring the wretches have appeared in droves, unabashedly hopping out of the underbrush and sitting in groups a short distance from me, watching me plant the garden they intend to ravish later. I wish I could catch more of them, but they're so clever.

All the animals are more plentiful, for some reason. There are groundscurries everywhere, and it's a pity they're not really worthwhile eating, since they're so much easier to catch. They are so stupid. Even if one of them manages to avoid getting its body caught in my traps, its bushy tail gets stuck. They tend to blunder about while getting the bait. I'm forever having to let them free and reset the trap for better game. Bounders seem to have learned how to extract it without getting snared.

Or maybe I'm also plagued with vermin. They're small enough to eat the bait and escape without tripping the mechanism. And there are certainly enough of those furry little beasts around and about. They've made their homes in the lodge.

The vermin seem to have settled in while they were at work on the contents of the lockers. I was up there at the end of Winter, and carpets were chewed and entry holes have appeared in various corners of the woodwork. The lodge now has the fetid smell of animals living, feeding, breeding, and dying—a smell I remember from the animal rooms in the School's biology section. That makes it unpleasant to go up there. The smell also reminds me vaguely of other things. The lodge has become a city for vermin.

I went up there again the other afternoon, nevertheless, because I thought to finally try the players I have, and not one of them, the cylinder or any of the ribbon players, works any longer. Conveniently, though, each does have a wiring diagram inside its case. I can begin disassembling the multiple carrier in the lodge for whatever parts I need to fix the players, since I know now the carrier is of no use whatever. I learned at last how to operate it, and there's nothing to be heard or viewed anywhere. Every frequency is silent, except for the usual static to be expected from solar interference.

But the sound ribbons and cylinders I have appear to be still intact. The synthetic material of the ribbons seems to be of the type that's virtually indestructible, another by-product of the Starship Project and compromiseable Dark

Owners. My only concern is whether or not the magnetic layer has been damaged, or the sound itself somehow distorted or obliterated. That can happen, I've read, but in circumstances I don't believe obtain here. I'll soon know. The cylinders are easier to assess—if they have no chips, cracks, or scratches, they're playable. For their age, the ones I have are in perfect condition, which is remarkable.

But once I repair the players, then Carath and I will have songs to hear in the evenings, and I can explain them to him and tell him something of what the world used to be like before he was born. I know he likes songs. I sang one for him, though badly, and he listened and listened, and squeaked and listened! I've never had a more attentive audience.

I have a companion.

Summer, Change 2: 2, 9506

It was more difficult than I thought, but I finally accomplished it. Obviously, a mass of knowledge, no matter how well learned, will not make a person adept in a profession. Nevertheless, one of the ribbon players works now, and we spend evenings listening to songs and talking about Athlan and all the people I knew, an inexhaustible subject, but one not nearly so easy to go into as I'd have thought.

Of course, the player looks a little odd, but esthetics are not my concern, if they're not Carath's. I had several things in my favor and one against me—there was no equipment with which to measure fractions of electrical potential, so I was reduced to pure replacement and trial. Most fortunately, though, the motor worked, and I couldn't have repaired it yet. I would have had to replace it with a motor from one of the other players, and I'm not certain I could have done that, since they're of simpler design. This one records as well as reproduces. I can see I'll have to study mechanics next.

Also fortunately, I was able to piece together a diagram of the multiple carrier, so I could determine the values of the various parts and what I could use of them for replace-

81

ment. I've almost completely dismantled that by now, and sorted, labeled, and stored the parts here. I'm not concerned that I took it apart. I certainly didn't need it.

The ribbons proved to be undamaged, and there are several unrecorded ones, too. And, at least by the listed titles, the cylinders are nothing but earlier versions of some of the songs on the ribbons, so I don't have to be concerned with that player at all. Comparison of performances was never of interest to me, as it was to people like Morin and Theras, so, good or bad, the way I hear the songs I will get used to. For Carath, naturally, if he's never exposed to a difference, he'll never know of one.

He appears to be quite pleased with the ribbon player, although I'm never quite sure what he thinks, since he often has an inscrutable look about him. Yet every evening now he chirrups and goes over to rub against the table on which the player rests, and when I turn it on, he climbs into my lap to make himself comfortable. He especially likes Sanse Karlin's work, which is fine, because so do I. So far we've listened to the ribbons of her singing more than to any of the others.

I recall having watched her perform once in The Place on the Embankment, *the* place for unaugmented singing. It was an enormous pleasure, though the evening itself was somewhat odd.

Sanse Karlin was a Dark, of the Family Larien, from Barenel, and the songs she sang and the way she sang them were very Old Style, almost excessively so. She only had two strings—one plucked and one drawn—and a single wind pipe to support her voice. No horns, no chimes, no blocks, no discs, and no special lighting, and not a single bell stalk. Yet I liked her songs. There was a simplicity in the way she sang them that made it seem as though there were more instruments behind her voice than there were. Perhaps that was the secret of her simplicity: that the plainer the rendition, the richer became the elements that were there.

She was enormously popular in Athlan, where otherwise hardly a voice was raised that didn't come equipped with at least twenty pieces in the ensemble and elaborate and diversified lighting. But then, street musicians were most popular in Athlan too, and they had to do without all this frippery.

I had seen her on Entertainment before and liked her then, but to see her in person—the experience was different, but not actually as though I suddenly liked her or her songs more. There was something about her presence that hadn't come across on the carrier, something more forceful, more direct and intimate.

I really hadn't wanted to go, I recall. The Place on the Embankment favored young professionals and their wives and friends, the people who worked on the various Projects. And they were all First Sons, of course, and that in every possible sense of the word. The Place was far too fashionable—for that I thought it almost pretentious. If First Sons set the styles for the rest of us, The Place on the Embankment was the location in which you could find the latest first on purpose.

And then, it was Morin who suggested going, certainly a rather good reason against the whole idea. But he argued: "Loren works this evening, and what would you be doing otherwise? You say you have no book in mind, and I'll tell you there's nothing of value on Entertainment. Not that for a ten-tenth I would imply you shouldn't watch Entertainment, but they're not showing anything with me in it. That's why I'm free this evening. And The Place on the Embankment is not so, shall we say, hazardous as another place might be. You see, Loren won't mind as long as you're not surrounded by predators. And you'll be with me and Theras, and we'll see to it that you behave yourself . . ." And so I went.

We arrived a bit early for the first of the singers and had to take a table in the front room to wait until the entertainment room was opened. There was a raucous crowd at the next table to us and, though Morin was initially being very subdued, the crowd seemed not unaware that we were second sons, or might be. I was apprehensive that one of them might say something that would prod Morin into responding accordingly, and so, apparently, was Theras, for he immediately began small talk on the singers we were to see.

"The starting group is called Perag," he said. "Ancil, why would they name themselves with an Imitator word?"

I shrugged. "Well, probably one of them has a cat named Perag." It was obvious he wanted me to go on, but I had no idea what he wanted to hear.

One of the crowd was glancing over at us with an inebriated half-smile on his face. Theras and I saw Morin catching the fellow at it for a second time.

"But that word means 'real,'" Theras stated quickly.

"No," I said equally quickly, waving my hand to distract Morin, who was peering at the fellow closely now with an expression suggesting the fellow was deranged. "It actually means 'unfading.'"

"What," Morin asked, "is the Imitator word for 'pest'?"

"I don't know," I replied warily.

"Suggest anything!" he commanded.

"*Ragath* means 'trash barrel,'" I said as helpfully as I could on the moment.

"That'll do."

"Trash barrel?" Theras asked hopefully. "Then an old friend of mine has a cat named 'trash barrel.'"

Morin glanced at the next table. "'Trash barrel' seems too good," he announced.

"What a terrible thing to name a cat!" Theras said rather desperately.

"Most people don't know that an Imitator word means anything at all," I responded and at Morin, hoping by that to dissuade him from being provocative.

"You two are really not making much sense," Morin informed us.

"I didn't know you were listening," I said.

"I am capable of doing two things at the same time, when one of them involves watching the antics of a mindless plant!" His last words were overloud.

Theras glanced at the doors to the entertainment room. They still weren't opened. "Why 'unfading' and not 'real'?" he asked. I didn't follow for a moment, and he added insistently, *"Perag."*

"Yes, Ancil, why?" Morin turned away from the fellow and his crowd as though they had suddenly ceased to exist. "Distract me." He watched me smile weakly. "Or did I just take all the fun out of it? Well, no matter. I've decided people like that just aren't worth my talents." He gestured broadly toward the crowd, and they seemed to lean away slightly, like young saplings before a strong wind. "But do explain," he continued, "since some people seem to be very interested in what we say." The people at the next table had become rather more quiet. "Ancil?" Morin said encouragingly. "Perform. It's easy."

"Well," I began uncomfortably, "the Imitators saw reality in two ways, that which can be touched and that which exists but can't be defined by physical senses." I sounded horribly boring outside of the lecture room, but I noticed that the people at the next table were listening. "*Perag* means the second, 'that which is real but without any physical attributes' or 'unfading' in the sense that, for example, the concept of shelter exists independent of the particular kind of shelter." The people at the next table, except the grinning fellow, were absorbed in the way I often wished my students would be. "*Perag* generally referred to the concepts of things and to abstractions."

"Like annoyance," Morin suggested pointedly. The grinning fellow grinned the more.

"No, it wasn't used for emotions. The Imitators considered emotions transitory."

"Oh," said Morin, "like the life of a First Son." And the grinning fellow's face twitched.

"Oh, look!" Theras ordered. "The doors are opening." He practically fled into the entertainment room. I could have made my way as fast as he, but I wanted to prevent Morin from making a parting comment.

Morin, however, went docilely and sat docilely with us at a table near the platform. "*Ragath*" was the only thing he said as we waited for the room to fill, but he said it with a certain stifled vengeance.

Carath, who had been sleeping on the couch, came over several tenths ago and has himself been sitting docilely on the desk beside me watching me write. He seems to be fascinated by the words I set down. He's staring at the page as though he were reading it. Are cats, I wonder, capable of readi—

No, he's more interested in the movement of my hand.

Back on the couch, whither I have banished him for a while, he sits staring sullenly at me. He does that sometimes and it makes me feel somehow uncomfortable, as though I were the one at fault, or at least as though I should know enough not to find fault with him. But there are differences between us.

He's already begun catching vermin. The first one was about half a change ago, and he brought it to me half dead, as though I were to share it with him. I congratulated him, of course, but explained that I didn't find such things particularly tasty. He went off in a corner, killed it, and ate it himself. Since then he's been supplementing his diet with them, probably a very good thing, and it relieves me, because I don't think a cat could survive forever on vegetables alone, no matter how well prepared. Still, for a while I had the odd recurring thought that I should have shared his first vermin with him.

But since he's been catching vermin, he also seems to be scaring off the bounders. I've developed a taste for them, not to mention a number of ways to cook them, but nowadays I don't trap any near the house, though I know they're plentiful around and about in the underbrush.

Carath doesn't care for them. It seems the meat is too tough and stringy. He tried several pieces, chewed on them for quite a while, then finally abandoned them in a mangled mass and went back to eating the mashed darts I'd given him. Now he'll sniff a piece and then just walk away, bothering only if the meat is reduced to the tiniest slivers.

I would imagine vermin to be equally tough, not to mention having to tear through their coarse grey fur, but he doesn't appear concerned about that at all. Yet he gets annoyed with me when I lecture him on the subject of bounders and how I'd like to catch more and how I wish he'd leave them alone for me.

But then, the differences between us are really immaterial. Carath doesn't remind me of Morin—actually, he rather reminds me of Lin. But I used to get annoyed with Morin at times, and he with me, and all that was immaterial over the long run.

Now Carath is getting impatient. He reaches his forelegs out, up, behind his ears, bending backward, claws extended curved and sharp, paws wide spread and grasping air. He's very unusual in that he only has four forward digits on each front paw instead of the usual five, and his fifth digit is positioned some distance back on the inside, as though it were vestigial. All the cats I've ever seen had a sixth digit that is an almost-but-not-quite thumb. The lack doesn't bother him in the least, I must say, and I didn't even notice it for a long time. I think it was the morning I playfully handed him a weed stalk and he didn't grasp it clumsily, the way cats do, but struck at it, played with the end of it, finally bit and crumpled it in his mouth, but never tried to take it from me or raise it up for a cat's careful inspection.

Perhaps that's how I came to have him: *He* was excluded from his litter for being different in such a radical way. I've not seen another cat around and about, though.

What would my colleagues at the School in biology say, especially those who always ranted against mutations? Someone would no doubt point out that animal mutations, when they did occur, never lived. But Carath seems quite healthy. As do I.

But Carath yawns. A squeak. He falls off the couch, straightens himself with some loss of dignity, heads for the table on which is the ribbon player. Another squeak.

I'll have to leave off writing for this evening.

Summer, Change 2: 9, 9506

I am much amused and not a little perplexed at Carath's clear interest in songs. His curiosity is quite like a man's—often, indeed, his expressions are quite like a man's, his face and sometimes the way he gestures or appears to. He is, of course, a cat, and much of the time he looks and acts like a cat. But when a ribbon is playing, or, for that matter, when I'm reading one of my father's books, or working in the garden or around the house, or doing anything he has not yet become familiar with, he has a questioning way, an interrogatory cry, a pose that conveys a demand to know, to be told, to have things explained. It's amusing in its way. I notice it most when we're listening to songs.

I haven't given a thought to the fact that I do explain. I've spoken freely to him from almost the moment I found him. I've read to him, shown him things, treated him as though he were like myself. And he more and more reminds me of Lin. It's even, I suppose, enjoyable.

Certainly, I've enjoyed having someone to speak at, if not talk to. But I only finally became fully aware of the absurdity of it yesterday's evening when I began a ribbon and casually mentioned that the songs were popular, as opposed to written or of a practice. Carath set up quite a bit of conscientious noise at that statement, literally being louder than the songs, until I stopped the player and demanded to know what was wrong. Then I realized he couldn't possibly tell me, but I also realized he had conveyed a question. That's very perplexing.

Yes, I've spoken to him, but has he really been able to understand me? It seems absurd. He's merely an animal. But there is the old verse:

> The cat sees into nothing
> And discerns the shape of things,
> Choosing among them the best,
> For only the best make proper playthings
> For this creature:
> The wise one, the visionary,
> He who steps carefully through time.

It's an ancient, ancient song, an Imitator song, actually, or derived from one, I can't quite recall which at the moment. But its phrase, "the shape of things," was originally *perag*—and I can see, glancing back, I was just writing of that word the other evening in a digression I never finished.

Yes, I've spoken to him, but is there any harm in that? I would never have dared do such a thing before. You never spoke to cats in the way an animal breeder might speak to his flock. It was said, if you spoke to a cat, you ran the risk of its answering you. At least, that's what children were always told. But now? Well, of course, I know that Carath doesn't answer, at least not directly. But is it that I find it embarrassing long after the circumstances which would have defined it as embarrassing have disappeared?

I'm sure he really can't understand me. He simply responds to the cadence of my voice, in much the same way that any cat responds better to strong consonantal sounds: *g, gh, k, kh, t,* and the like. And, of course, that's why cats bear Imitator names: Our language has few such sounds, while the Imitator language always seemed to me as though it must have sounded vowelless, like nothing but a series of stumblingly strong consonants.

Do I think I'm becoming deranged in that I choose to speak and direct my words at an animal? I think I probably do think that. But Carath is a different case, too. He's not like a bounder or a breathswift. He is my companion. The old ways hardly apply now. And they hardly applied before.

And I don't consider him entirely sentient, which is to say that at times I do consider him as the animal he is. I've been more and more inclined, for example, to go visit the Broadcast tower to strip it for spare parts, since it's occurred to me that the solar panels and other pieces of equipment I have in use will deteriorate faster from sheer exposure than ones I have carefully set aside protected for replacement. But what keeps me from going is Carath. How would he fend for himself here if some extreme situation arose while I was gone? He's only an animal, not a man. And I couldn't take him with me. He's still just a kitten, though getting almost visibly bigger with each day. He might get lost in the valley and not be able to find his way back home. And what would I do then?

He spends a good deal of time, at least a part of every day, up at the lodge hunting vermin. It's good for him and he's very respectful of the furnishings, something I can't claim for his prey up there. But several more windows have broken. I've had to move a great many things into more-protected rooms. And I'm always careful to remove all the jagged glass from the frames, because Carath takes delight in jumping in and out that way, and since he's not yet fully grown, there's always the possibility he won't get quite enough clearance and will injure himself. He is not regenerative, after all. And he still occasionally falls off the couch, instead of jumping, even though he can leap a decent height otherwise. It's the nature of his being a cat, and not a man, that prompts me to take these precautions.

Still, he does have an intelligent quality, several qualities that remind me even of myself at times. If I attend to those when they appear, and to Carath as a cat when he acts just like a cat, then I see no harm. And I may be only attributing to him those qualities which he does not in fact exhibit, which I would not see if I had the companionship of men.

In any event, he seems to want to know about songs. In the afternoon tomorrow I'll sit down and plan a lecture. It's been a long time since I've planned a lecture.

It will certainly demonstrate Carath's capacity for understanding.

But I won't make it too formal. I don't want him to think me a bore.

Summer, Change 2: 10, 9506

Songs: notes for a lecture for Carath.

Songs of practice, written family songs, written songs, popular.

I suppose I could make it easier for myself by comparing them with types of stories, both the acceptable ones and the sort I wrote, as limited as that comparison would be.

I can't put songs in order of importance, as that depends wholly on the period of history. I'll just have to speak to them as above, in their order of appearance historically.

But that requires mention, however minimal, of the sequence of history.

It doesn't seem as though I should start with songs directly at all.

Well, topic by topic—

A practice is a meeting of a family for the purpose of honoring the One.

"Family" can mean the family unit—the father, his wife and their children. Or it can mean the larger family group, such as lived together in a family block.

A family block typically consisted of the father and his immediate family, and his father, mother, brother, sisters if they were still unmarried, whatever paternal relatives were there besides, and occasionally a bit of overflow from the mother's family. But this lodging of maternal relatives generally occurred only if the lady had married well, or had originally come from another city.

But I suppose I should explain the immediate family in more detail: the father, the mother, the First Son, the Second Son, and however many daughters (up to three) it took to get those two sons. So a family block always had a First Son's house, a Second Son's house, and houses for each of the three daughters, whether there were that many children or not. A family block was of a set pattern.

And I suppose I should also explain in some detail the plan of a city—or, as they were first called, a Son-State. A city was a set of concentrically circular avenues crossed by the radials originating at the City Center, though Athlan was a semicircle with its actual City Center quite a ways from where it was supposed to be. But, as everyone used to joke: Wasn't half of Athlan already enough?

At the City Center was the House of the First Father of the city, which incorporated the House of the One of that city and the House of Council. And on the grounds at the head of the East Central Radial was the Jewel of the city in its enclosure.

I guess I must also explain what the Jewel of a city was, since it figured often enough in written songs.

But the One! I cannot believe I've written this verbiage.

But how do you explain who you are to someone who's never heard of you?

I never had to do this at the School. There those students I got came equipped with a knowledge of the terminology, at least. They knew what a family was and who was in it. They knew what a "family block" meant, and how a family block was arranged, in large part because they lived in them—unless they were of Athlan, in which case some of them might not know such Old Style details.

Outside the School I could say to anybody: "I have the rooms on the top floor of a third daughter's house on the Thirteenth Avenue South, Two Twenty-seven." And people knew exactly what I meant. But I can't give Carath even that much of my listing. He wouldn't understand the least part of it.

"Thirteenth Avenue South." Loren said it was isolated, but he hated to walk any great distance. I think he secretly wanted to have one of those private cars that new Owners amused themselves with on the driveways of Paragathi, though what he'd have done with it was a question. He certainly couldn't have reached my rooms with one.

He didn't much care for climbing stairs either. He'd arrive at my floor huffing and puffing, giving me baleful glances and refusing to be solaced for at least a fifth. But Aren didn't mind in the least.

But then, what was Athlan like from where I lived? How would I describe something even that general to Carath, who's never seen a usual city, much less Athlan?

Where I lived, the whole southern section in fact, was the last remaining untouched area from the first construction of Athlan at its confirmation as First Son-State at the New Year, 8971. It was all well built and meant to last. It had been envisioned as the only permanent residential area, and its rail lines were already installed by the time of the confirmation. It was intended to be so enduring that the School was established from the start in that section. What nobody realized, however, was that Ranoas would immediately purchase and settle most of it, thereby making the greater part automatically and perpetually the Workers' Section: ten of the largest radial lots permanently excluded from the other four Families.

My rooms were in the radial segment just next to the Workers' Section, in a location that by my time was virtually an isolated exhibit of Old Style architecture. The rest of the city had been rebuilt, and some parts of it several times over since the confirmation. I lived in one of the smallest houses in a family block. It was quite reasonably assumed that, if a third daughter hadn't married by the time she needed quarters of her own, then she probably never would marry and would never need very much space.

I expect my rooms were always let as rooms by Athlan, and I doubt any family ever occupied my block or any of the blocks in my segment. Who would have, with Ranoas so close by? Not even Paren, who tried to do the most for Ranoas, felt comfortable in their neighborhood. Ranoas saw to that by being so isolationist. So those who lived where I did had always been considered "new" thinkers. The area had that reputation for radicalism. Every one of my neighbors was young or youthful.

The top floor of an Old Style house was somewhat smaller than the others and a bit cramped in feeling, since it was cut back by the cants of the rooflines. But I was fortunate to have full-width rows of windows front and back, so there was that much more sensation of space than if I'd had to contend with nothing but two sloping walls with one window in each. I also had a great deal more light than usual.

But the floor was still set back somewhat at both ends.

I lost approximately eight thousandths altogether, though I didn't miss it. I've always felt a bit more secure in a confined room, particularly when I read or wrote. And entertaining rarely posed a problem, since I never did much of it. The cost aside, whom could I entice to my location, as a rule, especially after the workers started their disturbances?

My rooms were three, arranged around the staircase that ran up the center of one side of the house. At the back, overlooking the central garden, was my bedroom, and beside it my bath. At the front, overlooking the Thirteenth Avenue, was what Morin always jocularly referred to as my "public room"—my lounge—and to the side of it my kitchen. But the kitchen had no wall separating it from the lounge, so the rate I paid was for three rooms and not four. I can thank Theras for having found me not only suitable quarters, but quarters at a more suitable rate. What I received for lecturing was less than ample.

The central garden of my block was a delight, and the plantings on the Thirteenth Avenue were also exceptional. But that would naturally be so, with Ranoas so close by. The workers who gardened for City Services were always far more diligent in what they did close to their own section. Where I lived looked as extraordinary as the grounds of the School, or of the new City Center, and almost as fine at times as the Embankment itself. Because of Ranoas, also, I never worried about disturbances in my section. For all that they did do, Ranoas seemed quite careful to keep their violence away from their own blocks.

Otherwise, you might have thought, there would have been disturbances at the Market, when that structure was being re-created into a complex of shops, places, and pastime facilities. But there never were. The Market was on the Tenth Avenue South, running the entire length of the radial lot, right across from the Workers' Section. There was no doubt Ranoas didn't like it at all, drawing as it did so many of the rest of us almost into their very houses. But they did the work, and did it well, and never caused the slightest ruckus.

I thought my rooms were actually quite convenient, but I enjoy walking and would often walk even to Shopping in good weather. To get to the School I only had to go to the Toward the Land Radial, then in to the Eighth

Avenue South. And for an alternative I could take the pathway along the southern edge of the new section to the Eighth, and then over to Toward the Land.

The alternative was quicker, but I preferred the longer way, partly because going by the new section ran me the risk of meeting Salis, and partly because the longer way took me along the edge of the Workers' Section. I always enjoyed looking at the uniformly shuttered windows Ranoas presented to Toward the Land, and the high hedges that ran along their side of the radial, effectively blocking the view of their avenues. It always set my mind speculating on how they lived, an idle but always intriguing kind of thinking.

In bad weather, it was only a short walk to the South stop on the circumferential rail, no matter what Loren thought. He'd complain about the frequency of the rail lines, too, especially since we always had to change cars to another line to get into the city. But you had to anticipate a delay if you changed, even at Shopping and South, from which stop all the various schedules were reckoned, since arrivals and departures didn't always mesh. The practical mathematicians who supervised the rail service never seemed to be able to get everything to meet everything else coming and going. But when I'd point this out to Loren, he'd only get more sullen.

Despite all his complaints, it was much easier to get around and about Athlan than any other city on the planet. It had more rail lines, and being only half a circle, it had only two sets of listings—north and south—instead of the usual four. So even though Athlan was in reality larger than any other city, it was, all of it, more accessible. I tended to get lost and feel quite stranded in other cities. I got very lost once in Iceport, when I was there with my father. It all looked so much the same from quarter to quarter, and people whom I asked for directions, when they found I was of Athlan, considered my predicament hilarious. It was a rule that, if you were of Athlan in another city, you were wiser not to mention it.

I could tell Carath about the places in Athlan. The ones I frequented most were almost all near my rooms, between the Thirteenth and the Market. They were usually set in one of the corner buildings of a family block, where ideally, if not originally, were supposed to be the produce, meat, fish, and sundries shops. From the beginning of history family blocks were supposed to be virtually self-sustaining, and even in my time, in most cities but Athlan, these "corner shops" still existed. Only Athlan had gone on to establish centralized "markets" for each section and let the old corner shops out for other enterprises. I got what I ate from such a central facility—Glenellen's—of the new Owner to whom the city let the space, and who controlled the operation more with an eye to the esthetics of the surroundings than to the quality of his goods.

The places I liked, with only one exception, did not have entertainment. I rather suppose that's why I liked them. Places offering entertainment were generally more formal. This did not allow you to meet strangers so easily, something I always enjoyed doing. I'd rather an evening of decent conversation with somebody, whoever he might happen to be, than time spent being performed at, usually by aspiring singers and their equally incompletely trained musicians.

The one place I went regularly that did have entertainment, Kalenedden's Place on the Eleventh—or "Kal's"—always had very inspired performers who, I secretly suspected, drank dreamweed every chance they had. Certainly they made up in enthusiasm for whatever they lacked in specific training or talent. The singing was very energetic, sometimes almost to the point of frenzy.

The popular songs they sang, if heard elsewhere, would be unrecognizable if you were used to the way they managed them. And more often than not they even used drums in the accompaniment, a very morbid touch that still struck you as being anything but. Drums, according to the old ways, were supposed to be reserved exclusively for family songs at a death and at a marriage, and for the music of the New Year's procession.

Kal's catered to Second Sons, but the crowd it attracted was, despite that, not especially obnoxious as such a crowd might be at another place. There was, of course, the occasional incident, provoked always by homosexual stupidity and concluded with equal stupidity on the part of insecure Second Sons. But unless you made a nuisance of your interests, nobody especially cared, or even wondered about you. I personally felt that, since this conflict between second sons and Second Sons—and for that matter everyone else who took a side as well—was a matter of public information, then whoever transgressed the sensibilities of another got exactly what he deserved.

My opinion, of course, was in the minority, but as the issue was not something that had been presented by the Choice Program, I didn't consider myself special for thinking the way I did. And, being discreet, I made certain contacts there on occasion without any trouble. You simply had to be thoughtful.

I don't know, though, that Carath would understand the problem between Second Sons and second sons, since I don't know that I ever did. I know what bothered various people about us, and item by item I can understand the rationale, if not the logic. But all the issues taken together seemed to me to be just a collection of unrelated arguments that happened to focus on the same subject. Still, the part of this matter that I dealt with in *The Present Tense* was the only part I ever seriously examined and tried to comprehend.

That was the obvious issue: the similarity of epithet. The only distinguishing characteristic was the capitalization of the honored term, and in speech, which, of course, most people dealt in exclusively, that characteristic is irrelevant.

The common term arose about a thousand years ago and was started by Second Sons themselves. Until the Confederation, many Second Sons were also second sons. Even Paren wouldn't lift the restriction on marriage and fathering, though we did eliminate virtually all the other ones. Nevertheless, quite a few Second Sons weren't homosexually oriented, and on North, where they could at least engage in professions and establish an independent income for themselves, heterosexual Second Sons initiated the use of the lower-case version in the Daily Texts, specifically to distinguish themselves as heterosexual. There always remained the possibility that the First Son would somehow die young.

After the Confederation, when the last restrictions on Second Sons were finally removed—an action which devastated Darks as much as Athlan's sudden penchant for rebuilding itself—the honored term actually dropped out of currency for about a century, while the common term grew quite popular, particularly among Darks who reasoned conservatively: To allow both sons of a family to

96

marry would be to deviate from the way of the One, and most probably to endanger the Last Forming. Therefore, the Second Son should be prevented from marrying if at all possible. And what better way to do this than to raise him to be homosexual? And in the bargain Darks got to retain the term in use, even if in lower case. These things mattered to them.

Later, however, Second Sons had second thoughts when they realized fully what the very Dark were doing, so they turned about and insisted the honored term be revived, for legal reasons as well as for reasons of personal dignity. And of course there was instantaneous confusion among the clerks of Councils everywhere. Some Daily Texts were more cross-outs than legible words. And people in general began to be annoyed at helplessly erroneous confusions of address.

By then, though, the Confederation was secure enough under the dominance of Athlan and its social innovations that an attempt to accommodate all sides was made. Places were established exclusively for Second Sons, and patterns of activity emerged that allowed second sons to be at least socially distinguishable from heterosexuals. Even in my time there were still places in Athlan where it was tacitly understood that, if you were a second son in attendance, you behaved yourself. You went to them only with married friends or your parents, or with a congenial woman friend, never alone, and never with your companion, and never, ever in the company of such as Morin and Theras.

This adjustment worked well enough for a while, but at last another, ostensibly unrelated change that had been effected by the Confederation made matters worse again.

At about the same time that Second Sons had been released from their last obligations, women were also freed of theirs. In the old Light State some women had wanted to work, and several cities had allowed this, basing their reasoning on very slender historical precedents. But most Light State cities didn't, and the Dark State would never have allowed such a thing anywhere on its territory, even on Great Ocean. After the Confederation, however, anything seemed possible, so those women who wanted to work were able to force the removal of all their restrictions.

Yet hardly anything happened as a result of this for

quite a while. First Sons continued to marry without fail, while Second Sons were now also marrying if they chose to, which many did. In general, people still held to some old ways, if only for appearance's sake, so families still didn't amount to more than two sons and, at the most, three daughters—the approved ratio that reflects the average birth ratio among men. For a long while, then, there weren't a good many women to enter professions, except, of course, those hapless, unmarried third daughters.

About fifty years ago, however, biology researchers perfected a compound that guaranteed control of conception. This freed a great many married women to work if they wanted to, and they did. This also freed a great many women from accidental pregnancy, which, by their logic, freed them from the necessity for marriage. And they went to work. Almost all old ways lost even their value as a façade, and working women quickly developed their own sort of thinking:

They were now in competition with men for jobs that had for the most part previously been held exclusively by men. And they would defer to a First Son in this competition because he was still entitled to the deference. But they would not defer to Second Sons, who, they considered, were equals. The competition between women and Second Sons became fierce.

Meanwhile, unmarried women added a line to this thinking: While deliberately single, they had still been raised to consider marriage a desirable goal. So, as they worked alongside men, they naturally also took a moment now and then to consider one of their male colleagues as a potential husband. Working, for many women, quickly became as much of a social activity as a professional contribution.

Yet many women were finding themselves ill-equipped for the work they were doing. The rapid rush to employment, spurred by the ability to prevent conception, seemed to blind the average woman to the fact that she simply might not have all the training or the inclination to do a given assignment. I am absolutely no good at mathematics, but when I was twenty-two I wasn't especially aware of that. And had I been a twenty-two-year-old woman, thirty or forty years ago, I might well have gotten myself into a mathematically oriented profession in which I could only fail. Simply: No one thought then to do profiles of women, since the profile was still thought to be entirely a male necessity.

Certainly a good number of women succeeded nonetheless, but most managed only marginally, and some not at all. And those in the second and third categories made it a part of their business to find themselves husbands before they made complete fools of themselves. I suppose that's a practical consideration. We were such a practical sort. But it set an attitude toward working that young women entering professional life unfortunately continued to maintain, and herein lay the problem with second sons.

The Second Son, though he was competition, was alternatively marriageable. The second son, on the other hand, was just competition. But how was a woman to know who's what? Never in history had women had to worry about this before. And they became rather unsettled when dealing with an unmarried man.

If he called himself "second son," they had to know of which sort. If he was of the honored variety but didn't find a particular woman attractive, she could well retaliate by subtly, or not so subtly, accusing him of being homosexual. And everything else resulted from that.

Back came the old problem of the confusion of terminology. Second Sons began to develop an irritable attitude toward second sons, while women interested primarily in marriage looked down on second sons for quite different reasons. In addition, Darks were still enthusiastically raising their own second sons for their own reasons, which made Lights who automatically reacted against any Dark thinking begin to denounce homosexuality, as if it were something that could be so easily dealt with.

I was born into the middle of all this confusion, as a First Son of a father who was whatever my father actually was. And I thought the whole matter rather silly, since until just ten years or so before my birth there was nothing more or less than ordinary about being a second son. More than that: It's only been in the last thousand years that there's even been a term for homosexuals that wasn't strictly biological. How, then, to explain a growing, serious conflict that by and large was accidental, if not entirely artificial?

But this was to have been about songs, wasn't it?

Well, maybe I'll just play a song and explain a bit about it, and go along that way. Certainly, this kind of past detail hasn't anything at all to do with us now. Not even as a matter of curiosity, not even just my curiosity.

Chaos! It's a little after the first of evening already, and Carath has just come in, from an afternoon at the lodge, no doubt. I'll fix us a meal and then spend the evening really discussing songs.

There's an odd thing he does that I've never seen another cat do, that he's starting to do again now: He sits, as he is on the couch, and stretches out part way forward, as though half lying down, his forepaws separated more than usual, his body raised up a bit. Then he lowers his head between his forepaws until his forehead is touching ground. Now he begins to slowly extend and retract his front claws, pushing down and releasing with first one paw and then the other. He doesn't purr when he does this, though; otherwise I'd think he were mimicking nursing. His whole body rocks forward and back slowly, rocking as it were on his forehead.

There's something about it that reminds me of something, but I haven't been able to recall just what. It looks terribly uncomfortable, but he does it at least once every five days or so, five times a change, with such regularity that I can almost determine by his action how much of a change has passed.

But I remember what it is: It's a pose cats were often shown as taking in Imitator depictions of them. And Imitators did divide the year into eighty parts of five days a part, instead of sixteen changes of twenty-five days a change.

The Imitators did regard things quite differently than we. They had a much more complex system of measurements. There was a wholly unrelated set of standards and terms for distance, whereas we more simply define distance in terms of standardized times. There was also a wholly unrelated set of weights and measures, while we define those things in terms of our currency, which makes far more sense.

They did things quite differently: They seem to have had vast numbers of books, because remains of books have been found whose only reason for existence was to list

100

book titles. I suppose, then, their pets were entitled to do different things with them than with us.

But Carath seems to be reverting to "old ways," to misuse a phrase. But he couldn't possibly be mistaking me for an Imitator, could he? He couldn't possibly know what an Imitator is.

I wish he could speak. I wish I could question him. But I must call him "question" and leave it at that, I suppose.

Now he's stopped doing whatever that is that he does. He's crying loudly instead. He must be hungry. After all those vermin?

Summer, Change 2: 12, 9506

My lecture was only a moderate success, from an organizational point of view. But strangely, Carath seemed much more attentive than I'd have anticipated. I cannot help but wonder again whether I do project my imagination on him, or whether he really does exhibit traits like man's. Perhaps he's only modeling his actions and expressions on me, since he has no other cat whose example he can follow. But whatever, it's unsettling. And I also wonder again whether I should even worry. And that's unsettling as well.

As for the lecture, I kept noticing how much more I could say to virtually every word I did speak, and as a result I often lost my way momentarily. This never happened to me at the School.

History suddenly seems so much more convoluted than it ever did. The last two days, as I've gone about my routines, I've tried to determine why this should be so.

It was axiomatic that history was a linear progress of events. The Director of History at the School maintained that "history is the examination of the course of man's authority," a definition that satisfied me then, though now I'm not so sure he was right. Man's development on Ath— and of Ath and the whole planetary system containing it —went forward in a linear fashion. The first settlement was Athel, and Athel was settled by the first men, all of them, including, presumably, Ranoas, even if Ranoas doesn't have mention in the Daily Texts until around 3100.

Later, from Athel and its outlier, Paragathel, man expanded across the face of the planet—first throughout the Centrals and then on to the Islands to the east, and to Great Ocean and North to the west. And one event followed another, one Period another: of the First Fathers, of the Dispersion, of the Forty-Five, of the Consolidation, of the Two States, of the pre-Confederation, of the Confederation. And now of me.

But as I talked of songs it began to seem to me that they were not orderable in a linear fashion, or in any fashion. Their history is purely eccentric. The popularity or unpopularity of a song seems to have nothing to do with Light and Dark thinking in any way similar to an event.

An event takes place as a resolution of the two thinkings in conflict. But the acceptance of a song, or even a change in the sort of song, depends simply on the whim of a majority of people who are presented with it, no matter whether they're Light or Dark. I like Sanse Karlin, though her songs are Dark and I certainly am not. Songs seem not to have progress; they are merely in favor or not.

It is, I suspect, impossible to give a lecture on something like songs, and it would never have occurred to me, or to anyone, to do so at the School. I suppose the approach I had to take the other evening, however fragmented and halting, is the only approach—song by song. And for that, given the examples I have on ribbons, I suppose I did the best that could be done.

As for history itself, I think my attempts now to figure out what it actually is, or was, are just fatuous.

What caught Carath's fancy, or seemed to, though, surprised me. At one point early on as I was trying to understand for myself what might cause one song to be popular, while another is not, I told him of a fellow I knew, a sculptor, with whom I used to regularly converse in Kal's. Beskin claimed—and his wife always concurred with him, that if only all esthetic matters could be included as a part of the Choice Program, then songs, painting, his endeavors —and mine, as the two of them invariably pointed out— would be the far more consistently successful, because we would then have a good idea of what people actually wanted along these lines. As things stood, it was all sheerest guesswork. I suppose his was a point to be made, though I always found it hard to imagine asking people who didn't read what sort of books they'd like to have.

I merely mentioned the Choice Program, however, and Carath was suddenly all ears and vocalizations. I was startled at the intensity of his reaction.

Now, I wasn't sure it wasn't just my imagination, so I casually mentioned the Choice Program again some several tenths later, and again he reacted. I tried my tactic several times more during the evening, and each time I said the words "Choice Program," he responded. There are two D's, a T, and a K in the words, so that may well be it. But I didn't go into any detail at that moment because the Choice Program is a complicated subject and something I'm not sure I know enough about.

Still, I suppose I could explain what I can, even if all this is just the result of my own fancy. Keeping my mind occupied with such subjects does keep it from being occupied with others. Yesterday's night I dreamt badly, so badly that in the morning I remembered having the dream, though not what it was about. But I can guess. So all these narratives of mine may be perfectly pointless, yet they have a point if they divert me.

Theras was a designer for the Choice Program, and a respectable one. What I know of the matter I know from him, and therefore much of what I can explain to Carath is necessarily phrased Theras's way. And Salis, dear Salis, wrote for the Household Broadcast, so he might finally make some contribution of interest to me. But I shall rely primarily on Theras.

He designed clothing fabrics, wall coverings, carpets and draperies, and public interiors such as the main entrance halls of both the City Services Center and the Ath Services Coordination Center. He also did some packaging, primarily for cosmetics and medicinals, but also for children's toys. Besides this, on his own time he had designed interiors for several of the Entertainment Broadcasts in which Morin had a leading part. And, of course, he was responsible for the design of the presentation of the goods he worked on when they were displayed on Household.

He attended the Design Section of the School in Stes, one of only five such sections in Schools. Three of the others, as might be expected, were also in North cities, though I thought it was odd that there was none in Athlan. Theras remarked that that was the way the Choice Program Directors had always wanted it. For some unknown reason, Athlan was not suitable as a source for designers, though it was where almost all of them ended up working. These sections were staffed exclusively by people who had already worked on the Choice Program in some capacity, so the training in any of the five sections was uniformly excellent, even in the section in Amaria. And anybody who survived the entire course of training was able to work on the Choice Program at once.

But to apply, you had to be good to begin with, since the number of students accepted for this training was limited to the number of projected openings for them—in both the Choice Program and with those Owners who employed designers in certain capacities. Theras must have been good to begin with. I suppose it's my dislike of the Great Ocean style that would make me wonder about that even for an instant.

He was good. He was one of the better-known designers. You don't design public interiors if you're not, I suppose.

There were three elements of the Choice Program visible to most people: the Choice Catalogue itself, the range of periodic Opinion Pamphlets, and the Household Broadcast. The Choice Catalogue was given out Spring 1: 1 of every year and contained all the durables of whatever sort Owners had in mind to produce that year. It was divided into two sections: nonseasonal and seasonal. The nonseasonal section showed such items as clocks, players, general furniture, tools. The seasonal showed things appropriate for each of the times of year: heavier draperies for Fall, for example, or summer-lounge furniture. The object with either section was to mark those items you personally thought you'd like to have, and the color, the pattern, the size, whatever, you'd like to have them in. And then you could report your choices by carrier at the appropriate times, or you could return the proper section in person to the Choice Program Center in the new City Center.

You weren't obligated to accept any choice you'd made. You were only obligated to make your choices as honestly as you could. The Choice Program printed its homily on the front of every Catalogue and Pamphlet, and Household recited it at least once every hour: "The ways of man are interlocking. A man's falsehood returns to him."

The pamphlets showed clothing, cosmetics, and certain seasonal foods such as the meat of a breathswift, or northerly-grown fruits. They appeared at varying intervals during the course of a year, and with them also you were obligated to make choices, but not obligated to abide by them. The front half of the pamphlets was filled with photographs of what appeared to be exclusively First Sons and First Daughters, impeccable and impossibly earnest. The second half was designed to help set limits for the hunters, husbandmen, and farmers, such as Aren, and it contained not one single photograph of a person.

The Household Broadcast presented daily the items shown in the catalogue and in the pamphlets as most people had asked for them, with a limited list of variations also available. Each item to be shown appeared twice, once during the morning and once during the afternoon, for all twenty-five days of the change prior to the last choice day for that item. These, if you chose them, you received. Or you could go to Maronnen's—or Colabris's, I suppose— and see these things already made up, to order them your own way if you didn't like the available variations.

Theras rather liked Maronnen's:

"I shop there myself, you know. I don't dress entirely by the Choice Program. But we designers are not supposed to like it, not designers at my level at any rate. You see, I get a proportion of income from every item of mine that sells through Household, in addition to my regular rate. It comes from my position now on the Choice Program. So Maronnen's, in principle, reduces my total income. Still, I don't like some of the ways the things I design prove to be wanted in. Maronnen's gives me the chance to get it the way I intended it.

"However, I suppose I should change my thinking, since it is so often such a task to get something to look good enough on someone's carrier. For that I deserve the reward that Maronnen's reduces."

As it happened, Salis agreed on the problem of the presentation on the carrier. It was his job for Household to write the description of an item shown, so it could be better understood and ordered correctly, and he once complained: "I have only a certain amount of time to speak

105

to each object. And that's more limited by the readers—they speak so slowly that a sentence from them seems to take forever. And in that time I have to include material content, colors, sizes, cost, and the variations. And still most Owners, and not just the new Owners, supply me with a handwritten note—a handwritten note!—containing enough words of praise, all of which they expect me to use, to provide Morin with a full-scale Entertainment Broadcast."

On creating things for the Choice Program, I recall that Theras once wearily related:

"Let's say I'm going to design summer curtains. Owner Fribinil—they might as well all be named something that silly—dear Owner Fribinil will come to my office and say: 'I'd like something different this year. Something brighter. Bright for Summer. In a lightweight fabric that will look good in a mild breeze, you know, sensual, a kind of motion that seems to look refreshing in the hot weather. And it's time for a different sort of pattern, don't you think? Why don't we say'—and believe me, Ancil, I did have one Owner say something just like this to me—'something that will remind people of the stars and of the great space beyond our planets.'

"Can you imagine the sort of summer curtains that would result from that description? Well, I can't, but never mind.

"So dear Owner Fribinil goes his way at last, and I set to designing the way I was going to do it in the first place. And I come up with maybe six variations, maybe seven if I'm lucky, or if I haven't been out to a place the previous evening. And they range, as you might guess, from absolutely Dark, stark curtains to something so radical that even a demented Light would be repelled. But you may ask why I do so much.

"I could say I was told to do it this way at the School in Stes, and that's true. But in fact, the reason, as I have since found out by experience, is that if you put what you yourself like the best in the middle during preliminary presentations the two extremes will scare anybody who is not aberrant into making up his mind more or less the way you'd like him to. I have run across exceptions to this, but not very many. And the preference of every one of those exceptional Owners failed, I might add. My own preferences never seem to, though I suspect that's luck.

"But let's say this Fribinil fellow is a problem. He comes back, and out of my six designs he likes two, the next-to-most-radical and the one on the Dark side of the middle, say numbers three and five. So now he takes those numbers back to his house to show his wife, an ever-discerning person, let me tell you. And the One! if she doesn't rather like number five, but thinks it a bit too bright.

"Then she either strides into my office suddenly, while I'm in the midst of sketching a scent flask, and demands to see what her husband didn't like. Or she strides in and demands that at that instant I redesign number five to her liking.

"And of course, whatever happens, I do it. And whatever it is she wants, it cannot be done well enough to suit Lady Fribinil. Meanwhile, her husband is lagging behind in a corner looking as though he wished he had never involved this ever-seeking Arie. But you know that he's done just this before, and that he'll do just this again. The look he shows is a performance, and you lament he has no other talent.

"With what I go through with Owners of every sort on any normal day, I often wonder if the things people indicate they want and what they order from Household— I wonder if these things are really what they want. These things, by private agreement or by coercion on my part or somebody else's, are what the Choice Program wants people to want. There are a lot of things I design that no one's ever seen and no one's ever likely to see, interesting things, some very handsome if decidedly unusual fabric patterns, striking tableware, innovative things.

"And this question of mine I've heard other people in the Choice Program also ask. I know it's not something any of us would make a serious proposal concerning. It's a valid point to be raised, but the point rests so deeply in the core of the Choice Program itself that it hardly seems worthwhile to consider, since I doubt there is a thing that could be done about it. And anyway, the answer would no doubt be that for unusual things you should go to the craftsmen of Ranoas, which is no answer at all in terms of design.

"But the people who ask what I ask are all in innovative

areas. Many are designers like myself, others are researchers, some—as you might hope, Ancil—are writers or, as we call them, 'namers,' since they don't really write the way you do, but spend their hours and days thinking up that quick phrase or single word that will both typify the item and strike the ear of the listener as desirable.

"People with the capacity for innovation, I think, always ask 'why?' Most people only ask 'what?' And the 'why' that we ask isn't the 'why is this so?' That would be too easy. We ask, 'why isn't it something else?' That's the impossible question that, I suppose, keeps us going."

That's about as much as I know about the Choice Program. I really don't know how it was structured in detail, or how a given item progressed from imagination to production. Carath will have to be satisfied with this much.

On my own interests: I'm reading now on mechanics, and simultaneously more on architecture, material left over a year from what I was reading last Summer. I've just finished, for the second time, *The Primer of Building Design*, understanding it far better nowadays than I did some years ago when I read it as background for *The Present Tense*. In fact, it rather inspires me. It didn't inspire me before, much as I wished then it would.

But it has a whole section on model building, for display as well as for structural testing. It occurs to me to build a model of Athlan, as well as I can remember it, for Carath to look at. It'll keep me quite busy this Winter. And Carath will have at least some idea of what I go on about, when I go on so much about Athlan, which I've been doing a great deal lately.

The Choice Program. Theras claimed: "I'm convinced it's what keeps all of us safe. Judging by the Owners I've known, which are too many, the One only knows what they'd do to us and to each other if they didn't have the Choice Program to browbeat."

I've had a recurring bad dream, and I've finally been able to recall it. But at first it made no sense to me: I seemed to be up on the roof—I know because, looking up from where I was, I saw the Broadcast tower—and then suddenly I was falling. But then I still found myself on the roof, though I seemed to be starting to climb down shakily. And at that point I'd always awake.

I've been up on the roof several times since I've been here, though not that often. For a while I couldn't decide to which time the dream referred. I've never fallen.

A year ago, just about now, though, I did go up to fix the hole in the roof over the summer-lounge end of the house. I'd been putting it off because the instructions in *The Practical Woman* were so elaborately careful that they seemed almost impossible for me to follow, given the relatively few carpentry tools I have. But among my readings last Summer in architecture I came across *Building and Rebuilding: Better Ways with Better Materials*, which had a much simpler set of procedures.

It stood to reason to follow this book instead of *The Practical Woman*, because the materials I had to use came from the lodge and were new. *Building and Rebuilding* had information on how to use them correctly—and if I'd gone my own way, I would have used them incorrectly—while *The Practical Woman*, of course, doesn't mention them at all. Laminated planking wasn't created until after the Confederation.

Though it seemed unrealistic, I wondered if I hadn't been dreaming about that repair. Perhaps, as it was once claimed of certain people, you can occasionally see in your dreams beyond the moment. Perhaps I was envisioning, by my sense of falling, that my repair would fail. After all, it was the one instance in which I abandoned *The Practical Woman* for another reference that was easier to follow.

I do recall that the notion nagged me a bit at the time. And, of course, I'm not that good at carpentry anyway.

Loren would have sworn the truth of that, since he was the first and only person ever to see the contraption I intended as a counter between my kitchen and lounge. I dismantled it the moment he took his ridicule and left.

But now I suppose I must admit the matter:

I was on the roof that afternoon, and I happened to look off across the valley at the Broadcast tower. The sky was clear overhead, but around the distant peaks were wisps of clouds that formed and reformed, buffeted quickly around and about by the wind. But though I knew what they were and kept telling myself how they came to be there, I slowly became convinced they were smoke, not clouds. They looked like smoke—I thought there must be a fire, and I began to shake so badly that I wanted to get down from the roof, lest I fall down. But I didn't dare move, for fear I would fall. And I just stared at the clouds of smoke.

I saw myself back in the grove in The Land, by Aren's father's house. The sky in the distance, above Athlan, was filling with clouds, as though heralding a summer storm. And I thought the clouds must be smoke, but they gave out with great, furious flashes of lightning. There was no thunder. I remember I decided it was both smoke and clouds.

The entire city was on fire, after all. I knew that because we'd watched it being set on fire on Information for as long as the cameras continued to function without operators. We watched for as long as the broadcast continued, for as long as there was power available, for as long as we could. It seemed so remote, so unlikely. There were a few close views, though cameras in a position to get such views seemed to go off as quickly as they'd come on. And I thought, if there are enough close views, Morin will have his chance. It was just that amount of unreality that kept me watching, looking for Morin in scenes. It was just that that kept us all watching, I think, each of us waiting for some sign that this was not Information.

Great black plumes rose up from the Research Compound, from the whole new City Center, and from the old one at Shopping and South. The family blocks, the office section, the new section, and the Workers' Section and my rooms in between those two—even the Workers' Section, for a change—the School, Maronnen's, The Place on the Embankment, my father's house, everything was in flames glowing through soot. And high over Athlan loomed black

110

and white thunderheads, moisture coalescing from the heat below. It was a natural atmospheric reaction, I thought then, what would be expected. Ath itself was making the attempt to stop this aberration.

As though paltry drops of rain could have an effect! They never seemed to reach even halfway to the ground before exploding in tiny bursts of white steam that rose back up into the clouds, to condense and fall again, and again. That was what I saw: a huge white mound supported on night-black columns, the columns graced with small white dots like snow or stars. That was what I was determined to see, all I wanted to see, all I saw.

And then I ran—there was a single burst of great light —lightning or an explosion, but no sound or none I heard —and I started at it, and then I ran. Waves of black began rippling away from the city out in all directions, over the outliers, over The Land, darkening everything they covered. But I could see, I could still see enough to make my way, to see what I had to avoid.

There were fliers in bands like tiny pesters hovering here and there, descending, rising, darting about together, bands of them approaching or fleeing one another. When one came to alight somewhere, its occupants would pile out, set fire to whatever they found, jump about a while, and chant: "Glorious! Glorious! Burn the deviants!" They'd climb back in, the flier would rise up and away to somewhere else. Then it would land again, the men clamber out again, set their fires again, and sing their songs. Again and again.

A large farm was set afire that way, an Owner's farm, one of the sort that Aren disapproved of. Fliers came and went, leaving the central installations flaring. And out in the field was a solitary, lumbering piece of machinery, mindlessly proceeding up and down its assigned rows, doing whatever the automatic control center had most recently instructed it to do—harvesting, weeding, tilling, I don't know. I wanted to shout to it, stop it as it continued its task, completely oblivious. But it rumbled on regularly for a while, and I hid in a windbreak and watched it.

At last, smoothly as though newly instructed, it turned a bit off course and began to meander across the rows, over the crops it was to care for, flattening them. It seemed to have decided there was no purpose in continuing its instructions, there was no longer any purpose to anything remaining as it had been. So the machine proceeded a bit, but then began to move this way and that, indecisively. I saw the control center flare up. The machine jerked forward, then stopped. Its instructions had stopped. It didn't know what to do, so it did nothing. I felt bad about that, but I couldn't help. So I went on myself.

As I reached the river I realized that I hadn't known what direction I'd been going in. But, oriented now, I couldn't decide in what direction to continue. Still, I crossed the river, floating across, as much as possible, to look as much like a dead body as possible. I knew it wasn't wise to look alive. And by floating I was carried a ways downstream north, toward Athlan. I reached the opposite bank just as I was in sight of the junction of the Peripheral Road and the Embankment. But I didn't stop to look over there. I knew already what was over there. I just got out and made my way, northwest, I thought, intending to go between Telennin and Paragathi, and thus avoid them both. But I was too far south, too close to Telennin.

People were being herded onto the Peripheral Extension and shot in the face, each in his turn being made headless, like so many items in a manufacturing process being dealt with the same way, regularly, one at a time. Those doing the herding cheered with each shot. When there were no more people to be herded, the herdsmen piled the bodies together and set fire to the pile. Several private cars gotten from somewhere were set to propel themselves into the pile. There were explosions and the odors of electricity and flesh.

I made my way around this until, farther along the Peripheral Extension, I could cross without being seen. Ahead there were more explosions. There was more of the same thing everywhere.

Once I was finally beyond the outliers, I hid myself in the underbrush and slept, and woke and thought, and slept more and woke again. I seemed clearheaded, almost lightheaded. But I'd lost all track of time. Whenever I woke, the distant sights and sounds were the same. Whenever I woke, it seemed always to be the same time of day, the dimness between afternoon and evening on a stormy day. Perhaps I never slept at all. Perhaps everything lasted as long as all that. I didn't know. But then I thought of the

112

lodge and decided to come here. It seemed to me best to travel at night, as much as possible.

I did travel at night after that, but I don't know if it was best. There were always fires in every rural center. There was always burning, people being hunted and burned, people hunting and burning. And it always seemed to be happening at night. I suppose it happened during daylight, too. It was just more visible in darkness.

I don't know how I managed to get here. I really wasn't sure I was going in the right direction, so I sometimes stayed awake long enough to judge by the position of sunrise. But even that was hard to do through the thick grey haze that seemed to be everywhere. The sun, when it rose, was pale, bloodless, a dim and indistinct patch of the sallowness of Larien.

I remember I wondered sometimes where all the people who were doing the killing were coming from, so many were being killed. But the farther I went, as I came across centers that had not yet been destroyed, there seemed to be fewer and fewer people, killers and victims. But I don't suppose now that I was as clearheaded as I thought. I seemed to come across more centers than I know there were. Perhaps I was moving in a circle for a while, passing the same center again and again. Or perhaps, when I slept, I recalled in dreams the centers I'd passed that night, and thereby doubled and redoubled my memory of them. But once I reached the foothills of this range there were no more centers, of course, and no more people, and no reason to wonder. Still, I continued to be careful, to travel only at night.

Once in one center I saw a fellow's flier taken so it could be used to add to one of the fires. From where I was I thought the fellow seemed to protest. He called over to a woman who seemed to be pregnant. They were both shot headless, and both they and the flier were added to the flames.

I think now that I often got too close to centers. I was risking a great deal, but I don't think I could have done anything else. There's a fascination I can't name, a fascination that I felt in watching. I seemed compelled to watch. There are so many ways to kill a person, and often several were tried on the same person.

113

I'm glad Aren's circumstance was different. It was more private, and much simpler than most.

All I suffered from was hunger, and nausea when I did manage to find something to eat in the ruins I came upon. Everything had a terrible odor to it, rather like the odor in the lodge, and I smelled it for a long time after I entered the foothills and left the dead far behind. It was in my clothes and on my skin.

I recall so much, but it seems everything is disjointed, disconnected, like one story after another on Entertainment, with no relationship among them.

In one instance I saw people being assembled in a House of the One—being dragged up, pushed in, kept in by those who were collecting them. But somewhere else people were crowded onto a landing area.

When the House was so full that not another person could be shoved in, it was set afire. When the landing area was so crowded that there was space for no one else, marauders began shooting and shooting, creating limbless, seared torsos, and afterward taking the remains of the bodies and throwing them in a pond, until there were more bodies than water to cover them.

I don't know when each of these incidents took place, or where, or whether they didn't both happen in the same location, or in my mind. I'm not even really sure now just how I did leave Aren's father's house, or why. It just seems that was what I did—that that was what I had to do and, thus, the reason that I did so.

But it seems I'm not really remembering. These events are just occurring to me, out of sequence, out of reason, like old photographs of a strange place now hurled at me in a bunch. I pick them up one by one and look at them and try to puzzle how they go together, if they go together.

Their coming back to me disturbs me, and I often fight to keep them away from me. But their coming back as dreams disturbs me more. I can fight them more easily awake than asleep. And what disturbs me the most is what I can think happened that I never did see happen, what my imagination can provide for what my memory lacks. I never saw the rest of my friends being killed. I never saw them at all, only Aren. But it's so easy to know how they died, each one of them. I saw so many ways to die. Somewhere among the examples is what happened to Morin, and Theras, and Lin, and Loren, and everybody. I know how my father died. And no doubt my mother as well.

But I must not allow myself to be victimized by my delusions. I nearly did fall off the roof that day. That was just about a year ago. And the disturbance just about three years ago today.

And I remember something else: the face I saw in the mirror the time the old water pump broke down—it was much the same face I saw in the mirrored sides of the lodge's entry hall when I first reached it. Disreputable. Dishonorable. The face of something other than myself. The face I have now.

Fall, Change 2: 24, 9506

Earlier this change I went up to the old sap house, about a half hour's distance, because I thought I'd remembered some logging equipment stored there. If I ever need firewood, I'll need sturdier tools than a handsaw. I found Carath hunting groundscurries, and all the while I'd assumed he was up at the lodge. Apparently he's going farther afield as he gets older. If that's the case, then perhaps he and I can go to the Broadcast tower after all.

But I was wrong: There were only things for syrup reduction, which I guess I'd mistaken for logging equipment. I didn't know anything about either when I was younger.

I did, however, find a large stand of brainnut trees that I'd completely forgotten. The nuts were ripe, so I gathered quite a supply—more than I think I can use, but that's all right, since I'm not depriving anyone else in my greed. They'll keep at least through Winter and vary my diet. *The Practical Woman* says that nuts are a good source of nourishment, and she has a number of recipes for preparing them alone as well as with meats and vegetables. I also found another bed of marshpillars—they were most of them gone by, but it's a good location to remember—and I found a number of treefans, which I didn't think grew in this area. On the whole, treefans are a rather bland fungus, but they're filling and fine mixed with vegetables.

The Practical Woman lists quite a number of ways of preparing them, but mostly with ingredients I don't have. Even Carath has decided treefans are relatively edible, if worse comes to worst, though he indicated he wouldn't want them as a steady diet. And he has no use for nuts at all.

The sap house would be a good place to put up bounder traps, if I can get Carath to agree to let bounders alone. They never come near the house anymore, which is fine for the garden's sake, but difficult in terms of my meals. And I'll have to make more traps.

It never occurred to me to wonder before why my father should have had a sap house built. As long as I've known it to be there, I've never known it to be used. But it looks as though it had been used at some time or another. Perhaps it was my mother's industry, another of them, though I seem to recall reading or having once been told that the process of reduction required a number of people, at least five. And I never remember homemade sweetenings, though I never trespassed my mother's kitchen with the idea of assessing her stores.

I might go through my father's papers to see if I can find some record or at least an indication of why it's there. It's become a curiosity to me, especially since it, along with my house, is quite Old Style, whereas the lodge, of course, was New Style entirely. In fact, to look at the ensemble of buildings comprising this retreat, you might think my house and the sap house were considerably older than the lodge. Of course, that couldn't be so—the difference must have been a quirk of my father's. But I've been apprehensive about going through his papers ever since I ran across Heremis's notes on regeneration and on myself. I'm not quite sure what all I'd find if I looked further, or if I'd want to find what I might.

The weather's turned colder now, with light snow last night, which didn't last. Midday, when it's warmer, I'll have to go about sealing my windows against drafts. I wouldn't have to worry about this now, but last Summer I knocked over the entire group of cover windows while rummaging about the summer lounge. I suppose things happen that way, though. If I hadn't destroyed them all at once, I would have lost them one at a time. I've really irretrievably lost a good many things in the last several years by my own clumsiness, however, and I must be more careful. Still, I've tried to be more and more careful, perhaps too careful. I broke the cover windows while searching for the source of the musty smell in the summer lounge. And I didn't find that, for all my efforts.

A very odd thing—I've begun to masturbate again, and it's embarrassing. I'd stopped, I don't know when, because it seemed so futile, just as I'd stopped talking or doing anything that's usually done when there's contact with people. I couldn't even fantasize another man after a while; I was afraid, if I tried hard, I would do too good a job of it. But now I can masturbate again. It must be because of Carath. But it's embarrassing.

I feel myself growing tense evenings, the way I used to a few years ago, and I go hide! Initially I couldn't recognize my problem. I lock myself in the bathroom, which perturbs Carath no end, since he's just like every other cat I've ever known of—he hates a closed door. His paw keeps reaching under the door, and he whines and chirrups angrily. But I don't want him to see me. I don't want him to know.

I'm even uncomfortable describing it here, as much as I would be were I to do it openly. It's terribly silly of me, but it's something very private. I can't really explain it to him and he does demand an explanation. He wants to know what I do in there by myself and makes himself an enormous pest afterward, nudging my leg, whining, getting up on my lap and sniffing about. I hate to keep this secret from him, but I'm afraid I must. He's out somewhere this morning, or I wouldn't even write about it. Isn't that ridiculous?

The situation is a bit reminiscent of Aren. When he finally invited me to his father's house, he warned me strictly in advance that we would not be having any sex whatever.

"You never know who's going to walk in. And Elenie still thinks she's got permission everywhere in the house, like she did when she was young. I don't think you want that.

"And I don't suppose I care so much that my parents know about me, but it's not something I ought to throw in their faces. I've established myself on my land, so what I do with myself is my own business. And I am thirty-three —a little old for an only son to be unmarried. They probably know, but there's a difference between their knowing and my telling them. I think you understand."

I did. But I can't exactly make that sort of explanation now. And not to a cat.

It does make me feel more at ease. It tires me, but in a different sort of way. It's a pleasant weariness, almost the way I used to feel with Aren.

Sometimes it's a strain, sometimes I lose the feeling midway, and it becomes a hopeless, blankly determined struggle. Yet I know that afterward, no matter how difficult it was in the process, I'll feel better, relaxed and ready to sleep. Sometimes it's almost obsessive.

I never think of Aren physically, or anyone really, but there seems to be a vague image in my mind. I don't know what. Maybe that's why I go by myself and exclude Carath: I can't actually tell him why I'm doing this strange thing. It's not strange, though. It's just something man does. And how can I explain that to a cat?

I rather dislike doing it, in a way, because it makes me make him a cat. He is a cat, and only a cat. Yet he is a companion and sufferer of my monologues. He is my partner in all this as no one except probably Aren could have been. But he is not like me, however I consider him. Masturbating puts a distance between us, and that distance makes me feel uncomfortable. It makes me sad.

But he's back, looking satiated. He must have caught something to eat, since he's gone over to the couch to sit in the sunlight and clean himself. He always looks so handsome there, because the bright morning sun makes his fur glow a deep, rich brown. That's why I always think he looks like Lin.

I'd better put this away so he doesn't inquire.

Winter, Change 4: 6, 9506

I have Athlan almost complete after not a little difficulty. But I foolishly started on the wrong scale, so it's now rebuilt in fully one-half of the bedroom above the winter lounge. The model is only of the city itself; the four outliers would never fit. I can't even include the new development beyond the Peripheral Road.

Everything had to be rearranged. I still don't know where I'm going to store much of the stuff I've had to pile to one side and down the stairs. I suppose I can put a lot of it in the dining room. I never do take my meals there. And a lot of it can go in corners of my bedroom, too. This is a much larger task than I anticipated, and I hope Carath appreciates it.

It does pass Winter's changes well, though.

Carath, very curious about the model of Athlan, is yet very respectful of it. He doesn't get up on it, as I thought he would. Instead, he sits on the floor and stares up at the platform it's on, purring approvingly, or he crouches on my shoulder and gazes down on it. I think it's quite a good job myself. It's certainly the product of great inventiveness.

I thought it would be a good deal simpler, but the materials necessary—the lack of them, that is—posed an enormous problem. I decided on wood as the basic substance out of which to build the blocks and public buildings, since I have an unlimited supply of it around and about. It's much more difficult to work with than I'd supposed, however, so the first curves I chiseled out look rather erratic. But once I got used to it, it went rather better and more quickly. Models like this were always made of paperboard, not of stayalive. I haven't any paperboard, of course, though of course I now know why it was used.

Then there was paint.

The Practical Woman provides formulas for every conceivable color, but naturally the primary ingredients she uses I don't have and can't get. There are lists of alternatives for many of the substances—plants mostly, but some other things, like rust, copper corrosion, powdered stone— and I've been able to find many of them. But sadly, in some cases when alternatives are acceptable, a dye rather than a paint is produced, so I had to experiment with thickening my results until I could get something that adhered to a surface like a paint, rather than ran off or soaked in to disappear almost entirely. Still, at times it was amusing doing some of the things she recommended.

"BRIGHT YELLOW: To every whole-jewel of water necessary add five jewel-weights of wasteberries; boil until color is thorough, then add chloride of tin to desired brightness."

First I had to locate a wasteberry bush, which I did, rather uncomfortably far afield, near one of the blighted areas at the beginning of the wastelands two hours up the valley. I would never have gone such a distance except that my determination led me to lose track of time. But I secured a large quantity of berries so I wouldn't have to repeat my trip. Then I spent several days in a moderately successful attempt to dissolve part of a tin container in a cleanser having an indeterminate amount of hydrochloric acid, or what became hydrochloric acid when I added water. I put everything together as instructed and produced the most peculiar shade I've ever seen, a yellow that virtually glows in the dark, it is so bright. In strong light I'm not even certain it's yellow but, as happened with the origin of the terms Light and Dark, my eyes are registering an opposing color due to the intensity of whatever it really is. Oh, well, it seems yellow, and that's all that matters.

"SILVER GREY: Expose to the weather in an iron pot of four or five whole-jewels capacity old iron nails, useless machinery parts, or other such scraps, until all is covered with rust; afterward add one whole-jewel of clear cooking acid, two of water, and boil all together for an hour; put the object to be dyed in a solution of sulphate of iron, pour iron acid in, add four jewel-weights of powdered stonewood galls; then boil up more of the iron acid to renew the strength of the combination, boiling the combination itself 2 hours each day until the required color is obtained."

I did all that. I could barely stand the odor in the kitchen, and Carath spent as little time indoors as possible. The sulphate of iron I concocted with more old nails and a medicinal ointment of my mother's which certainly smelled as though it had sulphur in it. The One only knows why I should have eventually obtained a silver grey out of all this, let alone that it's such a lovely shade. But I now have it, and a great deal of it.

When I came to creating other colors, I did not make them in such large quantities. And that also helped to make the work much simpler.

Then there was glue, which wasn't difficult to produce, but was time-consuming and a nuisance to store so it wouldn't dry up by itself. And there were certain special wood tools I either had to locate among my stores or make improvisations of. And paintbrushes small enough for my purposes. And the means to sharpen my ever-dulling knife blades. I cursed out loud at one point, I was so frustrated with every new thing I needed, and I ranted about the house a whole day on the subject of things I couldn't have, couldn't make, things which no longer existed. I suddenly even wanted a drink; even plain distilled alcohol—I wouldn't have cared—seemed suddenly appealing, though I would never have dreamed of drinking such stuff un-mixed before. Virtually no one did, alcohol is so unpalat-able by itself.

But I calmed down eventually. Under the circumstances I don't really need anything ready-made. I've time enough to make most things myself, given the instructions. All I need is the patience.

Carath was mightily perturbed at my behavior, however, and when I was quiet once more, he began to deliver what seemed like a very stern dissertation on acting sensibly. At least he made a good many disapproving noises for a good length of time. I finally had to explain to him the problem, though cats have never been known to have such a prob-lem.

I've never realized how much I'd taken for granted. There were so many staples in life—like glues—that were so basic they weren't even included in the Choice Program. You could simply get them anywhere, even in food shops. Paints weren't a matter of Choice, either. You just had a color made up when you wanted it. Paper supplies weren't, perhaps, so common—though I recall seeing paperboard around and about in what, I suppose, were unlikely places, like markets. But I knew just where to go to get whatever I needed, or I contacted City Services to ask where it might be found.

Everything could be found in Athlan. I always assumed the same was true of the other cities as well, though I sup-pose it wasn't quite true. Theras, I recall, and even Loren mentioned now and then something they hadn't been able to get when they were younger. But I never knew such a lack. Almost by definition, Athlan lacked nothing.

More than that, though, with so many New Owners so ready to make their reputations, you could get certain special things if you wished, just by specifying what you had in mind. This was always done with jewelry, and the cost was only slightly more, unless you were extravagant in your desires. And, of course, the craftsmen of Ranoas would make things up for you completely by hand, though only very Old Style things.

A model such as I'm making would probably have been quite expensive to buy, but that's due to its size as much as to anything. There were toy cities for children, I recall —replicas of smaller cities such as Heremia, or Lakeside on Great Ocean—and even a model of the whole Lesser Island of Corona, but the scale was much tinier and the detail far less than I've tried to achieve.

I miss having all that. I do. It's not that I'm not interested in doing for myself. What else is there to do with my time, outside of my regular chores? It's just that I'm inexperienced—though I'm sure I'll improve as time goes on— and my inexperience in so many things makes them all seem so much harder to accomplish, even to imagine attempting. But I've built this model, of all things—and isn't it intrinsically useless? And I've done it for a cat! Well, but I don't know that I'm capable of doing anything strictly for myself, anything like this.

That comes of writing books, I suppose. I never could envision myself just making my own way through the world like everyone else, doing my work to collect my rate so that, afterward, I could afford to do something entirely different. I have to have someone to write to—I have to have someone to do things for, beyond my own survival. So I've made that someone Carath.

Aren once said that he could appreciate the way Ranoas held to the very oldest ways: "What they do, they do for everyone, not just for themselves. The plantings, all that they do under City Services, the farming, the old things they make—as much as I personally dislike workers, I often admire them. Nowadays they don't have to do that kind of work. There are machines that can do a lot of it, though I hate those machines myself. And a lot of it is just pretty: the plantings on the Embankment, along the avenues and radials—no one notices how carefully those are done, though people would notice if they weren't done carefully. But to Ranoas this kind of work matters, the care matters, and I guess the results matter, though they never stay around to enjoy what they've done. I figure they do it all because that's the way they think—it's for everyone. If you left it to Galien, the world would be a mess in no time."

I surely hope Carath appreciates what I've done.

Winter, Change 5: 1, 9506

Besides closed doors, Carath seems to have taken a dislike to anything he cannot get at. He opens any book I leave on a table top, pulling back the cover and pushing his way through the pages, one after another in impatient haste, as though, with each one turned, something hidden would be revealed. When he reaches the end, he turns the back cover over to close the book, then pushes it off the table top in great, annoyed disappointment at not having discovered anything other than a sheaf of paper with lines of black marks everywhere. If only he could read. Or if only I could convey to him that that's what books are for. But of course, I cannot: To him books are for telling, for being read from out loud, to provide his enjoyment. I suppose he assumes there are things in them from which I draw my descriptions, rather than words and words about things. He grows irate that he cannot play with words. I must sympathize; even I have trouble doing that sometimes.

And now he insists on opening drawers, all drawers, everywhere. He will spend hours prying away at one until he finds a way to get it open. Then he noses about inside, sometimes removing one thing or another to the floor, where he examines it or tries to eat it, sometimes tumbling things out as he burrows deeper in his search for the quintessential plaything. I found the kitchen littered with utensils after one of his quests. Another time he'd spread all my shirts and undergarments about my bedroom. He's also upset the careful order inside my desk, and that rather often. That's especially a nuisance, but he does have a particular fascination for those supplies—paper fasteners, which he loves to rattle about the floor; erasers, which he loves to gnaw on and will often hide under the corner of a

123

carpet; gummed labels, the taste of which appeals to him; cloth-backed reinforcing strips, which he holds down by one end while shredding from the other.

I can't really blame him. Under other circumstances I, too, might do the same thing. I often suspect myself of just such a careless pastime as his when it comes to the technological devices I now tinker with. But, though I've never been a person concerned with great neatness—my mind has to be the most disarrayed object in the universe—I've always felt the need to put almost everything in order around and about myself, simply so I can find it when I want it. Should it occur to me suddenly to have a particular color of ink or a particular binder or something as basic as mending strips, I want to be able to locate it immediately. If I must search, quite often I will eventually run across the thing in question, only to find I've forgotten why I wanted it. Then I must sit and consider the cause of my searching. This is a waste of time.

Wasting time is something I've always been good at. My foremost ability, however, takes a different complexion nowadays.

It's also quite frustrating, especially if I'm in the midst of writing something. I'll lose that well-modulated phrase, or the sequence of my argument, or even the whole concept, if I must endure the bother of hunting for some ridiculous item. And when I'm reading, especially when I'm reading all this inordinately complex scientific material, I lose my mental place if I'm too long away from the text. Then I must return to the start of the section, sometimes to the previous section. And sometimes, while I'm off looking for whatever it is I want, Carath will pull out my bookmark. He's fiendish that way.

He's also disturbed my tools in the past so that, if I need something quickly because the task at hand requires a certain precise timing, or it's a delicate operation that I cannot abandon even for a ten-tenth, but I cannot find what I want, I must virtually begin all over again. This always seems to happen when I'm fusing wires, or when I've reached an enigmatic junction on a circuit sheet. It is infuriating.

But I've solved that problem to an extent by securing my tools in wood boxes I've made, into which he cannot get, or by shutting him out of the room in which I'm working

—the latter something which infuriates him. I often have a sense of perverse pleasure in doing that, though I don't know why.

He is so extraordinarily inquisitive, I occasionally find it almost stimulating to keep a project from his prying. My mind nearly literally tingles; I feel myself breathing more rapidly; a sense like excitement or anticipation rises physically from my abdomen. It's a peculiar reaction to a measure so completely pragmatic, and I've sometimes considered that it might be just that I never had a cat before, nor did my parents have one, so I'm only still reacting to the personal newness of the experience of Carath. I haven't had him a year yet. But I really do think it's the result of my having been so long without contact with people and without the normal reactions that go with it. I haven't had that for three and a half years. Such things must build up without the usual outlets and then begin to manifest themselves suddenly, unexpectedly, aberrantly.

I know I've succumbed to fits of hysterical laughter over occurrences which, while amusing or ridiculous, aren't all that funny. The morning Carath first was out in a snowfall, snapping at the flakes as though they were pesters—it was laughable, but I giggled for nearly one whole hour.

That reminds, me, though, of the first time he discovered snow existed. That wasn't quite so funny.

It was late evening, and we were listening to a ribbon, and I was reflecting absently on a whole host of things as usual. Carath abruptly jumped to his feet and dashed for the door to the side yard. He all but bashed into it, and began jumping up and down at it, as though trying to catch something. I was startled, and I stared a good long moment, until I decided he had lost his mind. He has no more contact with his own kind than I have with mine, and that's bound to have its results. But he chattered and squeaked and leapt and pawed, so I finally went to see what was the matter.

I opened the door and found a snow flurry; Carath, seeing the bits of swirling white, instantly went to hide. But he must have seen the snow, "seen" it through a solid door. It was the following morning I tossed him out into the middle of it, much to my enjoyment. Then he accustomed himself to it, as only a cat can, by trying to overwhelm it.

Now, I know cats see far into the infrared. After I'd

considered it a bit, I realized he must have "seen" the snow through the door as flickering against a background, the warmer door itself. But it bothered me because, knowing cats should be able to do this, I'd yet never witnessed the ability before. I was only cognizant that they can see perfectly well in the dark, which is no mean feat, to be sure, but an easier fact to grasp than their being able to "see" through solid objects. "The cat sees into nothing / And discerns the shape of things," but I'd never thought of it that way. Small wonder Imitators found cats so useful, and a pity man never sought to capitalize on this talent.

But then, how do you get a cat to do what you want it to do? There's a great deal of evidence the Imitators had persuasive means of some sort, and a great deal of evidence that I absolutely do not. Animals do have ways of communicating with one another which have nothing to do with sound, sight, or smell. This has been demonstrated. But what those means might be was never determined. Nobody bothered finding out, for the means would be useless, since man does not share them. It was sufficient to know that such a thing happened, as it aided animal husbandry and hunting techniques. But, of course, it does make Imitators more "animal."

On the other hand, in the earliest Daily Texts, there were references to certain "honored men" who apparently had the capacity for something or another like this: the Thinkers of the One, "they who draw out the wisdom of the stories for us, and who see things together which many men cannot but they must be shown"; the Speakers of the One, "they who can explain things by touching them, and who can reach outward to the One and bring back present wisdom"; the Eyes of the One, "they who can see beyond into what may be and bring back future wisdom." Such persons seemed to have talents similar to those cited in Imitator texts, talents which were considered everyday occurrences by Imitators and were spoken of only when a particular Imitator didn't possess them. Imitators referred to such unfortunates among them as "retarded" or "atavistic," depending upon your preference of translation.

But as far as men are concerned, we don't know what these talents amounted to specifically, other than what they were said to accomplish. And such "honored men" were entirely discredited soon enough, anyway. They were considered charlatans and were even referred to as "Imitators" themselves. In fact, at least at the earliest times, they may well have been Imitators, if they weren't always Imitators. Such "honored men" fell into disrepute at around the same time that we exterminated the Imitators.

However, none of this sounds like anything that would help a person get a cat to follow a particular order. And anyway, "Cats have no whims," Morin used to say as his cat would stalk about his rooms, "they have plans, plans for everything. And if something doesn't fit into their plans, it's a whim, and they'll have nothing to do with it. Men have whims—the only thing men have are whims. And cats know this, and they tolerate it, but only barely. The sooner we know it too, the better off, I think, we'll all be."

But this is way off my present problem.

From a drawer recently Carath extracted my standard set of tablets, pried the box open, and spread them across the floor of the winter lounge. He didn't chew on any of them, thank the One! He wandered about inspecting each one.

When I entered the room, he promptly sat down in the midst of them and started squalling, indicating he wanted to know what they were. My first reaction was despair—I do so treasure that set, even though I'm really no good at tablets. Aren was. But after I'd collected and counted them to make sure the set was intact, I felt better.

Carath has since made a nuisance of himself about them, though. He goes to the drawer in which they're kept and paws at it repeatedly. I've secured the drawer against him with a thin wedge of wood, and he doesn't like that a bit. But I can't determine how to explain them. Tablets as played is a complicated enough subject, even if I refrain from going into what they connote besides in a family practice.

But perhaps I can avoid explaining them, if I just explain tablet games as being pastimes. Tablets was the only pastime shared by both second sons and Second Sons, and no one else played them except daughters who preferred the much simpler games with the five set. First Sons considered tablet games to be vulgar. And the One only knows if Ranoas indulged in them. Neither Nata nor Lin could remember.

Explaining pastimes in general is even easier—even if I

never indulged in them much myself, unless you consider my writing, as my father did. Most often I preferred to watch. I guess I've always preferred watching to participating, which is either less strenuous or less expensive.

The pastimes of Second Sons besides tablets were very arduous: ocean fishing, hunting, and the running sports. But they were, after all, the representatives of their Families in the ancient Judgment Games. I went ocean fishing just once, from Port South, in the company of three second sons of my acquaintance on Great Ocean and upwards of forty Second Sons, who anyone might have gathered were all drinking-and-relay associates.

It was all very boorish, though I was alleged to have caught a respectably sized jumper—I was never sure, since it was struggling at the end of a tangle of lines that merely included mine. But I was awarded it, and we had it dressed and cooked for us after the sortie. Otherwise, the event consisted mainly of Second Sons, rather sotted on slow-foam, wielding gaffs, nets, and poles, and talking of their athletic and sexual prowesses. They none of them really looked capable of either.

The pastimes of second sons, however, required little physical effort. Chiefly they amounted to gaming of one sort or another. Second Sons did wager on their footraces, but we wagered on things we didn't have to do much about, like casting sticks or the chance tables. I didn't do either, since I never had the money.

The most activity a second son got was on shore walks or in bed. Shore walks in the evening under the stars by a placid ocean always struck me as something that should have been heterosexual, though it never was. I didn't like walking on sand, when there was sand, and along most shorelines I would invariably trip on the rocks. There is nothing more disastrous for the casual encounter than a display of great ungracefulness. When I was on the Islands, I always tried to stay back to listen to singers.

The other ordinary pastimes—music, painting, sculpture —were indulged in by many, including an increasing number of Second Sons like Beskin Elarin. The results were rarely better than mediocre, though. Like writing, I thought, you had to have some ability, though no one, except people like Theras, agreed with me on that. The best work in those areas was usually accomplished by women.

128

Of my sort of fellows the best that could be said was that their efforts didn't appear to be frivolous, though they yearned to be said to be earnest. That was considered a high compliment.

Yes, I think I will explain tablets in this context. It's easier, both on Carath and on me. And this way I won't have to try to explain the origin of the terms "Light" and "Dark," which I would if I got into the family colors of the tablets. Even the most intelligent would balk at Galien being "Dark" when their color was gold, and Paren being "Light" when ours was black. To make sense I'd have to go into the history of the Judgment Games and all that. I'd rather not just now. Those were not pastimes.

But I see I'm starting to second-guess what Carath is likely to want to know more about, or at least what he's liable to make the most noise over. How ever could I assume I could do that? I guess I'm just trying to limit the range of my disquisitions so I won't ramble on. No one has ever known what's on a cat's mind, let alone in advance of something coming to his mind.

Winter, Change 5: 12, 9506

I'm preparing for the New Year. Carath has stimulated me into this project, and it should be at least interesting, as long as I have the time to get everything ready. It's just half a change away.

There are still occasional flurries, but most snow has already melted. This last change has been exceptionally warm and, barring another storm of midwinter proportions, Spring will be under way before the first day of it. Already the yellow clarion and white horn have sent up shoots. They should be in bloom by Spring, 1: 1, as they were every year in Athlan, unless a severe freeze sets in. I think those two survive simple frosts.

In the woods the endurance-of-man is up and also the stench leaf. But the stench leaf is the first before anything, according to *The Practical Woman*:

"This plant would seem useless, it has so many disagreeable aspects. The odor of it is nearly unbearable, smelling like the corners of a market two days after the last produce has been sold. Pesters of all sorts swarm about its leaves when they are bruised. Yet the stench leaf does good, in addition: It has the ability to generate enormous quantities of heat from the beginnings of its growth, which is the reason that, when you walk through a woods still deep in snow, you will see pits melted out, from which glows a radiant green in bright sunlight.

"This has always been encouraging to man weary of long Winter who wishes reassurance that the world will be verdant once more. This also provides warmth to the ground just about the plant, thereby providing the element most essential to the early arising of the endurance-of-man, which comes up to surround each stench-leaf plant with its chalices of leaves, from the centers of which reach forth stems bearing the delicate and delicately scented purple blossoms. In this you can see how the world attempts to provide good qualities for bad things, and how it further makes even the worst give comfort to the better.

"As for the endurance-of-man, it is so named because, when conditions are harsh, each plant is male, as it was with our First Father before the creation of woman. Only the male has strength to endure adverse conditions; the feminine is thus protected, as it should be. When circumstances improve sufficiently around and about the plant, it becomes female and fertile, ensuring the continuance of its kind in the best possible situation.

"But you must be warned not to tamper with the ways of this plant, as you should know not to try to alter the ways of the world and of the One. Should you desire these in your own garden, know that transplanting will cause the endurance-of-man to revert to its maleness again, even if it be in the full of its female aspect. And it will remain male, often for years, until it once again senses that its environment is comfortable enough for its feminine form to appear. So it is also with women in the progress toward the Last Forming: They will always be fewer than men until all the world follow the way of the One together. Then shall men and women be born equally and the Last Forming commence."

I often feel sorry for *The Practical Woman* in her devotion to the way of the One. Otherwise, I would be overcome by a peryerse amusement at her hopes.

If Spring comes before its time, I must be prepared to begin my garden again. This year I must also cultivate those parts of the woods where I've found berry bushes, to make certain they flourish for me. Not that I doubt they would without my help. They've obviously grown by themselves for years. But if I can make them grow better, my provisions increase.

The only limit to my provisions is the extent of my means of storing them. I must figure the number of preserving containers I have—glass and synthetic—and the amount of space in my freezers here. And also the amount I can store in the cold room in the cellar below the dining room. Fallfruit, darts, and weepers will keep there quite a while.

But I'm really coming to hate darts and fallfruit. It's just that they are so filling and grow so well. I wish I had a way of getting sweet fat or some other such flavoring for them. But there are no wobblers—I don't know that they ever were wild. And bred as they were for plumpness, I doubt any survived without man's care. They could no longer fly, if they ever could, and I don't think they'd have known how to nest if it weren't in a man-made roost.

Well, but even if Spring is here early, I can still find time to arrange a New Year procession in Athlan for Carath. I've many of the details already made. I've even a small piece of crystal suitable to represent the Great Jewel of Athlan on the Embankment. And there will be songs, of course, though far from the proper ones. I'll have to supply the drumming somehow, which will make Sanse Karlin in particular sound most strange. But there'll be no Heralds, and no pursuers, and no crowds along the Embankment.

But he'll have the idea, the sense of it all. And I'll make crowds for him out of my memories of them. In fact, I'll have him witness the last New Year in Athlan, the one I recall the best. I can use words to create what I can't reconstruct by hand. Isn't that, after all, what you can do with words?

At 9503 there was a crowd of us: Morin and Theras, of course, and Theras's latest, a little fellow named Benjorin somebody, who looked like Salis, naturally, but was smarter. Loren was there with two friends, the companions

131

Hansin Selemis and Keneris whatever-his-family-was. And, of course, there was Paras. What would an event be without Paras, if Loren attended? And Heller, the ever-present, enigmatic Heller, he was with us, too.

We were among the first there, arriving while it was still morning, bearing the parts of the extravagant "small" meal Theras had prepared for us, saving room for passing friends and watching Morin apologize for our continual intrusion on nearby strangers with his solemn: "It's the way of the One, my friends. You won't mind."

Soon there came by a friend of mine, Sor Devlin, a second son who lectured biology at the School. And two of his colleagues came with him, a Second Son and a First Son, of all sorts of people to bring into our midst. But they proved to be quite pleasant people, and when Morin discovered that they found him genuinely funny, then nothing mattered, even when Paras hinted rudely that he admired one of them. Morin explained that Paras was congenitally blind, which solved the problem by shutting Paras up.

Beskin and Mila joined us too, after a while. Mila thought we were all adorable, and she and Theras gossipped designs and styles for hours. Beskin allowed that he could see the attraction we had for one another, and in general was very jovial. "If you were all just Second Sons," he told me, "you'd all be drunk by now, and I'd be bored."

They brought with them another couple like themselves whose names I've long since forgotten, but who seemed to be quite pleasant people. Beskin and Mila as a pair were rather the heterosexual Theras: forever dragging out into public married couples they knew who'd never been here or there, and who often didn't know what to make of where they were.

As that morning went on—as we ate our way through it, that is—even more people joined us, friends and then friends of friends. By the first hour of Midday there must have been thirty-five or forty of us in a sizable oasis of food and drink. Most of them, like Theras, came with "small meals" ample enough for quite a number.

Around us were thousands, some in small groups, but no group as large as ours. Most were there as families. And we were positioned directly in front of the enclosure for the Great Jewel of Athlan, right in the center of the Embankment. Thus, we could see a great distance in each direction, but we still enjoyed front table for the Destruction of the Imitators. That would be the high moment, something that had to be seen up close.

At last, at the second hour of Midday, the procession began. Two formations of four hundred Heralds danced toward one another from the ends of the Embankment. Each half of the procession was the same: a band of Heralds for each of the four Families, every band divided into ranks for each Family's secondaries. In the lead was Galien. Its golden banner was the first thing you saw in the distance. And the first thing you heard was the bright sound of the Heralds' bell stalks, their silver bells chiming frantically as the dancers bore them forward, stepping and spinning, in those eccentric movements that were our parody of the way Imitators were supposed to have walked.

Galien's dance was measured, staid, extravagantly elegant, but of stately patterns that showed more attention to the progress of the Family's ranks than to the virtuosity of the individuals who made up those ranks. Galien and its secondaries—Heremis, Barenillen, and Akaror—came toward us haughtily from both sides. Those of Galien in the crowd along the pathway shouted greetings. Paras did, and Loren started to, but he stopped when Paras became overloud, as though trying to outshout his twin. He seemed too obvious about it. There were so few of Galien in Athlan that their shouts were more like lone cries than encouragement, and the more exuberant you were, the more you stood out. Osir Heremis, I suppose, was shouting, too, but I didn't have to see him that day.

Behind Galien—and after each of the four Families—were musicians and singers performing the appropriate Family songs. This music came up from the distance, muted at first by the sound of the bell stalks, but louder and louder until the bell stalks returned to being merely another instrument in the ensemble. Galien's songs were most solemn—they were said to be the oldest in form. They amounted to chord progressions that shifted along the scale, and their words made simple statements of the intentions for man and of the way of the One.

Next came Larien with its orange banner fluttering and its ranks of secondaries for Sarandor and Amaris, the whole Family appearing, at least to me, like a poor copy of its superior. Even the chiming from it sounded weaker. Salis, of course, gave a shout, or tried to, but he only managed to sputter through a mouthful. He ate almost compulsively and never gained weight, a feature which Theras envied. But Salis had black hair.

Larien's dances, like their songs, were meticulously rendered and might have been even exciting. But like Larien itself, the performance of them lacked a certain energy. It made the sentiments sung seem lackluster, as though Larien didn't believe the thinking it espoused. I was glad to have them pass behind the enclosure and fall in line next to Galien along the city side of the pathway.

Then Menes came forward. Its crimson banner waved wildly. Its Heralds danced with that peculiar to-and-fro motion that made me always think they were actually on a boat. Their songs had that rolling cadence, too. And the ranks of Orkanis, Larsanis, and Fargas broke apart from one another at every intersection of an avenue to step out in movements peculiar to each. The Family and its secondaries appeared to be as individual from one another as each of the four Families. And as Menes was a fairly large proportion of Athlan's population, the shouts flowed along the length of the crowd like ripples returning to where a stone had been dropped.

Behind the musicians of Menes was Paren, my Family. I actually cheered to see the black banner held aloft, though I had never been involved with the Family to such an extent. I think it was the moment and the slow-foam. And Morin began to cheer with me at the sight of Mekthedden itself. At that, I stood, and he stood too, and we shouted and shouted in foolish glee, even after Mekthedden passed and we were encouraging Seternis.

Our music, of course, I liked the best. It was the loudest and boldest, the newest in form and the most compatible in sentiment. It used far more horns and more resounding drums and could be heard from such a distance that it sounded even over the last of the songs of Menes. To be truthful, now, the songs of Paren sounded a good deal like the music that could sometimes introduce and conclude an Entertainment Broadcast, but even so, it moved me most. But isn't that what a Family's songs were supposed to do? Or was I merely trained without my knowing it to respond to them because they were of my Family?

134

All this was impressive, to be sure, but we were actually waiting for Paren's musicians to finally pass behind the enclosure, because then would come the Rout of the Imitators and the Destruction before the Great Jewel. This was history: a stylized representation of the assault and burning of En-Marab-i-Bar, the Imitator city on the Eastern Sea. That was the chief event in the ancient destruction, though the last of the Imitators were actually forced into the water, where they drowned. But the majority were burned with their city.

It's a most vile history. I never realized that until now. At the time, at that New Year, it was an entertainment.

During the Rout, men dressed in furs as Imitators were chased in a zigzag course along the Embankment, often through sections of the watching crowd, pursued by others dressed in the colors of the four Families. There were musicians who walked along the center of the pathway, but no singers, and they played quite loudly together in a form of music never heard otherwise. It was said to be Imitator music, but I doubt that. I know Imitators never used instruments like ours, and I feel quite certain even the melodies themselves did not come from that source. But the music did fit the scene: alien, unsettling, and not entirely harmonious.

Those of the Families bore fire-red clubs with which they mimicked the beating and burning of the adversary. When the whole ensemble reached the steps of the enclosure, the Imitators sought refuge, and one by one they were touched by the clubs and "burned to death." At each touch an "Imitator" crumpled.

When the last of them was killed, the dome of the enclosure opened to reveal the Great Jewel, a stupendous piece of crystal that sparkled fiercely in the Midday sun. If all had gone well, this happened at the middle of the third hour of Midday when the sun was directly overhead. The refractions cast multicolored light great distances in every direction. My father said that this was the one evidence of man that could be seen from the void, and that at that moment at Midday, as Midday progressed from Athlan west around the world, you could see the slow progression of sparks like flashes of stars across the face of Ath.

Last in the procession was the Family Ranoas. Actually, none of Ranoas would take part, so they were represented by men of Paren. There was the single pink banner, but there were no secondaries—or none that we knew of—but just a single group of Heralds bearing bell stalks, who danced the most complex and beautiful steps by far. They crossed among themselves in interweaving patterns—now a circle, now a square, now a triangle, now in turn each of the initials of the four Families.

When they reached the enclosure, they each took an Imitator and led him away, cleaning up, as it were, after their superiors. And with that the procession was done, the New Year inaugurated with much beating of drums and death.

I can't avoid mentioning the Imitators. I hope Carath doesn't take umbrage. I hope he doesn't even know what I'm talking about.

The New Year of Athlan was the only one shown on Information in that time area. Those processions of Inland, North, Westland, and Stes, and of Port South and Lakeside on Great Ocean, were, as a consequence, rather meager in comparison and less attended. And it was reshown in every succeeding time area on Entertainment, as the middle of the third hour of Midday reached those places. More people saw ours than saw their own.

If only I had a visual ribbon of it, then I could show Carath a sample of the reality. But my description will convey the impressiveness of it adequately. I'm sure he'll have an idea. And I simply won't tell him what all of it means.

Spring, Change 2: 14, 9507

The garden is planted once more. I've enlarged it into the side yard by the winter lounge for no other reason than that I had the extra seeds and tubers. It means a good deal more work, but a good deal more food, too, and I have all Summer to plan for its storage.

For a moment I thought it a little extravagant, since I could never eat everything I'll grow, over next Winter, even with Carath's help. But the more there is, perhaps, the better the possibility of attracting bounders back to the vicinity. Now they seem not to frequent even the woods nearby, though a fair number have been caught in my traps out by the sap house. I've spoken to Carath about this, but he appears to deny any responsibility for their shying away.

I'm beginning plans for a watercourse from the lodge's well. The water is there, and if I can't get it out by bringing it up, I can start digging horizontally into the wellspring, downslope from the lodge, to draw it out by gravity, then build a course to my house across the small depression between. That way I can set up a sort of irrigation system for the enlarged garden, a system which will be less work to maintain than the greater effort I must now make to water it from my own supply. Additionally, I may one day need such a facility for my own use, when I can no longer bring water up from my own well. That possibility, of course, is real, however much I tend to forget about it.

The other day I examined myself in the bathroom mirror again. I'm still twenty-eight years old. There is not a sign of difference. I'm not getting old, although I'm now nearly thirty-two—I will be on Summer 4: 19. I felt like avoiding the mirror ever after, but I need it, of course, to trim my hair and beard. I'll just have to avoid looking at myself. I look like someone else for looking exactly the same as I did about four years ago.

Curiously, I have a new weed sprouting in the garden. It's not really a new one—I know what it is. I've just never seen it here before, and I can't imagine where it came from. According to *The Practical Woman*, who gives it short shrift, "This nameless growth has no value to man whatever, but is said to have been a staple vegetable of Imitators and other animals. However, not even a herder will nibble at it. Further, it is not good ground cover, as its stems break easily even in a light wind, laying bare the earth to erosion. If you find it, rid yourself of it immediately. It is pernicious."

Since I came here from Aren's father's house, I might have inadvertently brought a seed or a seed pod, which had gotten trapped in some fold of my clothing that morning Aren and I walked through his field. That weed intruded on some of his land. But that presupposes a rather unbelievable chain of fortuitous circumstances which I am not prepared to believe. In my trek, I should think, nothing like that could have remained with me. My clothing was

137

tattered when I arrived here. There was hardly enough of it left to have folds for trapping.

Or the seeds might have been brought here windborne, I suppose. They're certainly lightweight enough. But what's especially curious is that, where it's already established, it looks as though it had been planted there purposely, right along the edge of my garden, like a hedge.

It's also occurred to me ridiculously that, since I have attempted to model my garden as best I can on what I remember of Aren's far larger land, the weed has appeared out of nothing, has been created out of my imagination, as it were, in order that my garden have an even closer resemblance to my model.

But that is absurd in the extreme. As Heremis might put it: "Nothing is spontaneously generated."

I'll have to keep it in check, but I don't think I'll try to eradicate it, contrary to *The Practical Woman*'s advice, and much, I'm sure, to what would be Aren's horror. He did so emphatically dislike it. It is, after all, rather appropriate to its setting. Though of all things that might remind me of Aren this must certainly be the most ludicrous.

In any event, I cannot discover the weed elsewhere in the area. However it's started, this seems to be where it has started, and that suggests that I ought not interfere with it, which is equally ludicrous, if pleasantly enough sentimental.

I dislike sentimentality. Writers always relied on it, but Darks were generally prone to it. Women and second sons, who were the only people who ever read much, adored it as a rule. It gets in the way of sense. And certainly, had I been sentimentally obsessed, I should never have accomplished even what little I've done here. I should have been crushed at my experience.

But perhaps a little sentimentality isn't such a bad thing, so long as it's oblique enough not to cloud my thinking. If I keep the plant in check—if I can—I see no harm in it. And maybe it will attract bounders. *The Practical Woman* does call it "a staple vegetable of Imitators and *other animals*."

I don't suppose my garden really does look like Aren's land, though. I only had the one opportunity to examine his field—that morning—even if I can—and do—remember every detail of all those hours. But I have in my own way tried to utilize the techniques I observed or that he told me of. And I seem to have had success, even though the terrain is rather different.

His land was divided into plots separated from one another by earthen mounds running the length and breadth of the area. Each plot was exactly the same size. Each consisted of neat, equally spaced furrows, between which were flourishing mature plants, one sort in each plot except where "helpers," as he called them, were intermixed. As space has permitted, I've tried to duplicate this same meticulous measuring of ground, though in my garden the plots are more like terraces because of the slope of the land.

He said he rotated his plants from year to year and explained briefly what that meant. *The Practical Woman* has given me much more information on this subject, but unhappily I haven't the variety of vegetables that would make such rotation thoroughly successful, though I've attempted it just the same. And, of course, I have no helpers except the dome-of-spikes, which does keep at least flying insects away. But while it would be nice to have others like sweetsmoke, if for no other reason than the flavorings they provide, my garden seems to do well without them. All my plants have done well every year so far.

What makes my garden other than Aren's land, I'm afraid, is the sensation I get from it, or, rather, the sensation I don't get from it. On Aren's land the air smelled of growing and the odor was penetrating, not just around and about. You had a feeling of growth too, and the sight of it, and more, a physical sensation, as though, like your own blood pumping, you could feel everything straining upward, enlarging and ripening.

Here in Summer there is the strong though not unpleasant scent of stayalives everywhere that masks the garden's odors, unless you bend down to just above the plants. I am in the mountains of North, after all, where stayalives are as plentiful as any tree. And there is also a general odor to the surroundings, but of the growing wilderness to which my garden is actually an alien addition. I do not get here the kind of truly positive feeling of growth I had on Aren's land. But Aren's field was in its proper context.

It was in The Land, among other cultivated fields. My

139

garden is exceptional to its context and should, perhaps, by rights be as wild as the stands of berry bushes and clusters of marshpillars growing out toward the sap house. But if my garden were wild, it would not exist at all.

I think I should assume I'm so directly involved in the growth that I'm too close to notice it. That morning with Aren I was an observer, not a participant, and I know only too well that a person sees less when he's involved in something than when he's detached. My involvement with Loren exemplifies that.

I don't know if I should let that weed remain or not. Aren spoke so strongly against it. "This stuff grows in an instant," he said. "And see these seed pods? The very first thing that happens with this is that these seed pods form. The plant doesn't flower first. It doesn't flower at all, in fact. It doesn't even bother to put out leaves until its seeds are ready. I guess that way the plant's done its work, whether it continues to live or not.

"And each of these little pods . . . see how each one has a line around its middle like a brainnut? Well, they break open there at just a touch, and there are about a hundred seeds inside all ready to go. Every one of them is ready to sprout. You could put them on the ground and watch. Let the stuff go and it'll cover a whole field like mine in half a change. And it'll choke out even mature plants. It puts out a chemical into the soil that kills other plants, so you've got to keep after it constantly. Even the littlest sprout of it in a furrow in one day's morning will take over the end of a row just by the end of the following afternoon."

He also claimed workers ate it. "They think this stuff's a delicacy. I tasted some once. It's a little like soggy stewed clothing. I don't know if you're supposed to cook it or not. Workers don't talk about the way they do things. But I can't imagine what it'd be like cooked." And he curled his upper lip. "If you cooked stewed clothing, what would it taste like?" he joked.

Perhaps I should leave it, as a joke. I should decide soon.

Meanwhile I have plans to begin drawing up for my watercourse. I'll spend the rest of this evening on them and decide on the weed tomorrow. With the amount of time I have to spend getting rid of it, tomorrow is soon enough to worry about it.

The lodge is rapidly falling to ruins. It's as though, without people to care about it, the whole structure has given itself over to collapse. Almost all the windows are broken, the floors around them warped. Walls show signs of water leaks. The roof is damaged in places from who knows what causes. When I went to turn on the electricity—a foolish mistake had I thought about it, but something I just did automatically—the switch terminals promptly burned out with a great display of sparks.

The lodge is dead.

That great expanse of lawn leading down to the stone landing area has become a densely overgrown field that no longer looks as steep an incline as it actually is. The landing area itself now looks like something alien—a large stone terrace set into a hillside, the purpose of which would seem mysterious to anyone who had never seen a flier. And my mother's carefully tended plantings that once bordered the now-hidden steps from the landing area up to the lodge have disappeared entirely in a tangle of green studded with seasonal colors that can hardly be called flowers any longer. Remarkably, I found grass growing in two places in my father's study.

I've taken everything remaining of any value whatever, and the rest may now be abandoned to natural forces. But there's so little left: only a shell enclosing an old chair, a broken drawer from a table that somehow has been reduced to splinters, some useless sculptures—hardly even a shell, now that I'm done with it. I systematically removed all the piping, all the plumbing fixtures, and as much of the wiring as I could get in useful lengths. There's hardly an interior wall that hasn't been ripped open, hardly a part of the floor that hasn't been chopped up, hardly a section of ceiling not pulled down. There was hardly any reason not to wreak such havoc, since I knew that, if I didn't do it to some purpose, it would be done anyway, and to no useful end at all.

I've started digging out an access to the lodge's well, a tunnel that, according to my measurements, should intersect with the well just below the water line. But I've also devised a hand-pump mechanism out of the most incongruous parts. This hand pump works rather well, but requires water for operation, according to the age-old logic that getting something demands having something to begin with.

My pipeline, should I actually accomplish the monumental task I've set myself, will be my ready alternative when the makeshift electric pump fails. The hand pump is my alternative to the pipeline, which, even if it doesn't function as I suppose it ought, will still serve as a handy supply of water with which to get more water.

Of course, unless I devise some means of insulation, the pipeline will freeze in Winter. Thus, I would have to drain it seasonally or suffer irreparable ruptures in irreplaceable materials. Because of that, my hand pump becomes more than just a standby. And no matter what I do, the pipes will eventually be destroyed by simple chemical action over the years. So my third alternative, so far, is to build a tank for catching rainwater. There are so many ways of doing the same thing, and I'm determined to find them all, just in case. Of course, I will ultimately be able to determine which is the longest lasting and most efficient. And I may come upon yet another system in the meantime.

I collected my courage at the beginning of this season and struck out into the area to see what I could find. Downslope from here are more berry bushes—drops-of-night, drops-of-blood, and puckerberry. Much as I used to like them, puckerberries are useless without a great deal of sweetening, which I no longer have. I thought of refining sweetsap for syrup, but *The Practical Woman* has advised me against that. It does take several people to do the job, as I'd thought, people who in late Winter and early Spring have nothing else to do. At those times of the year I have plenty to do in my garden. Drops-of-night and drops-of-blood, however, I can prepare and store as condiments. I also found several patches of groundberries, a little bitter for being wild, but edible nevertheless, and certainly not as acid as puckerberries.

Very peculiarly, I discovered distinct plots of palegrain, cottagekernals, nutgrain, and fieldgrain on the land at the

142

foot of this slope. The plots looked cultivated, although weed-infested. I had a sudden, frightened feeling that there were others around and about who were living as I, whom I had never seen because I hadn't ventured so far from my house before, yet who must know I exist, if only because of the lights in my house at night. Later, though, I realized the explanation: My father must have been using parts of this area for agricultural experiments, the growing of foodstuffs under adverse circumstances, in order to test and determine hardy varieties. In one of the volumes of *Starship Planning* I browsed through it says:

"There must be preparation for encountering less-than-favorable circumstances for settlement, and this preparation must include research on minimal conditions for survival of living things. Speculation suggests that a substantial number of ideal planets would already have indigenous intelligent life of some sort, and that, as likely as not, we would readily encounter such planets, which would be unsuitable for us. Therefore, we must be prepared to make the best of conditions less than those existing on Ath.

"Osir Heremis's group has been directed to develop strong breeds in all areas, which either can readily adapt or are already adapted to a wide range of inferior possibilities. And there are already successful plant variants capable of producing during shorter Summers and of enduring harsh Winters, as well as variants requiring less moisture, less sunlight, and a range of different balances of soil nutrients.

"Of these, fieldgrain seems the most promising, as it has been proven capable of growing in some manner under all but completely sterile circumstances: It can be reverted toward its hardier original to quite some degree without substantially losing its value as a foodstuff. Experiments are ongoing in various remote locations to determine, as much as possible on Ath, the viable limits."

Once I remembered having read this, I felt safe going back downslope to tend the plots, so now I have a source of grains and kernals from which I can make a great many things to eat. This Fall, when I harvest, I can set aside some kernals of each sort to plant near the house next year. An hour's distance is much too far, and I can certainly enlarge my garden some more, since I need no one's permission. Whom would I petition for Growing Right, as Aren

143

had to do for the fallow land next to his? There is something to be said for the way I live now.

I also really ought to take time to read all the *Planning* volumes but the 310 of them are in a developmental sequence across the entire range of research, and not divided into categories. It would be massively repetitive reading for one thing, though the volumes are divided into fifteen and a half temporal subsets beginning with the year 9458. But I'd only be able to comprehend a handful of the twenty volumes in each subset, and probably only a relatively small portion of those. As far as I can tell, most of any given subset deals with research on propulsion systems, Starship support systems, potentially encounterable life forms, astronomy in general and likely directions in which to launch the Starship from Pleistar, none of which is in any way relevant to me.

On the other hand, there is a topic index for each subset, so I suppose I could read through that and make a list of those parts of each volume which might be of use or of interest to me. But that would take quite a bit of time just now. And the one volume I did browse through was, one half of it, results of the three prior years, and the other half directives for the three coming ones. All of it seemed to read: "We did, we will, we did, we will." Somehow, I don't think I will, at least not in the immediate future. But I did get the impression that the *Planning* volumes do have a more practical orientation to them than the technological books I've been reading so far. Maybe I'll get to them this Winter.

Carath has gone with me on all my outings and hasn't managed to get lost, so perhaps we'll try to visit the Broadcast tower after all. He comes when I call to him, in itself something remarkable for what I've known of cats. And he rarely goes far out of my sight, anyway. When he does venture off, it's with a crouch and a slinking, a careful, methodical testing of the area with each step, his whiskers bristling, his ears laid back flat. He's a sight when he does this. He seems to feel, as I do, that unfamiliar territory can hold unexpected surprises.

We also went uphill to the low crest just before the start of the mountain slope back behind here. From there can be seen most of the valley, nearly as far as the beginning of the plain stretching southeast eighty days to Athlan, or where Athlan was. There was no activity of any sort—nor had I expected any. But I was relieved to have this confirmed.

Toward the northwest I could just see the beginning of the dense vegetation at the edge of the wasteland up there. A wasteland is said to glow at night, though I've never seen this. I doubt Carath and I will make an expedition back up to the crest at night just to verify this. Still, it's also reassuring to know that the wasteland is there. At least that's one direction from which I don't have to anticipate the unexpected. Nothing can live in a wasteland, and very few animals in the vegetation surrounding one.

I'm not sure how I'd feel if I happened to meet another person now. I'm not sure I'd want to, though I'm not sure I wouldn't. My old fear of marauders has vanished. Still, there is a nagging apprehension of such an encounter that persists. What would I do? Sometimes I cannot believe I am totally alone, but sometimes that I could ever see again a familiar face or form.

The apprehension comes, I think, from the possibility that, at long last, I would see someone I know rather than just another man. In fact, I think a stranger would be more acceptable than a friend. It would be horrible to encounter Morin or Theras or the twins. My stomach knots even now at the thought. A stranger would be simply strange, while somebody I was once acquainted with would be bound to be stranger than that. I suspect this is one of the great restraints on my venturing off around and about here—manlikes, Carath, and my own laggardliness aside.

Meanwhile, Carath has taken to racing about in a rage on occasion. No doubt he's beginning to sense his masculinity and he's looking for some viable outlet. I don't expect he'll find one, but then, there must be other cats in the area, whether I've seen them or not, and one of them must be female. Or so it would seem at a brief thought about it. The poor thing, how distraught he must feel, how frustrating must his life be. Well, if I can manage, he can too; which is crass, I suppose, but the only practical way of looking at it. There remains some question in my mind, however, whether a cat has any of our sense of practicality.

In the near future I must do something about the summer-lounge section of the house. My earlier repairs of the roof have been to no avail, as I suspected that dream I

145

had once was indicating would be the case. The whole section is beginning to rot. My foot went through a floorboard recently, and the lounge's ceiling has begun to sag. I'll have to tear the whole section down or the rot will spread. I'll also have to devise some feasible way of protecting the wall I'll be exposing so that the rest of the house remains protected.

The bedroom above my kitchen is floor to ceiling, wall to wall possessions: furniture, equipment, fabric, and clothing, everything I have no immediate use for and that I had to remove from the other upstairs bedroom for the sake of Athlan built in there. The other entry hall next to the summer-lounge section is stacked with the various materials I extracted at the last from the lodge. There's also some of that salvaged stuff in the dining room, which is now completely unusable.

But the only buffer between the things I have stored and the now-rotting section is the far wall of that other entry hall, which, being a part of what my father added on, was never a prepared exterior wall as the near wall was. I don't know how I'm going to convert that wall to withstand exposure, but I certainly can't tear it down. Sometimes I feel as though I'm living in a storage depot and not a house at all.

I think my end of this house will be all right, since there is the cellar underneath it, which provides adequate ventilation. As I remember, my father never extended the cellar when he had the summer-lounge section added, because there is a large boulder in the ground there. Probably it was not my repair of the roof that was at fault so much, but moisture that had already entered the section before I could make the repair and which never entirely dried up because of the lack of ventilation from below.

Maybe I can build a retaining wall of rock of some sort, founded on the boulder, to face the exterior of that far wall in the hallway. In the cellar, now that I go look, I find that part of that boulder can be seen, incorporated into the main foundation. If the boulder was built upon that way originally, I don't see why I can't build upon it further the way I have in mind. I'll have to think about it further.

I can well understand Carath's curious little rages. I myself have been increasingly tense all Summer, and nothing —my project, my routine work, sleeping, masturbation, exhaustion, rest—nothing relieves the tension.

I've been digging out the tunnel, which is surely an effort. I ignorantly had not anticipated the rockiness of the earth and so far have extracted enough small boulders to construct a house wall. Still the tunnel is not yet very deep, really no farther in than I am tall. I'm in a quandary whether to move all the rocks I've unearthed to the house for the retaining wall I have in mind, or to use them on the site as the foundation for the pipeline. My plan was to support the pipe on wooden pilings, in effect to build a bridge between the side of the lodge's hill and this knoll. Wood, however, is not as durable as rock. But I cannot make up my mind. I cannot seem to concentrate on the relative merits of the alternatives.

The distance between the tunnel and my house I gauge at a fifth, or a fifth and a tenth. I haven't actually timed it out exactly, which would be hard to do in any event since the underbrush would slow me down considerably. Thus, even taking the slopes of the depression into account as a factor in the rate, I would still arrive at entirely the wrong distance. How I wish I had a whole set of measuring equipment instead of just two depth rods and a distance ribbon. I wish, I wish.

However, in a direct path it appears to be about a fifth or a little over. If I compensate for the depression of the path, a straight airline between the two points would likely be six or seven tenths. From that, then, if I conceptualize a triangle with the vertices at my house, the tunnel, and the lowest point on the ground between them, I can compute the height of my pipeline. After that, deciding how wide I would want a stone construction to be, I can estimate its volume.

Assuming an average volume for the boulders I'm unearthing, I can finally judge how many I'll need to construct what I envision in the proportions I've determined. This I can set against the number of pilings that would be required if I built it out of wood. Further, I can estimate the amount of time it would take to chop down and trim trees for the pilings, to dig the holes and set the pilings, to attach the construction together with cross braces. This result, then, could be compared to the estimated amount of time construction would take with the boulders.

All this calculation would provide me with factors I could weigh against the questions of durability, repair, and replacement, and the obvious chief deficiency of each proposal. If I made the bridge of wood, and if the pilings weren't set properly, or if one rotted quickly or was otherwise broken, then the bridge would collapse and damage the piping. But if I made it of stone, then: either winter freezes could heave the construction, collapsing the bridge and damaging the piping, or, unless I also installed proper drainage, I would in time form a small pond in the depression between the two elevations.

Such a pond would not necessarily be a bad idea. It would be another water source. But it would also put undue pressure on the stonework, meaning that a stone bridge would have to be considerably wider than a wooden one.

There is also the problem of accessory materials. For wood I'd need nails or something similar—bolts, for example. I wonder if such things could be gotten from the lodge's construction. Or I could peg the cross braces to the pilings in the ancient way, or I could rabbet them together in the way Menes once built their temporary fishing shelters.

For stone I'd need mortar—I am certainly in no position to finish each boulder to fit them together without mortar, unless, of course, by virtue of the necessary extra width, the stones could simply be piled securely with the gaps between them filled by rubble. Then, though, I'd have to taper the bridge toward the top, and, designed that way, it would get progressively weaker as the height increased.

But wouldn't the pressure of weight from my hypothetical pond be on the bridge's base primarily? I could limit the height of the pond by installing sluices somewhat below the pipeline.

Now an additional advantage of stonework occurs to

me: I could more easily insulate the pipeline against Winter. With wood, such protection would have to be far more elaborate, since the piping would be much more exposed. And I suppose I could even make mortar of some sort. I think the stone façade on the front of the lodge is of the sort of material that can be reduced by heat to amalgam compound. It shows signs of weathering, so it may be that material. However, I'm not sure I can produce the kind of heat *The Practical Woman* says is necessary. Although I could build a kiln. But that's just one more complication if I use stone.

But whether or not, I yet cannot concentrate enough on any of this to perform the basic mathematics involved, let alone to determine which is the better way. Every time I examine alternatives, another ramification appears. Just now it strikes me that I could eventually construct a sort of hydraulic system utilizing sluices, either for electricity generation, had I the additional parts for that sort of device, or for a mill to grind the grains I expect to harvest, which would also require extra parts.

On another aspect, I now wonder if by using the lodge's façade for mortar for the bridge I wouldn't be foolishly wasting an essential resource I could better use elsewhere, for instance on the retaining wall I'm to build after I tear down the summer-lounge section of the house. But could I actually get the rocks I'm unearthing up the slope to this house if I decided to use them for the retaining wall?

It's all options and alternatives and possibilities and this and that. I can't narrow anything down to reasonable, manageable terms. It seems as though I've learned too much of all the information I've been trying so hard to learn. As though there is more in my head than my head should reasonably be expected to hold. But isn't there a great deal more of the brain than man ever actually uses? Or perhaps, having started to teach myself how to develop alternatives to everything, I have yet to learn how to discriminate among alternatives sensibly.

In Heremis's notes on regeneration, he explains that nerve cells in general normally regenerate as any other cell would, unlike the nerve cells of a nonregenerative. And he goes on to say:

"Brain cells, while not regenerated, are still present in such number that they would seem capable of storing thou-

149

sands and thousands of years' worth of information, though no one has lived so long as to try this potential. It may be that actual storage of information is limited, however generous the limitation, or in fact unlimited. We still do not even know whether the individual brain cell retains a single item of information or several related items, or many related and unrelated together, or how a brain cell effects the retention, in specific terms. Nevertheless, there still remain two perfectly possible extremes, even partial manifestations of which imply a great deal.

"First, it may be that over the course of time information of perceived greater value would systematically replace information of perceived lesser value. In basic example: What's useful to know today is substituted automatically for what was useful to know yesterday. Then yesterday's information would be erased completely from the mind.

"Or it may be that all information accumulates without fail. Nothing would be lost. Everything would always be retrievable for all time, whether that retrieval could be disciplined or not. And this raises the additional question of mental discipline among regeneratives in general.

"In the first case, we would then expect eventual, irrevocable change of attitudes and behavior over time, unless absolutely everything were kept static. And this change would be of indeterminable value: It could be for the good, or it could prove disastrous. In the second case, however, the possibilities are ungaugeable, ranging from immense wisdom to immense madness. We know so little in this area that in a general discussion only extremes can be considered, for only they can be defined to any specific extent.

"However, it seems to have been a natural development among us to avoid remembering extraneous information, recording it rather in writing or on ribbons for reference as necessary. This is the chief reason that I have proposed elsewhere that a substantial portion of the Starship be allotted for mnemonic material and devices.

"Still, this development does not suggest that either of the two cases mentioned is the actual one. We could as well be instinctively providing against our innate forgetfulness as protecting against the prospect of madness. But certainly regeneratives have been noticed to suffer more frequently from indecision and confusion than nonregeneratives, when they do not take full advantage of mnemonic materials and devices. And again this does not suggest the basic reason for the problem. It only describes a symptom, which could be due to either alternative."

I may indeed be exhibiting something of one of those extremes, though which one? I have only myself by which to gauge myself.

But perhaps this indecision of mine is the source of my tension. It could well be, though there are other perplexing things about this tension that would seem to have nothing to do with my indecisiveness or with my memory. For example, on occasion my eyesight becomes fogged, or wavers as though I were looking through a sheet of water. And on occasion I hear things that even Carath seems not to hear, a kind of roaring as though from a Starship shuttle flier heard at some distance.

It's perfectly possible, though, that I'm simply trying to plan and do too much all at once, as though I absolutely had to do everything quickly. That's the result, I'm sure, of having been raised to die instead of to be what I am, though knowing that is, I'm sure, far different from changing my perspective now. If that's not the source of my tension, the frantic pace it engenders must at least be contributory. And the side effects must be just that.

Still, however I try to tell myself that I have time enough to think and act calmly, I sometimes become absolutely obsessed with a feeling that I ought to be doing something, though I can never figure out at those times what it is I ought to be doing. Then I search about. I wander to and fro. I look at this and that. Nothing is right. Nothing satisfies my mysterious urge. And I cannot think rationally at all.

At those times Carath stares and stares at me, intensely, totally dumbfounded, convinced I've gone completely aberrant. I mutter to myself. I move things about. In desperation I finally fling myself into a chair, hoping, I suppose, to knock my breath out, thereby immobilizing myself until the feeling passes. Or maybe by that I'm trying to cause myself enough pain to obliterate the one feeling with another, the way a person might dig his nails into his palms when he stubs his toe, to make the toe hurt less. The One knows the feeling itself is a "painful" one, though nothing

151

physical I can locate. At last I go lock myself in the bathroom, at which point Carath picks up where I left off.

About the only time I can rid myself of this pointless obsession comes when I sit down, grab Carath, and hold him to my chest. He squirms at this, and I can't blame him, but it has its effect. It's as though there were someone else with me, a comforting. It's not, I think, sexual, certainly not in terms of Carath. There were moments I remember when just holding Aren was similarly comforting, though my distraction was never so great as this then. At those times it was merely after some days without seeing him, or after an encounter with a particularly frustrating student. In fact, I wasn't noticeably tense then, though I must have had tension, or I wouldn't have gotten the sensation of relaxing. But when I held Aren at those times, there was no sexual implication, just a consoling fondness. And there is also none now. I am sure of that.

Well, but I must reach some decision about my plans for my pipeline. And I must do so relatively soon, at least so that over this Winter I can spend my idle hours making detailed calculations. I would hate to be mindlessly obsessed on a frigid, grey winter afternoon alone in these mountains.

In the meantime, the garden still flourishes. That is no worry at all and, I guess, some consolation. The weed is apparently quite healthy, though I really don't know how it should look "healthy." But where it grows, it grows profusely. And curiously, it's not spreading. I find a shoot of it here and there in the rest of the garden, and I uproot one when I find it. But it's rare that I do. Where it grows along the edge of the garden is just where the plant stays confined. It shouldn't be like that, but that's hardly cause for complaint, after all.

The individual plants of it seem to have gotten a certain size and no larger. It actually resembles a low hedge, and a neat one at that. In fact, it looks tended. I am not tending it. But I'm pleased at its restraint.

It occurs to me that if the weed, as Aren said, sends out a chemical through its roots that kills other plants, it's perfectly possible the other plants in my garden have developed a defense—even, perhaps, a counter-chemical they use to keep the weed in check. After all, I don't know the source of the seeds I used to start the garden three years ago. They may have come from Heremis's experiments, too, and for that they might be capable of anything.

But why shouldn't they change or develop an extra characteristic by themselves? Carath has a total of five digits on each forepaw instead of the normal six. He's a change. And I'm regenerative. That's a change. Why should plants be deprived of the same opportunity for change? If nothing else, that would be unfair.

It's no more absurd a thought than the ancient thinking that being a Light was an inheritable characteristic. Some still believed that long after the Confederation, just as some still believed that man's appearance on Ath had nothing at all to do with any of the other life on the planet. I can understand the cause of that last thinking, though, since most people were never aware that Imitators were pre-bearing animals and thus, reproductively, totally unlike us. Otherwise, we could be construed as their descendants, which we absolutely aren't.

But my explanation for the weed, while it might not be the right one, is an interesting enough explanation. I can find none better, nor, I think, shall I try to. I concern myself with too much speculation as it is.

Summer, Change 3: 24, 9507

My most crucial doubt is resolved: The pipeline idea will work. After tunneling far enough into the hillside to reach a point near what I thought must be the side of the well, I managed to force a piece of piping through the earth the remaining distance. After a moment, water came out of the pipe at me. For some reason I'd begun to suspect that wouldn't happen. But it did.

The pressure is low. Nevertheless the source is usable. Of course I hadn't really thought things through, so my tunnel is presently unbelievably muddy. But while it's slightly downsloping into the hillside, it isn't filling up, so there must be some sort of drainage. Judging by the way the water comes out of the pipe in very slight surges, it seems there is some sort of underground stream or well-

153

spring rather than just a catchbasin. The water may be seeping back into its source.

Actually, the idea of tapping the well is what has proved feasible. The more I consider it, the more it seems to me a pipeline itself will not be the means. Likely, the top of my bridge will have to be a trough, with gravity as the force for transport. That means the position of my tunnel on the lodge's hill had better be higher than the place at which I intend the water to arrive on the house's hill. It also means my bridge will be stone, the better material in the long run.

There are plenty of stones. The lodge's hill seems to be composed of little else but stones held together by roots, with only thin buffers of dirt between things. That's proved to be fortunate, for my tunneling looks to remain stable. Had there been more dirt, the water coming into it would have sooner or later caused it to collapse. I still don't know if there'll be enough stones. But that doesn't matter so much, as I can always dig out more.

This Fall I'll clear all the underbrush between the tunnel and the house. Then I'll have a much better view of the circumstances. After that, for as long as the weather remains even marginally temperate, I can begin building the bridge. And now I'm beginning to realize there's no necessity for such elaborate planning as I'd been imagining. I can deal with each problem as it arises. I can adjust or correct as things happen. The bridge may look odd when completed, but appearances are of no concern to me.

I see now that in all these books I've read, however concentrated they are on the technical thinking, there is always consideration of the appearance of the finished product. That stands to reason: Everything always had to look like the product of man, had to conform to our esthetics as well as to its function, simply because the mind of man required it. We seem to have needed the reassurance of the look of continuity, even in things that were radically different from what had come before them. That is, I suppose, what made Theras's question so impossible: Practically speaking, people who did not make an object still had to be able to tell what it was, what it did, or had to be able to use it easily. It had to look as though it belonged to them and belonged with all the other things they had.

Now, however, with what I make for myself, there is no

154

such consideration. I will be the only one who ever has to look at or use my own creations. If they're different, odd-looking, if they would be totally alien in the sight of someone else, that matters not at all, as there are no other people. I know what I've made, how it works, how I can use it. If the bridge functions, then, though it look like a flier or a rail stop or some Imitator creation, it will still bring water. I needn't be bound to conform or to make anything conform to previous standards, especially if it would be inconvenient or impossible to do. I can, as I once childishly claimed, be Light forever, or Dark, or neither, at my own convenience.

The hand pump would be totally unrecognizable to anyone else.

And I've managed to construct a kiln of sorts in the large stone hearth of the summer lounge, which kiln more resembles a miniature of the Research Compound in Athlan. But it can reduce the lodge's stone façade to amalgam compound easily. Now I can make mortar. Additionally, the kiln has taken out all the dampness in that section, not that that's of any help now.

I wish I'd thought to do something like this last year. But it will likely retard deterioration sufficiently to let me wait until next year to tear the section down. I'll do it next Spring. It won't take long.

It seems, however, that I completely misinterpreted everything in planning repairs to the roof of that section. I'd disregarded *The Practical Woman*'s advice in favor of what appeared to be more efficient, more practical, better. And I used the right methods for the materials from the lodge, but they were the wrong materials, not intended for the use I put them to. I must remember that my present cleverness is no substitute for someone else's past experience.

As for the sample of amalgam compound I've produced for mortar, it's inordinately caustic. Without a moment's hesitation I spread it around with my fingers and promptly suffered some terrible burns. The burns vanished quickly enough, but it was a most unpleasant sensation at the time, not one I'm likely to want to repeat.

It was distinctly unpleasant to watch myself heal—not that it was revolting, but it was distasteful to see happening while knowing some of the whys and wherefores. It

155

itched furiously, at one stage, as much as it had hurt before that. I can't imagine why it itched—Heremis's notes say nothing about that—but on reflection I suppose the process of healing must have some sensation to it. But such a maddening sensation!

It could have been worse: I mightn't have known I'm regenerative. Then it would have been revolting to watch my flesh actually grow back. It would seem unnatural. This was the first time I've had such noticeable damage done to myself since I arrived here.

On the way here, certainly, I suffered innumerable cuts and bruises, all of which dutifully and speedily healed without a trace, but which I was scarcely aware of. By and large I know I'd gotten hurt because there was dried blood on my clothes, not because I recalled a particular accident.

I'll have to be more cautious, though. I'd rather not repeat the episode.

I thought about the lodge today, my father's favorite retreat, now an almost unrecognizable shambles. I feel sorry for it in a peculiar way. I can't honestly say I didn't find a little pleasure in dismantling the place, but it's not as though I hated it—I didn't. And it's not as though I hated my father so much, either, though we always had such a distance between us—one far greater than I knew.

I've always by nature simply dismissed people I didn't especially care for. I dismissed my father, for the most part, while he was alive. And I guess I always dismissed the lodge as well, preferring the guesthouse, *my* house, where I always felt more as though I could be my own person. Still, my feelings about the lodge in the past probably came more from its being much too big. Nine couples could stay there in addition to my parents.

It certainly seems even bigger now that each room is nothing but a barren enclosed space. My kitchen here is rather large, as such rooms go in houses like this, but the kitchen up there, especially bare of all equipment save the frivolities, seems the size of a public lounge. A meal could be prepared for forty in it—and sometimes was, as I recall.

Perhaps I'm getting some satisfaction in overcoming its size, outlasting its apparently more durable New Style lines, putting it to better use as a resource for my house than as a house.

Perhaps I'm also doing something of this sort with the

things of my father, with him in a way—putting him to better use for myself than he was before. And in a way putting myself to better use in his terms, by his things. There's that.

Well, all this aside, I think everything is beginning to assume a sort of logic. I'm starting to conceive of planning for things over a longer term than before. There's less of the urge in me to rush everything to completion than I felt even during the past change. That's no guarantee I'll feel better about everything I do, but it does suggest that everything will work out more reasonably than I'd thought. It does make me feel calmer, which, Carath agrees, is preferable.

His raging seems to have passed too, at least for the moment, or for the season.

Winter, Change 1: 4, 9507

The brush has been cleared, and now I can see that I've managed to make the right decisions despite myself:

My tunnel is just a bit higher than the level of ground on which my house stands.

Stone is the best material, whatever its perceived drawbacks might have been.

A pond of some sort will form—water from the rains of the last change of Fall has made a large puddle behind the foundation I laid at the bottom of the depression. And since I cannot utilize a holding tank for the transported water after all, because the difference in height between the two ends is not that great, such a pond will serve the purpose well, perhaps better.

All in all, I'm pleased with my good fortune, and a bit chagrined I had to rely so much on the fortunate. This for my inflated pretensions.

The stones I've already excavated are nearly used up and the foundation is only about as high as I am tall. The topography of the depression is irregular, but by eye I'd estimate what I've built so far spans about a third of the linear distance. The higher it gets the more stones I'll need, even though the higher it gets the narrower it will be. I started it, perhaps unwisely, in excess, at about a ten-tenth and two thousandths wide, a rough estimate. It's approximately twice as wide as I am tall. But I'd rather err in excess and be sure the bridge is sturdy. As for the rest of the stones I'll need, I can actually get many of them from just under the surface of the depression itself.

I turned up quite a number when I cleared the brush. It would probably be a good idea to clear out the rest of the depression behind the bridge, so that the water won't be fouled by rotting plants. That's sure to yield a quantity of boulders, perhaps enough, but whether or not makes little difference, as the ground is turning out to be incredibly rocky.

Odd that it isn't rocky around and about the lodge or my house, but then, my father could very well have had the land for both cleared of rocks and covered with special topsoil. In any event, since it never occurred to me to dig deep into the land before, there's hardly any reason that I should be surprised it turns out the way it is. But perhaps the land around the house and the lodge is the way it is naturally. What do I know about geology?

I must say that what makes this project of mine seem to be going more easily now, at least in retrospect, is that I have only myself to consider. I don't have to ask any Council's permission for any of my plans. Even before, this land wasn't owned by a city. I suppose my father never had to pay any rate for it, or consult anyone about what he planned to do with it. But I suspect eventually—and I would have lived long enough to see this—some city, most likely Inland, would have extended its claim to this area. Or perhaps there would have been a new city built not far from this valley.

It's difficult to imagine which would have happened, since I never followed that controversy closely. But the valley below me would have been an ideal place for a facility of some sort, or even for farming, what with Heremis's hardier strains of plants available.

How much simpler things are now without men. I wonder if any Council would ever have approved of my designs on the land around and about me. I was hardly the sort who was interested in approval from anyone but those closest to me. But that I usually got, even from Loren eventually.

I'd better get back to the planning that interests me, or the planning that I can manage. And I'd better absorb myself in the work, as I find now my distracted feelings of earlier this year returning once more.

They're rather like the sensations I used to get whenever I tried to keep some project of mine from Carath's prying paws. There's an annoying tingle at the base of my skull, in my mind, as it were. And my breathing becomes so rapid that I nearly hyperventilate. My vision becomes clouded. My hands even shake at times. My stomach becomes unsettled and I feel as though I want to laugh, but not because anything is amusing. My urge to laugh is pure nervousness.

Can this be some result of regeneration? Heremis mentions nothing of the sort, and you'd think he would. Is it loneliness? I do have Carath, though he is a poor substitute for a man most times. Is it fright? But of what? My earlier fears have all but vanished. I expect no intruders, hostile or not. What can cause this? It is most disturbing.

But it's no doubt due to my reminiscing, which is the inevitable outgrowth of the idleness of this time of year. Just imagine my considering something as absurd as whether someone might have approved of my method of survival. Why would I care to think about that? I would never have thought of it before. I wrote books, after all.

One day I hope to dispense with such thoughts entirely and thus with the discomfort they bring me. One day I expect to be so far removed from them that I'll never need think of the past again, at least not that past.

Winter, Change 3: 9, 9507

I've never felt such distress. I've never done anything so ridiculous as a result of any sort of tension.

That dismaying nervousness of last Summer grew to be so overwhelming by the beginning of this change that my whole body was actually shaking, shaking so badly I could do nothing at all but sit in one place. I felt as though I were fighting something nameless and unknowable. I was so distraught that I found myself entertaining suicidal thoughts for the first time in my life.

Suicide is such a rare phenomenon, except for that time in history toward the end of the Dark State, that, had I not been a historian, I should probably not have known just what I was considering. I certainly never dreamed of experiencing the aberration myself. But I was seriously wishing I were dead, rather than continue in such confusion.

I suppose what stopped me from attempting it was the consideration that for me suicide is nearly impossible. The lengths to which I would have to go, or the length of time I would need to prepare for less complex methods, portend either failure or self-dissuasion. If I didn't succeed in severing my head, I would endure agony while I inevitably healed. Burning myself, poison, drowning—these things are too slowly painful or too slow readying the means for. I would have too much time to reconsider. Suicide must be both swift and sure. Such nonsense was the extent of my upset.

What did I do instead? I went about insanely searching for something to occupy my mind. I was so impatient that I produced quite a good deal of disorder in the house, pulling things out, looking at them dumbly, dropping them, leaving a trail of worthless solutions—kitchen utensils, papers, sound ribbons, photographs, electronic parts—ultimately rummaging through the storage room upstairs one whole day without sleep.

Then, suddenly, I was obsessed with an item I at long last came across—a book, of all the absurd things. And not just any book—not something I'd never read before—but one with which I'm already nearly overfamiliar, on a subject so pointless now that it would not have been in the least worth saving. I can only assume I brought it over from the lodge as mindlessly as I brought over so much else. It's the *Compendium of the Imitators by the North Central Wastelands near Eastern Sea*. And it's the first version of 9481, at that.

I worked on part of the fourth version myself while I was at the School, retranslating and reassorting much of the material that comprised *Conversations,* by Amsochr

160

the Wise One. I drew a good deal from that particular piece for my chronology *The One*. But the version I have here and now is the original thoughtless assembly of photographs of Imitator documents found at one particular site, all out of their logical order, each accompanied by a highly erroneous translation and particularly facetious commentary.

Yet, when I laid hands on it, it was as though I knew I had found something in which I could become absorbed, even though a rational part of my mind recognized that the book is inherently worthless. I felt it was something that would distract me from being distracted. And so it proved to be. I read it almost uninterruptedly and with enormous concentration for the next four days, stopping only for an occasional meal when my hunger was so great that my vision blurred, or dozing off for an hour or two when I was absolutely incapable of forcing myself to remain awake any longer.

Now it seems perhaps the choice was not so ludicrous, was not so devoid of all reason. That's only a speculation on my part, however, and not really a very good one at that. Perhaps, because I am so familiar with the book, I could concentrate on it better, literally fix my mind on it, as though it were a safe routine to be followed when all else has become completely chaotic. But I know the contents of the book in their fourth version, not in such a disorganized format as this. It hardly stands to reason that I grasped at it because it would be so familiar, or because it might return me mentally to a time in my life when things were normal. And, in fact, the book's effect was to demonstrate a totally different sort of familiarity, one that I would certainly not have called normal when I was younger.

I have routines to fall back on at times like this, even now in Winter. There are basic things to do around and about, things so common I don't believe I've ever mentioned them in these pages. Cleaning myself and cleaning up after myself—those are regular duties. Checking my stores of food, maintaining the heating system and cleaning its filters, washing down the solar panels, or even writing here, which I consider as much a duty, even if I'm not too regular about it, as an impulse. Or masturbating, which I could describe just as I do writing. Things like these should have offered me some solace, not a carelessly

161

compiled and out-of-date book. Still, I felt, the moment I picked it up, that it would be entirely appropriate. I even felt calmer at once, just holding it. But I would never have anticipated the various effects the book has had on me. Who could have? And though I suppose there's an explanation, I'm still just bewildered enough to be unable to discover it.

Most strangely, while I was adept at reading the Imitator language—at least better at it than anyone else, though I still read it relatively slowly and not without the occasional difficulty—and while it's been over four years since I've taken up any Imitator texts to read, the documents themselves were crystal clear. They were as plain and as readable as a three-word declarative sentence in Aten. But the Aten commentary, while certainly fallacious enough to present problems of comprehension to me, proved to be virtually incomprehensible, so much so in fact that I shortly began skipping over it entirely. I found the only way I could have my own language make any sense to me was to painstakingly read it aloud and listen to myself speaking, something so laborious that I quickly grew tired of doing it. Moreover, the Imitator documents might as well have been wholly new material, so remarkably different in interpretation did they appear. It was as though I suddenly and completely understood the Imitators—their language, their thinking, as much as their very being. Quite honestly, it was as though I myself were suddenly an Imitator.

This comprehension is almost frightening to consider, although I didn't think an instant about it at the time. Since then I've pondered the problem and decided that I most likely was always so familiar with the Imitator language and thinking, but that before I was inhibited from acknowledging my familiarity to myself. So few could read Imitator at all—only a few more were aware that it could be read. And those of us who did recognize it as a language were generally derided by most of our colleagues as attributing too much order to Chaos. How silly that consideration seems now. I thought it silly before, but, as the few others like myself, I contained my opinion as much as I could.

The notion was that Imitator documents were exercises in design and carried meaning by the nature of the design and by the placement of the details of it. (In fact, this is true, even more true than was assumed.) But Imitator was not to be considered a language. There was only one real language, ours, while what the Imitators accomplished was a sophisticated but still "animal" endeavor, like their penchant for dancing, or their habit of standing "mute as grazing animals." Certain birds, it was argued, like the false speaker, exhibited "language." The false speaker could recite words it was trained to remember, and could even devise real sentences of those words, though it was plain the false speaker hadn't the slightest notion what it was actually doing. Likewise, the croaker could be made to utter cats' names—in effect, Imitator. Yet given these examples, most claimed that the Imitator efforts were similarly false. Such works could be interpreted, they said, only because Imitators were more advanced than false speakers.

The capacity for design was dismissed by drawing similar animal comparisons. Didn't the cultivator bird grow a tiny garden? But that was not for food, but to impress its potential mate. Didn't the seamster make its roost by sewing leaves together with fibers gotten from the stalks of the floss plant, the very plant from which we obtained our natural fibers? Many animals were craftsmanlike, many of their results apparently inspired. That the Imitators' writing was so much more deliberate was again attributed to their more-advanced animal development.

Even that it could be demonstrated that the Imitators' language made sense, that that sense could be translated into our terms, that the sense was expressed in a way comparable to our language—all these things were equally dismissed, though now for more sinister reasons. Weren't the Imitators the agents of Chaos? As that, they were intended to seem like men. The goal of Chaos, according to the thinking, was to create a system that appeared to be a duplicate of the way of the One, but which was opposed to the way of the One in every detail. Implied by this was the universal struggle between Chaos and the One for dominance in the realm of reality. Thus, naturally, the Imitators would seem to have a language that meant something. The Imitators were called as they were because they were supposed to be like men, but diametrically opposed to men.

Well, I knew differently before. I suppose those like myself also knew differently. But we never explicitly said anything, because who would dare? It was enough to refer to Imitator as a "language," to say that they had a "culture" and a "thinking." To try to assert that Imitators had an intelligence as valid as our own was to run the risk of public condemnation, even in 9503 when it was widely accepted that "the One" and "Chaos" actually represented merely the extreme terms of the continual attempts by the material universe to balance matter and energy. Thus, that I knew differently still was restrained by what would be the result if I, or anyone, tried to assert such knowledge.

Nowadays there is no such restraint on me. I've already recognized that "the ways of man" are exactly and only what I decide they are. Thus, I suppose, it stands to reason that my fluency in the Imitator language, which was always good, should now be superlative. I no longer have to be careful. I no longer have to privately suppress my abilities, my reactions, or my results. Hence the apparently sudden clarity of the documents I was reading.

The things I've learned, each by itself, are, I suppose, rather irrelevant to me. Certainly I've had quite radically new insights into certain matters that may be of some use to me. I've a concept now of being calm, of making myself calm in an entirely alien way, or, at least, in a way men never thought of before. I've a new concept of relating aspects of the world around and about myself to each other and to me, a concept which cannot even be termed "opposite" to the thinkings of man, but just quite different. The idea of opposites itself now seems stringently limiting, even foolhardy. The distinctions Imitators made between the material and the abstract appear to be more sensible means for categorizing and assessing than simply to declare that for each positive element there's a negative, for each item there is only a single counter-item.

But what matters more, or appears to as far as I'm concerned, is that, first of all, I've learned the linguistics of the Imitators, how they expressed themselves. And then I've learned how to come to comprehend the expression of the world in terms other than my own, other than man's.

It would seem more important to understand facts than to understand the way those facts are presented. But it seems I consider it more important to understand the viewpoint than what's being viewed. This awareness seems even exhilarating, though from the practical standpoint—man's inevitable standpoint—I must admit such knowledge is supremely useless. There are no Imitators, there are no men, and what I so gloriously know will never go farther than myself. The best I can hope for is to achieve an empathy with Carath. But I have that virtually already. Otherwise the only substantial result is that the exercise seems to have calmed me down.

Still, there's something that nags me. How did I arrive at such an enlightenment? I do know that before, when I read Imitator materials, I was always perplexed that the Imitators should have bothered with such abstracted considerations. I was always interested primarily in what facts could be gleaned, not what concerns were being argued. I might guess, though, that the primary factor for me was my at last realizing all three aspects of Imitator communication and how those aspects stood in relation to one another. No one ever deduced one of those aspects—in part, I'm sure, because we have no such concept and no words in our language to communicate it. And no one ever unraveled the relationship between written and spoken Imitator, or, rather, the lack of one.

Imitator speech was less than basic. Their vocal apparatus was extraordinarily simple by comparison to a man's. The sounds they could utter and the combinations of those sounds, while words, had more significance as conveyors of the emotional component of meaning than as absolute meaning itself.

But they communicated one to another by a quite different method, one for which the only even remotely adequate word in Aten is "Thinking" as the ancient, honored term. Thus, it's quite plain to me now why it was written that: "The Imitators are not like men. Their speech is rough and simple, unlike the smooth sound of a man's voice, and they say they talk among themselves without sound, which is to say they gesture with their bodies like animals, except that none have ever seen this. When they are together they stand mute as grazing animals."

Of course: They were "Thinking" at one another. There's apparently nothing to see of that process. Sounds were actually emphasis, like punctuation among us, in a way. But if their speech was so confined, their writing was absolutely boundless in its range of employment.

They wrote not sentence by sentence or section by section, but in terms of each entire page, everything on that page set down in a design so that at first glance a page was a pattern, a carefully balanced organization of characters. And that first glance would be as crucial to meaning as any word or phrase extracted from the pattern.

It was always assumed this was nothing more than an inordinate skill in design that was peculiarly Imitator. There were ten such patterns, and whatever was written was conformed to one of those ten. We thought it was just esthetic. But each of those patterns, I know now, conveyed a very specific attitude toward the verbal content that made up each pattern, spanning a range from complete approval of what was being said to complete disapproval. The instant the eye saw a page, the mind would know whether the writer was expounding what he considered a pure truth or, as they established the opposite, a pure evil, or any of the eight shades of attitude between those two. In effect, the layout of a page was the written equivalent of a sound uttered during the course of an Imitator "conversation."

Thus, an Imitator page might be written in two counter-spirals, or in a star pattern, words being syntactically distinguished by structural positioning, letters often heavily diacriticized in addition, not as punctuation, but as a function of positioning and shade of meaning. And their letters were exquisitely fluid, capable of a good deal of distortion without necessarily losing their ability to be recognized. Ours are quite clumsy to write out, and the script form, which is easier, is often quite difficult to read if the hand isn't especially careful.

For that, written Aten would seem to have been conscientiously devised to prevent writing. Carriers and their dominant importance in communication from early times aside, no wonder people objected so strenuously to most writing and reading. Imitator, not conveniently speakable, makes up in written form for the vocal difficulties by sheerly beautiful graphic eloquence. An Imitator text, no matter what its subject, is perfectly lovely to look at, though that's my point of view and perhaps not theirs at all.

But, then, the vocabulary! So many words for colors, when we have so few even though colors were so important to us. And so many adjectives—so many of all sorts of words. We defined new concepts by compounding old words. Imitator had a different word for each different idea, and each word by itself was really no part of speech at all, but assumed its full value only in its given position. There's an inherent linguistic variety so lacking in Aten that I could be envious of the concepts which can be expressed so easily in Imitator, while they're so difficult as to sometimes be nearly impossible to express in my language. And there are so many discrete abstractions, concepts no man ever thought of and distinctions no man ever thought to make. What a wealth!

The letters themselves have a particular peculiarity I recall no one ever really comprehending, though it's quite plain to understand now: Simply, written Imitator has nothing whatever to do with "spoken" Imitator. It made no sense to us for it not to be correspondable, letter to sound, even though there obviously were far more letters than possible sounds. But it's quite clear why the two aspects of their language had no connection to one another, when it's realized that their speech wasn't "speech" at all. But I can by no means comprehend this "Thinking" of theirs, as I have never myself experienced anything even remotely like it, so I have no way of knowing if their letters didn't have some sort of correspondence to it.

It's rather sad to consider, incidentally, that our firm notion that there had to be some correspondence between their speaking and writing came from what must plainly have been their concession to us in the earliest times, before we destroyed them all. They must have mechanically assigned letters to sounds because we were incapable of understanding in any other way than that.

There arises an intriguing thought, too, that spoken words of Imitators as recorded in early daily texts and other writings must have been in spoken Imitator, our first fathers also speaking Imitator as best they could. Our speech would have been quite impossible for an Imitator to manage, while theirs could have been crudely rendered by man. The recorded dialogues are, therefore, translations, and undoubtedly untrustworthy ones at that.

But out of this pile of facts, how did I see beyond the facts? I don't know by what means I've come to so deeply understand the Imitator mentality, nor what point there is in doing so now. It's just happened. But it has seemed to calm me.

Perhaps it's the historian in me that has gone so long unpracticed. If it's my nature to make such analyses, and if I have—as I obviously have—repressed that nature, then it will have its own revenge, I suppose.

Still, better this than what I could be analyzing. Even if there is no more point to it than as a mental exercise, at least it's a safer course. Its goal is so much more remote from my emotions.

Spring, Change 3: 15, 9508

It's been an especially clear Spring, so I've taken advantage of the fine weather to dismantle the summer-lounge section. The only thing left standing is the chimneywork for my makeshift kiln. I think that sometime in the future I'll use the wood left over from the section to build a shed around the kiln. That's not an immediate concern, though.

Meanwhile, I've already used some of the wood as a temporary facing for the wall I had to leave to protect the other hallway. The rest I've stacked on blocks, the way I've seen it done by building-materials suppliers. If that kept wood from damage for them for a season or so, it will for me.

In consultation with *The Practical Woman* I've sorted out all the other bits and pieces of materials for future use. That's all in the other hallway too—no longer a hallway, I'm afraid. Everything is reusable, something again so obvious, yet something I could easily have failed to remember. All the waste from Athlan was, after all, sent to East Athlan for sorting and reuse. Every city had a reclamation center in an outlier. But I might not have thought to bother saving such things as bent or broken nails, had *The Practical Woman* not alerted me in her section, "Uses for Useless Things." Where else would I get metal now if not from the metal I have? I'm always astonished at times like this to discover how much of life I simply overlooked, took for granted, didn't bother con-

168

sidering, when it was directly before me to see and know about. One day I'll set to reading on metallurgy, and if I can manage it even in small, I'll establish a forge for myself in conjunction with my kiln.

I've begun again on my watercourse—my dam, which is what it really amounts to. I'll use up the remaining stones I have first, then begin clearing behind the construction to get more, then build more, then get more. By doing one thing and then the other, back and forth, I'll manage to create a bit of variety where none really exists. The work is tiring and somewhat tedious, and I'm rather sore of arm and leg after having been so idle all Winter only to begin again as though there had been no hiatus. Regeneration keeps me healthy, but I must keep my muscles exercised myself.

From the height where I left off last year, progress seems much slower and sense of accomplishment far less demonstrable. The length of the dam grows as the height goes up, so even though the amount of effort remains constant, it appears I'm making less headway because there are now fewer finished layers produced over the same amount of time. I suppose it's only to be expected, but I've become annoyed with the expected in the past. Time is the factor, and I find it very difficult to judge time nowadays.

Before, I could usually gauge an hour when it had passed, but before, there were ways of determining time. The routines of my neighbors in my building, the routines of the city around me—all these gave me reference points. Now I have only sunlight or starlight, the position of the sun or the progress of star clusters across the night sky. It occurred to me to have a clock nearby, but that's ludicrous, and I haven't the wire to bring one out such a distance anyway. Why do I feel concerned about how much time something takes? What do I have to do but what I'm doing? What appointments are scheduled? What meetings planned?

The large puddle that had formed behind the construction did finally drain away. Whether it soaked into the ground or perhaps evaporated instead I don't know, but I do know it didn't leak through the foundation. I guess my barrier of rocks and rubble needs no mortar, though the lack of significant rain so far this season has given me no opportunity to make further observations on this

169

part of my scheme. But it has given me the chance to get things done that I've been meaning to do, so I can't complain.

The lack of rain seems not to have hampered the garden's sprouting. Of course I've watered regularly, but *The Practical Woman* comments that one of the generally unconsidered benefits of rain is that it washes off dust and dirt from leaves and makes them, therefore, the healthier. I cannot provide that service, but so far there's been no noticeable difference between this Spring and previous ones in terms of initial growth, so perhaps "healthier" in this case is a superfluous degree of improvement. And the weed is doing fine, looking quite lush and remaining just as confined and well groomed as before. I really ought, one day, to try eating it. If Aren didn't like its taste raw, then perhaps cooking makes the difference. I know most ordinary vegetables have an awful flavor uncooked.

Carath has been raging most of Spring, and I sometimes can't help but find his antics funny, and pathetic too. He'll sit and chortle on the brink of the downslope into the depression, then instantly race away, turning this way and that in tight curves like some new Owner who's finally been able to make enough to resettle from Athlan to Paragathi, purchase a private car, and run it wildly along the driveways terrorizing his more sedate neighbors. Occasionally, too, Carath's first flying leap takes him right over the edge of the depression by mistake. Then he tumbles and howls, legs frantically waving, claws extended in the hope of catching onto anything to stop his plunge, until he careens directly into some shrub. Once he landed on top of me as I was bending over to hoist up a rock. He often exhibits the worst sense of balance I've ever seen in a cat. In fact, I can't remember ever knowing of a cat with such a dreadful sense of balance. But it might again be a function of his odd paws.

The more I think on it, the more convinced I become that somewhere nearby there must be a mature female. Where I don't know, but you'd think Carath would know. He had to come from someplace. "Nothing is spontaneously generated"—particularly a cat.

Of course, it's also possible that, being different, he is rejected as a potential mate. I recall thinking that's likely how I ended up with him: His mother rejected him from

170

her litter. I wouldn't imagine the number of digits on a paw to be a crucial factor in acceptance, but that obvious change could imply other less obvious ones, or ones less obvious to me but strikingly plain to a cat.

Well, but when you get aroused, you don't want to have to consider your acceptability, I suppose. If you must, then it will be a great source of irritation—hence, perhaps, Carath's raging. I know I would have been enormously reluctant to be with Aren had I known I was regenerative, since at that time regeneration was considered contractable. It was called "the Disease" in those pamphlets, though I now know it certainly is not. And that reluctance would have angered me the more, since the disease I was supposed to be carrying was not deadly, but in fact brings unending life.

I suspect Carath will be in his frenzy for a while longer. It's a shame because I can't talk to him at times like this.

But it will go by. Things do.

Summer, Change 5: 21, 9508

The system works.

The dam is complete. I dug out the tunnel to let the water escape, and now it flows nicely along the trough across the depression. Apparently the lodge's supply is a stream, rather than just a pocket of water: It issues in such a larger quantity than when its outlet was just a piece of piping. Of course, since I dug directly into the source, I got drenched, and when I emerged from the hole dripping, Carath, who'd been eagerly watching the opening into which I'd disappeared, took fright and leapt away directly into the water's path. So he got drenched too.

Naturally, the flow was muddy at first. Though there is not much actual soil in that hillside, there certainly appears to have been the promise of a good deal of erosion. But I lined the bottom of the tunnel out to the dam with extra stones and then temporarily diverted the water down behind the dam while I mortared together a low wall on the valley side of the opening. Otherwise, the water would have gone right over the front and down into the valley, where I certainly don't need it. This isn't as good a solution as it could have been, had I recognized the problem in advance, but it's completely effective. The water comes out fairly clearly now, and it gets clearer by the day. What sediment is still carried will settle out.

The pond is forming. Approximately four or five thousandths below the trough, I built a line of thousandth-wide openings as sluices. They were fun to build, my having to carefully assess the size and shape of each stone to be used for the sides of them so that each sluice would hold together firmly without mortar. In time the flow will wear away even stone, and I do want this thing to have the best chance of lasting as long as possible without repair, so I wanted to avoid using mortar on the sluices. Mortar would erode much more quickly. Still, I had to mortar the trough to make it watertight. We'll see how long it takes before that begins to leak.

Though most of the work on this dam was purely arduous, finishing it—making the sluices and the trough—was truly enjoyable. It gave me a great sense of professionalism and accomplishment. And the whole construction looks quite professionally done, or I assume it does. I choose to believe it does and will hear no argument to the contrary. That's certain.

The depression becomes a gully a short distance in front of the dam. When the pond is full, a new stream will begin down the gully and meander its way until it joins the stream running along the center of the valley. That stream will then increase in size and flow out southeast into the Inland River, which then joins the North River. That flows past North into the ocean, its waters further combined with those of the South Inland Branch that passes by Athlan. I will have changed the face of Ath here, and my change will have further effects, however small, all along the way. It's a peculiar thought that the work I'm doing has such far-reaching consequences, if only slight ones. Some would call the thought aberrant.

The pond fills at an even pace. At its deepest point it will be about three ten-tenths. In the last four days it has already risen one ten-tenth and five thousandths. Four more days and the stream begins.

Presently the water flows across the entire distance and

172

then is turned to the side and down behind the dam. The next thing to do is dig my irrigation channels, line them with stone, construct a gate of some sort by which to regulate the flow through my garden, and then find out if that part of my plan works, or if I've just engaged in a massive construction project, the only point of which is to create a place where I can bathe myself on hot summer days.

There's no reason that it shouldn't work, though, as the grade along the side of the house and through the other part of the garden is reasonably even. However, I'll likely need additional gates at various points to channel the water this way or that. And it's quite possible, no matter how many clever pathways I provide, that the water will choose its own way and ignore the rest. But if things go as I wish, the water will, too. And one esthetic result will be that I'll have a series of miniature waterfalls before my house as the water progresses from one terraced level to the next. How delightful that will be.

Finally, I'll have to cut an exit at the bottom of the garden, to take the surplus to the stream that will be forming shortly. This is all very orderly, what I have in mind, exquisitely so, I think. If I can only get it all to happen in as orderly a fashion as I can dream it.

I've become quite engaged in planning and doing all this, to the complete exclusion of everything else, except the mandatory care of the garden and feeding Carath and myself. I even think I'll make the effort to get the statuary in the lodge, which up to now I've dismissed as so useless that I haven't even thought about it, and put it around the garden in various spots by the irrigation channels. It will look so terribly Great Ocean, such a landscaped plot as I imagine, except that the statuary is all New-Style and not representational at all. To be Great Ocean there should be figures of people and animals, not fluid shapes and geometric constructs. But who will know? And the less it looks of Great Ocean, the better.

I don't know—it strikes me as a rather fussy thing to do. On the other hand, I do have the statuary available, and I suppose it's a shame to let it go to waste in a ruined building. It's almost all of it stone, so it shouldn't be affected by weather. Even the metal pieces are of iron alloy that doesn't rust. I'll think about it.

But I suspect, what with all my ideas for this project, that I'll have no chance this year to build the stone retaining wall in place of the temporary wooden one I erected this past Spring to cover the outside wall of the hallway. But the wooden one seems sturdy enough to last until next Spring without there being any significant damage done. However, I've said something like that about other things in the past, I believe, and been unfortunately proven wrong. Still, I have little choice but to believe my supposition, unless there's enduring good weather this Fall during which I can do the work.

Carath, who has long since calmed down again, or become temporarily resigned to his isolation again, adores the dam. He walks back and forth across it along one edge of the trough as though he were responsible for its being. He'll sit down and stare into the water as it courses past, reaching out to grab at it on occasion, seeming to try to stop it or to arrest some of it. He has more than once fallen into it. But the trough is not deep, only two of my handspans, and while he can't quite touch the bottom of it, except toward its sides, he's not likely to drown in it. The sides do slope rather sharply, though, so being able to touch at those points still does not mean being able to gain footing.

In his frantic efforts to escape the trough, it's possible, I suppose, he could fall over one side of the dam or the other. Then he'd either be in the pond or in some unfortunate condition on solid ground far below. I wouldn't want the latter to happen—the former he can probably get out of reasonably safely—but the distance is enough that during his fall he ought to be able to accomplish what cats as a matter of course can accomplish, to right himself and land crouched on his feet, the impact cushioned. Loren had a cat that once fell out of a third-floor window with no harm done. But Carath's not always very good at that for brief distances. I hope that's only a matter of the distance and not of him.

He's still astonishingly clumsy at times. I can't figure out why. I'd thought, when he was younger, that it was just inexperience. Yet he continues to be clumsy, almost deliberately so. Aren would probably say, as he said of Ranoas, that Carath is "rock-bottom stupid." But I don't think it's that. Carath does often have an expression on his face that suggests he has something on his mind which is distracting him from paying attention to where he is and what he's about to do. I can only wonder what, however.

Still, sometimes while I'm hard at work my own mind goes off into all kinds of irrelevant speculation. For a matter of embarrassment, I was wondering recently why I continue bothering to wear clothes of any sort on hot summer days. It's hardly a matter of propriety now.

I suppose my genitals require some shielding in some circumstances, but for the most part what clothes I wear when it's especially warm—really just old pants that I've cut off the legs of—are just uncomfortable enough, even so, that I could do better without them. Yet the thought of being completely naked, even here and now, somehow disturbs me. I suppose in my mind I consider that not wearing any clothes at all, however more practical, puts me totally on an animal level, and that does disturb me.

On the other hand, going without clothes would soon enough eliminate the extraordinarily ridiculous-looking patch of lighter skin from my waist to my thighs that has been covered from the sun by my cut-off pants. When I regard myself in the mirror, I look half Larien, and in the worst possible place. The rest of me looks half wild, particularly because of my beard and long hair.

Well, I'd better continue to wear something. If my friends could only see me with my skin so much darker—never mind with the beard—they would be appalled. But to me, I guess, the contrast with my blond hair seems somewhat attractive, if alien. In any event, I'm used to it.

So this is the sort of thing I consider as I work. But it doesn't make me clumsy. I suppose, though, that while there's not much thinking to most manual labor, my mind insists on thinking anyway as a sort of pastime. For me it's perfectly harmless. It's just that the topics are sometimes rather peculiar. For Carath, on the other hand, if he does think idly like this, it seems it could be hazardous.

But that's a meaningless bit of imagination on my part, and I shouldn't waste the paper writing out such stuff. My supply is, after all, limited.

Perhaps I will go without clothes entirely one day and discover what it actually makes me feel like. I am, after all, unquestionably a man, even stark naked. At least I know that.

175

I had thought this past Fall, while I was putting up the stone retaining wall, that to prevent a recurrence of last Winter's upsets I should find an absorbing project. But what? What is the real cause of this malady, and what have I done since I've been here that has absorbed me?

Well, the retaining wall took enough time and was mindless enough work so that I could, as I've found I can under such circumstances, devote all my thinking to my problem. These mental meanderings of mine had been pointless before just because I'd not given them any point. After I did, though, I soon enough came up with reasonable answers and what seemed to be a reasonable solution.

I've been trying very hard for the last five years not to remember a great many things, and I still do not wish to remember them. I do not care to recall exactly how Aren and his family died. Even as I write that sentence I begin to, and I notice myself mentally straining to avoid it.

I do not care to recall what I saw of others dying, and not because I had any of the feeling for them that I did for Aren, but because I'm afraid it would lead me to consider how those that I did care about but never saw again might have died. I have a wonderful imagination that must somehow be kept restrained.

I've also tried very hard to avoid seeking reasons for what happened. To arrive at answers you must pose questions of substance, and it's that substance I want to evade. But in part this is also due to my suspicion that I'm incapable of determining the reasons. I don't know that I have the necessary information, or if I do have it, that I'm in a position to make sense of it.

Yet, I'm supposed to be a historian by profession, and even though I'm quite certain now that our historical perspective was always just so much nonsense, the penchant for a perspective of some sort is there. Or perhaps I have a penchant for being the kind of historian none of us ever were, but should have been.

Perhaps that's what made me the writer that I am. Surely, for not being true, *Tales of the Forty-Five, One of Each,* and *The Present Tense* each in its own way has the very sort of "historical perspective" I have now come to see historians should have had. Or perhaps being the writer that I am inevitably led me, though lately, to recognizing my concept of a "historical perspective." I doubt that the word "perspective" applies to anything any historian did before.

But by trying so hard to avoid these things I've obviously put myself under a great deal of stress. It must be, then, that from time to time this stress becomes too great to bear. Thus I become agitated. But by refusing to recognize the sources of this stress, my agitation is accompanied by complete bewilderment, hence the hysterical nature of my agitation.

This even explains my suicidal feelings—didn't my people commit suicide, after all? That's exactly what happened: Mankind deliberately killed itself. So either it's in our nature, and thus in mine, though I strongly doubt this, or I was merely grasping at a solution to my problem that is, in fact, one of the parts of the problem I refuse to consider. Because everyone else did it, it came to me that I, too, should do it. That seems most likely.

Still, after thinking this through last Fall, I was faced with the question: How do I continue avoiding what I want to avoid without suffering for doing so? It's not that I'll avoid it all forever. I think one day I must seriously consider these things, just for my own well-being. The One knows there's no real purpose in my doing so, for having the answers now is far too late to have them matter in the least. They won't prevent what's already happened, and the world, now devoid of men save for myself, is not likely to face such a crisis again. But for the time being it's still too soon. If, when I think of Aren's death, I still want to cry, it's still too soon.

But what could I do to take my mind away from it all? What project could I devise to so deliberately mislead myself? So many things bring so many things to mind. My little world here, all the things I have and truly want to have, the things I truly need, these just by themselves bring back so much.

And I have to continue with them.

So I considered: What have I done since I've been here that's been simply fun? That's banal, but banality is, I suspect, my only escape.

There is my dam, of course. What an engrossing project that was for me. But I can't do something like that in Winter. For next Summer I've already devised quite a number of similar projects, from establishing my forge to fully landscaping and planting with flowers the entire area around my pond. This is all the world I have left, so there's no reason not to indulge in it completely. In fact, I have so many alternative projects in mind for Summers that I can probably keep myself occupied that way for the next ten or twenty years before I have to devise any more.

But for Winters—well, but I know what kept me occupied one Winter. I built the model of Athlan and enjoyed doing it immensely. So why, I thought, don't I build another model like it? But, then, of what? And I deliberated the possibilities, not to mention the question of where I would embark on such a project.

Athlan still sits upstairs in half the bedroom gathering dust. I haven't the will to dismantle it. I worked so hard, it would seem a shame. But I've no more room in this house, so much is stored everywhere.

Yet I decided a model was the answer, at least for this Winter. I would simply use a smaller scale, and if I had to sacrifice some detail, so be it.

Then I had what I thought was a real inspiration: I'd reconstruct old Athel, man's first city. What could be more perfect, particularly for the historian in me? And the size of the model would naturally be less, since the city was considerably smaller than any of the later ones.

But it was burned to the ground by Port Athel in 6559, the event that marks the beginning of the Period of Consolidation. The two cities were in conflict for supremacy on the Centrals, and Port Athel resolved the conflict quite simply. After that incident the Judgment Games were established to settle all subsequent problems by more rational means. This history gave me pause, and I decided my idea was not so inspiring.

As I thought further on the problem, though, I decided on a solution despite the history of it: I would build as best I could a model of En Marab-i-Bar, the city of the

178

Imitators. It certainly would be a challenge, so I set to work on it with the first lasting snowfall.

The obvious problem was finding source material that describes En Marab-i-Bar. And the first source was my own book, *The One*, in which I cited completely *The Generation of Athel*, restoring to that piece its often-deleted section, "The Building of the Lower City":

"The lower city was on the delta of Atheril where it flows to the Central Sea. En Marab-i-Bar, the new city of the great sea, was the place of the Imitators. And it was totally against the order of all things around and about Ath. It was corrupted to its very foundations.

"The lower city had no even boundary, but spread across the land without stopping, as some evil disease covers the skin of the unfortunate. The pathways were in no particular direction, but turned now this way, now that, without seeming to come from anywhere or to go anywhere. Each pathway, moreover, became a great circle in mockery of the One at every certain distance. These circles were numerous within the city, some larger, some smaller, arranged in no particular plan that could be seen from above. And as the city spread, so did these aimless circles increase also.

"There was no order or even distribution of places for the Imitators to get of others' goods, but that all grown food was had in one section, all game in another, all fish in a third, all articles of adornment in a fourth, and thusly. There was no order or even distribution of places for the Imitators to meet with one another, but that some large places were here together, some there together, some other, smaller places in still another section, often those next to or with the places for food and other things. There were no regular gardens, except that flowering plants sprouted everywhere without regard to order or plan. Sun-rays and starflowers and ruffle vines and dewcups were as crowds along the pathways, and open-mouths and shades-of-evening and pious friends and chalices grew together. And poisons grew with medicines, and all manner of plants were in En Marab-i-Bar, also called 'The City of the Flowers' for this reason.

"Between the pathways rose dwellings such as shame the ways of the One. Each was taller than the others, as though to reach above the clouds, and they were enclosed completely from the outside, but the inside was open to the

179

air like a stone cup. It was said that in the north the inside was covered over with a transparent top to keep out cold, but in the south such a thing was not needed. Couples dwelled severally within each, some on one layer, some above or below. None were together as a single family except they have sons or daughters too young to be sent away, yet they spoke in their own tongue of family, of husband and wife, father and mother, children as sons and daughters, in the ways of men, while they were not men."

Unfortunately, while this is a very evocative description to me, it evokes, I think, the wrong things. En Marab-i-Bar sounds rather like Athlan, even in the lack of a distinct city plan. The new section side-by-side with the new City Center of Athlan occupied an enormous portion of the city and completely obliterated the semicircular street pattern as well as most of two radials and a not insubstantial portion of a third. Furthermore, where my father's house was, at the north end of the city, that whole section likewise altered the city pattern. Eventually, I suspect, Athlan would have borne no resemblance to the way it was originally laid out.

But En Marab-i-Bar couldn't have been at all like Athlan. Just the buildings described in that passage that were "open to the air like a stone cup" suggest a quite different architecture. I felt it would be an untrustworthy thing to rely very much on "The Building of the Lower City" for facts, as much as the description does call to mind. So I set about finding and reading all the books I have of any sort that have to do with Imitators, five altogether besides the *Compendium*—three similar to that book, and the other two rather uncertain catalogues of Imitator artifacts with explanations of those artifacts. I'm not surprised my father had the books. I'm only a little surprised he didn't have more. I would have thought he would, since he did so like to joke about Imitators in such a pseudoserious way.

The four collections of Imitator documents, including the *Compendium,* were fascinating reading, to be sure. I learned from them what I could never have imagined before my sudden fluency in Imitator manifested itself. Two of the additional books I knew and had previously read, the third I'd known of. But now reading them, I discovered the extent and density of Imitator thinking. These creatures, whom I'd long known to be interested in abstruse speculation, now appear to have been absolutely obsessed with it, almost to the complete exclusion of any sort of facts.

They questioned the nature of the universe. We were only curious about the physical ordering of it. They questioned the nature of life itself. Our interest in life was only whether or not it was proceeding in the direction we assumed it was intended to go—toward the Last Forming, what I know now to be a perfectly silly notion, as we conceived of it. They speculated on the distinction between the mind and the body. I don't think we ever thought there was much of a distinction. They were enthralled by arguments over the nature and purpose of intelligence, as well as of what they called "intellect" and "creativity," though what they meant by those terms was wholly abstracted. They even had speculations of their own concerning intelligent forms of life other than themselves, all sorts of forms, many of which I could not conceive of even though they were extensively expounded on.

In short, while man was pragmatic in outlook and practical in his affairs, the Imitators were esthetic in outlook, if I can use that word—I can think of none in my language that comes closer to their term—and completely without regard for materiality in and of itself. The real world seems to have been for them rather more of a convenience than a necessity. And they seemed to somehow take reality as being very much more malleable than we, as if the structure of reality could be so easily rearranged whenever and however they liked that it was secondary. What they called "the principles of reality" was their foremost concern.

Well, but I got no details of En Marab-i-Bar or anything physical out of those books. And the two books on the artifacts are, I strongly suspect, untrustworthy, if only because they were written by men who had no knowledge of Imitator thinking. I don't have a complete comprehension of it myself, it's true. But I only needed to see a photograph of what a man called a "chance wheel" to know that I would do as well devising my own definitions for the objects shown. Imitators did not indulge in gaming. In fact, the notions of randomness and simultaneity were matters of very serious concern to them. I got the impression they stood in awe of these notions. And the "chance wheel" was, in any event, a document, the letters cut-outs of one sort of metal on a large, thin disc of some other sort. The workmanship was exquisite, the photograph too poor for me to read more than a word here and a phrase there.

So, finally, this project of mine turned out to be a project in preparation for a project. I've spent the whole Winter reading. And it's proved a fruitless project in the bargain. I have no way of building a model of En Marab-i-Bar, because I have no sufficiently detailed descriptions. But now, I suppose, it doesn't matter, as Winter is nearly over.

However, one thing I will say for all my endeavors: All the reading and all the thinking seem to have kept me busy enough. I've had no attacks of the anxiety I've felt before, and I feel now as though I won't have any, at least in the near future. So I got the result I wanted, even if in a different way than I expected. I won't complain except to note that I wish I had more Imitator documents to read. I'm fascinated by what Imitators are proving to have been, and certainly not a little dismayed that they now no longer exist.

It occurs to me to think that, if man and the Imitator had only established some sort of cooperative relationship, what wouldn't have been possible! That's something I would never have dared even think before. But before, I wouldn't have known enough to think it. And even then it would have been a useless thought. But had I the chance for such a relationship now, would I want it? That would take some thinking, quite some thinking.

Winter, Change 5: 10, 9508

It has rained unceasingly for the past five days. It's been unseasonably warm, too, even humid, which is abnormal for this time of year. The ground is soaked, and if this keeps up much longer, I'll surely have to delay planting. Usually around this time I can at least turn the soil over in the garden and tidy up the rest of the area, but the garden presently is mud. Thank the One it's terraced mud, or I think the whole area before my house would presently be oozing slowly down into the valley.

My irrigation channels are all tiny, swift-running streams ending in waterfalls. I found I had to open all the secondary gates because, closed, they forced all this water to back up and overflow into my plots, some of it actually beginning to seep into the cellar below the winter lounge. But that's stopped and, though I had to have the heat on a day to dry out the moisture down there, which made the house almost unbearably uncomfortable, there seems to be no damage done.

Between my water source in the lodge's hill and the rain, the pond is merrily flowing through the sluices. The stream below is nearly a regular river, and the wider channel it's been cutting for itself has already undermined two small trees, which finally toppled yesterday to land right across the stream. I had to go out and pull them away to one side, else the water, which was starting to back up, might have started to erode the base of my hill. It has already caused a small landslide farther down, washing away the soil on the face of what I'd taken to be a small outcropping of rock, but which now proves to be quite a ledge instead. Without the soil that masked its true character, it's become the edge of something of a waterfall itself. With that and with my ever-running faucet in the kitchen, and the tiny cascades in the garden, and the falls I built, and the rain, I feel completely inundated. Add the racket of the water pump and you have the impression I'm residing in a facility of some sort.

I've looked thoroughly for more books on Imitators, but there are none. I don't want to read any more technology just now—I have been reading about metallurgy and chemistry, both of which are truly dull subjects. I think I'd really love to write a book, though I have no idea what sort of story I could tell, or why I'd bother. But I have the urge to write.

I'm edgy, not anxious as in the past, but just eager to be doing something instead of sitting here watching it pour.

I've talked to Carath, but it's all been aimless remarks. He knows it. He even fell asleep on me. I wish Morin and Theras were here. They'd know how to enliven a dull day, though they both might flag if they had to enliven five of them. For that, thank the One that Loren isn't here. He'd

183

just fidget. He always abhorred doing nothing, while generally I could do nothing with great ease. This is a bit too much nothing, though. So, of course, I'm writing here.

I'll write on a subject: my childhood. It was exceptional, but in all the wrong ways, even discounting what I know now was so wrong about those ways. I never had a Ranoas wet nurse. I'm of Paren, and Paren dropped that custom millennia ago, unless the mother was somehow ill. But my mother was of Galien. You'd have thought I'd have had one.

Morin's family still employed them. His nephew had had one. "Now, I can't say for certain myself," he remarked, "since I've made an effort to forget those days when my talent lay undeveloped. But I suspect, Ancil, that much of your difficulty now has its basis in your not having been nursed by a woman of Ranoas. Take my brother's First Son, for example. Left alone he does nothing but squall. It ruins a gathering and jars my nerves. I cannot bear children, nor do I have to concern myself about that. I suspect I wouldn't have been able to tolerate myself. But put little Kelvin in the arms of his Sena, and out flops her breast, and smack go his lips, and in a ten-tenth he's as silent as a snowflake. I think that if we could station a few women of Ranoas in strategic locations in our favorite places we could deal very effectively with some of the more annoying of our acquaintances. I wonder, would it work if you substituted a man of Ranoas? Ancil, you should know about that. You've been with one."

My childhood was solitary. I read a great deal. In those days I read everything: packaging, the Choice Catalogue from front to back, regulations and instructions for appliances, those terribly maudlin Dark story collections. As I recall, my mother used to get those Dark books, but I don't think she ever read them, or if she did, she must have read them very carefully. When I got to them they were as if unopened. But she couldn't have gotten them especially for me. Why would she have done such a thing?

I read historical summaries by the cartageweight. I learned Imitator that way, when I was eleven, from a book on their documents by a man who lectured history at the School in Far Westland, Foril Pentelis. I met him many years later, only to discover, much to my surprise, that he couldn't—or at least he said he couldn't—read Imitator

184

at all. He said it couldn't be done. Yet at the conference I attended at the School in Athlan, which is when I met him, even though he claimed an Imitator page could only be interpreted in terms of its design, he proceeded to demonstrate how to "interpret" such a page by actually reading it.

I know now he was lying. Then I was very confused and perturbed at him, since I could read it too, and that courtesy of his instruction in his book. But I was never able to locate a copy of that book afterward. I suppose, like most such books, its number of printed copies was only five hundred. But I'd have thought the History Section at the School would have had one. I seem to have assumed a great many things in my life that proved not to be true, or rather that there seemed not to be any proof of whenever I decided to take a second look.

I remember when I first got my great leather chair and foot rest. I was thirteen. When it arrived, my father harrumphed and said it looked as though it would be more suitable for an Owner than for an adolescent. My mother chose it for me for my birthday. I loved it, even though Summers, when it was hot and I sat in it with no pullover on, my sweaty back stuck to the leather. I even remember the sound that was made when I'd pull my bare back away from the chair—the sound of a piece of soft fabric being ripped apart at a distance. And it felt as though a layer of skin were being pulled off my back, though without any pain. I miss that chair. I wonder what happened to it.

I had no chums when I was young. There weren't many First Sons my age in that section of Athlan, and those that were there were insufferable, I thought. They were perfect First Sons. Maybe that's when I decided not to be one. I did have a brief acquaintance, though, with a Second Son nearby. His father put a stop to that, even in that year, though the family was, I believe, of Larien. I'm not sure, as I didn't really pay attention to Family distinctions until I had to at the School, studying them. I suppose my father would have put a stop to it himself, if he'd known. I don't know.

There's so little I really do know, when I start examining the details of my life, though the major events seem plain enough.

That episode with the Second Son later became the basis

for my story, *Foolish Friends*, the juvenile book about just such a relationship between a First and a Second Son, though I set it in the Centrals during the end of the Period of the Two States, just as I did *One of Each*. *Foolish Friends* did well enough as a juvenile book. Because of it, I seriously considered writing only juvenile books. And perhaps I should have done that.

Now there's a question I see as I look back on the last two paragraphs. How did I decide to be a second son? I suppose I had the inclination. You do or you don't, no matter what sort of Son you are. But the first experience I had was on a trip with my father, that time I got lost in Iceport. That's why I got lost.

The fellow I encountered lived in another quarter of the city, and I was so intrigued by the situation I just never paid attention to where I was going with him or how to get back. What was his name? Did I even know it? Probably, but I don't think it made an impression. What did was what happened. It was nothing like what I would have supposed, though, looking back on it, I have to say it was as good as nothing in terms of the mechanics involved. I didn't know what I was supposed to do. I wonder what impression I left with whoever he was. I'd hate to think.

Well, I'm tired. I'm tired of this rain. Carath is sleeping on the couch, but I think I'll displace him.

It's curious that he won't sleep with me, as cats I've known of have always done. Loren's cat used to sleep between us when I stayed the night at his rooms. Carath prefers to sleep next to my bed, not on it, when I'm on it. Likewise, he prefers to sit on a chair near me when I'm eating and watch. Other cats sit right by you and beg. Morin's used to claw my pants until I'd feed him. Carath has strange habits, but really, what does he know about being a cat? And he won't listen to me when I try to instruct him. At those times he regards me as though I were aberrant. And at those times I suppose I probably am. Really, why should he be a cat, after all? Let him be what he wants, as if it were my position to so give him leave!

This past half-year has been remarkably uneventful. It was as though everything were methodically regulated, as though all my efforts were merely a part of this regulating. It was as though it ought to have been boring, but it didn't seem to be, nor did anything seem interesting as I look back. I could even suspect it didn't occur, this last half-year, were it not for the evidence—the vegetables, berries, grains, and the like that I've harvested and stored; the land-scaping around the pond, which I can see from the window here. These things have been done, but I cannot say with certainty that I did them. I have no feeling about them.

The landscaping appears, even at the end of this season, to be quite an accomplished job. Behind the pond is a flat terrace of stones, and from that, around the water's edge and down to the dam, there's a stone walk with occasional steps where the grade of the land drops a ten-tenth sharply. From the dam there's a stone walk over to my door.

Along these walks are plantings, now all gone by, of sun-rays and starflowers, of all sorts of blossoms—all rescued from the tangle of my mother's plantings. And where the stonewood tree casts its shadow, plantings of star-pointers, ladies'-scent, and shades-of-evening, the last still carrying a few of their faded purple flowers even now. It all seems quite pleasant—I recall at the height of Summer it was lovely—but did I actually do it? The effort seems as remote from me as if it had been done by Ranoas.

More than the distance between myself and these things, there's a feeling I have strongly that I did nothing else, either. But I've read a great deal more since the end of last year. I know a great deal more about various things—my proof that I must have studied them. I've read voraciously, in fact, until late every evening, this past Summer, and I remember noting that the reading quite rapidly grew easier and easier, almost abruptly so, as I found myself experiencing an increasing familiarity with technical terminology. This had to happen eventually, I suppose. Now it seems hardly believable that I should once have been so apprehensive about scientific matters. And now it seems quite absurd that I should have lauded myself last year for my professionalism in building the dam.

There's no "professionalism" to anything I did, only the doing itself, and that correctly or incorrectly. "Professionalism" is only a consideration when there are others working, by whose efforts you can judge your own. I suppose a pretension to professionalism was helpful in a way, though —it provided me a sort of impetus to continue, to keep trying, and to keep learning, and to become more skilled. Still, it's nothing but a pretension, and now the pretension has no more use. My impetus to accomplish whatever I have in mind is present in and of itself. I needn't any longer pride myself in order to stimulate myself. I need only think in order to do something, and for much, it would seem, I hardly even need think about it any longer. Even the landscaping, for all its pleasantness, was rather routine.

I have no worry about surviving any longer. I will survive, no question, and even without much of what I've had from the start, when those things fail irreparably. It was fortunate I had them all, I suppose. Everything was a solace, a collection of advantages to rely upon; and a catalyst, a means of forcing me into learning how to repair it all, replace it all, do without it, go beyond it. Or the fear of losing it all was the catalyst. But I've now brought everything into a set routine, a pattern of this and then that and then a third thing and then a fourth, each in its proper time, everything in a sequence, in an expected, dependable, almost automatic, whole-year, repetitive chain of events.

This cycle I've established allows me time to think about other things than what I'm doing, and time to accomplish the frivolities, like all this landscaping. There's time for my reading and learning, and time to consider what I can do with all this knowledge I'm accumulating. Thus my world expands even as my cycle continues. Or, my cycle expands to include every new bit of knowledge I acquire and every use to which I put it. As self-contained as my world is, therefore, it does enlarge. That's why, I guess, I don't find this all boring, when it seems as though I should.

Memories, when they come to me, as they still often do, have no more impact now, it seems, than a dream might.

I am still interested one day in determining somehow, as best I can, why things happened the way they did, and how I could have come to where I am. But it's no longer an interest driven by fear or frustration or the blind, pathetic demand to know absolutely, to have finally every last answer to every possible question, as though doing so were some final tribute to the Aten, or to my friends, or to the past. Knowing isn't going to change anything. I suspect I must have had some hope it might. Knowing isn't going to change me. Nothing, in fact, actually will.

I've begun reading books on this planetary system and on the stars, books that were given out by and large for use on the Starship Project. Most of them aren't really even books, but merely photocopies of mechanical-writer pages bound in sets, and loosely bound at that, as though certain things were expected to be revised from time to time, new pages written and inserted in place of other less-precise ones. That's probably the case. It seems a quite sensible system.

Ah, and, to be sure, it's a pastime for me to read them, but, I have the feeling, a not unimportant one. They contain a good deal of speculation, not on strictly scientific matters, but on life and its general origins, and on the forms life could take other than our own, and on different or alternative organizations of life in the control of intelligence. It's all what could be reasonably inferred from known biological facts as applied to conceivable circumstances the Starship might encounter. This is intriguing in and of itself, a kind of speculation it would never have occurred to me to be necessary, and one that was certainly not mentioned publicly as being done.

The Imitators, I know, engaged in this sort of speculation also, perhaps centuries before man appeared on Ath, or perhaps because man did appear. But theirs was an abstracted sort—how an alternative intelligence might think, how it might speculate, given differing circumstances. Our version of this speculation concerns itself strictly with how other life forms might live—under what physical circumstances, under what social organizations, with what sort of technology. Ours was the pragmatic viewpoint. Imitator speculation would seem to have no practical application at all.

It's clear this speculation would have to be done. There

189

is, I suppose, no reason to assume that man is the only likely intelligent life form to appear, though that's what people did assume. I guess even I would have assumed this, had I thought about it, but that was before I came to recognize that the Imitators were also an intelligent life form, or before I allowed myself to recognize this fully. I know most people felt that the Starship would discover either planets exactly like Ath but without any men on them, or planets like Ath with people exactly like us. One or the other—it was obviously the way of the One. But it's obviously nonsense.

I can only wonder what would have happened if the Starship had been launched and had subsequently discovered an intelligent life form other than our own. Or worse, if it had discovered other beings like us, but who did not give credence to the thinking of the One. How would they have reported the discovery? How would we have reacted to it? Even now the possibility strikes me as demeaning, though why it should I have no idea.

Once I'm through these books, I can start to read through all three hundred and ten of the *Planning* volumes with a good deal more comprehension. I've been avoiding them, not because so much is speculative, but because the speculation is so specific to the kinds of conditions to be tested. With the general background in what was being considered that I'm now acquiring, the specifics will make much more sense. And of course, my technical knowledge is now much better than before, though I'd yet never qualify as a practical mathematician of any sort.

I've progressed through chemistry and metallurgy, and I'm currently also reading about emission generation, usage, and containment. This subject rather neatly relates the divisions of science to one another, and incidentally it clearly explains why nothing can live in a wasteland where the level of emissions is fatally high. The material also, however, deals with much that is strictly hypothetical, much that is, perhaps, beyond the realm of possibility in the hands of man.

Carath was very good this Spring and Summer. He seems to have fallen into some sort of routine as well. His pattern consists primarily of sitting and watching intently as I go about what I do—the garden, the landscaping, keeping the house, reading, even sleeping. More than once

I've awakened earlier than usual to find his great yellow eyes fixed on me. I can't imagine what he finds so interesting. But at least he's no longer as boisterous and noisy and clumsy as before. Yet I miss all that at times. It was noticeable activity, however random and ridiculous.

As I think about it, there has been a distinct lack of activity around and about, too. The animals in the area are probably no more or less numerous than before. I still trap bounders regularly. But I seem to see them less and hear them less. The manlikes that I've come to expect to be roused by, nights in Spring and Fall, haven't made their appearance this year. They're not gone away, however, as I've seen them individually or in small groups far out in the valley, lumbering off in some direction or another. But it has been quieter than usual.

Perhaps I and my establishment have just come to be accepted as part of the surroundings, like an outcropping or a stonewood tree. Not that I think animals accept or reject —Carath, of course, does, but I've long since abandoned the notion of considering him an animal or actually anything other than what he is: most basically a "Carath." He's neither one thing nor another, but himself.

But there's no reason not to suppose animals notice, and then get used to, and at last cease to take notice of things which are destined to remain permanent in their environment. Even an alien life form like myself. Things seem strange and frightening only on the first encounter. Later they become commonplace, even ignorable. And, perhaps, that's the way I now reply to my life, and why these past two seasons have gone by without much notice.

Fall, 1: 24, 9510

It's been nearly a year since I've written anything here. I'd have thought this couldn't be true, but I recall having been similarly deluded before, some years ago. And I see that the last entry stands a half-year away from the one before that. Are things indeed becoming so dull, or am I coming to rely so much on Carath for my communication? Perhaps it's an effect of my being regenerative. I know I've come to disregard time entirely, preferring instead to mark my existence by associating events with events rather than with the abstracted measurement of hours and days and changes, and seasons as collections of changes. I've reckoned the date today—and I have continued to reckon the passing days—solely to mark this entry in my record here. I suppose I should continue to mark the days as they pass, but it seems so pointless. Days come and go—what matters far more is what I do with those days.

But what have I done this past year? The garden grows and produces as always. I've read through a third of the *Starship Planning* volumes. In one book there is a discussion of hybridization, and for a moment I feared for my garden because of the discussion.

I'd come to assume that the seeds with which I'd started my garden were the results of Heremis's experimentations. Each Fall I'd set aside some seeds from the crop to plant the following Spring, but the particular *Planning* volume remarks that the seeds of hybrids, if they are fertile, won't produce truly, but tend instead to grow reversions. I thought: Have the plants in my garden been slowly reverting, and I've just not been noticing? That seems to be false. My crops remain unchanged in kind—even the grains I've grown up here from the seeds from the plots I found downslope. So my original seeds must not have been from hybrids. They must have come from my mother's own efforts.

I've also enlarged the landscaped area around the pond and built by my stone terrace a small summer shelter, where I've slept on hot nights this past season. It's more comfortable to sleep out than in my house when it's so warm and humid, and it's idyllic to waken in the early morning and bathe in the pond. It would be a luxury, if I couldn't do it whenever I like. As it is, I think nothing of doing what I do—I even think nothing of no longer wearing clothes Summers—though at moments my style of life still gives me brief pause when I consider the way I lived before. It's not, however, as though I worry about what people might have said; no, at moments now I wonder how I could have lived the way I did.

I've even tried my hand at sculpture. Who's to know if it's good or not? But it's not good. I have no ability at that. My efforts, all in "New Style," as I would never be able to accomplish a representational figure of anything, have a distinctly uninspiredly functional appearance, as though each one ought to be something else or do something. The One only knows what. But if one of my four lackluster creations were abruptly to begin producing tableware or food sticks, I shouldn't be surprised. They each look more mechanistic than geometric. Yet they grace my summer terrace, and Carath, at least, seems continually astonished by them.

I've not yet constructed a forge, though I should. I've not yet needed anything new of metal, nor am I sure I could produce even the simplest of items if I had to. If my sculpture is any indication, I'll never be able to. But I should have the forge in any event, just in case such work does not require talent. The future will no doubt require the facility.

I haven't, I think, become complacent, but my life is no doubt more mechanical than ever. The seasons and their various weathers dictate much of my activity, just as day and night do. I seem to know now just when to plant, and when I have free time for other activities, and when I must tend to other chores. And everything gets accomplished, and, apparently, on schedule. I've suffered no losses or inconveniences. I haven't even glanced at a clock for what seems several years. My day now starts in the morning when I wake up and ends with sunset, a much more reasonable way of marking the day than the old way, at Midday—to be precise, at the middle of the third hour of Midday. I suppose there must have been some reason for our having done that for nearly ten thousand years, when otherwise a half hour is solely a measure of distance and not of time, but I've never known that reason. Who would have thought to ask why such basic things were the way they were?

This disregard for time as a measure does have one remarkably beneficial result: I am free of the dependence upon and worry over the powerful phrases, "how long" and "how soon." I am no longer impatient—"patience" itself is made irrelevant. I feel I have more latitude to my activities because I no longer have a strict temporal restraint upon any one of them. But I suppose I also feel somewhat adrift from existence, unhindered by it, yet somewhat unconnected to it.

193

I often have the feeling that I float through the world around me like the leaves on the surface of my pond. At those moments I touch myself to make sure I'm still a substantial being. But such moments happen infrequently. I imagine that the only reason they happen at all is that I still, by habit, feel the need to mark events by time. That is, after all, just what I do in these pages, though I'm doing it less now.

But, in fact, there is one great "clock" by which I can measure the progress of everything. There is a standard which, no matter what else happens, I can always be sure will remain exactly the same in its cycle every day, every year, forever, for as long as "forever" amounts to. There are the planets and the stars in their cycles above me. Carath and I have long watched the procession of them evenings and nights—the infinitely great, infinitely dependable turn of events, in the most precise sense of that phrase. I can follow their movements and mark mine by theirs. Certainly when my man-made clocks are gone, the night sky will remain as always.

I need only three planets to tell the seasons: Nar, which rises and sets in Winter; Narath, which rises and sets in Summer; Pleistar, which hovers low on the horizon Fall evenings and also Spring mornings. And if the passage of daytime can be marked by the progress of the sun across the sky, so the passage of nighttime can be marked in Winters by the passing cold gaze of the Eyes of the One, those two vast star clusters of a hundred million stars apiece; and Summers by the flight of the Swarm across the southern horizon, itself a separate galaxy. These time my life sufficiently. Fifths of an hour, tenths and ten-tenths —these are distinctions that now make little difference to me. Hours, in fact, are irrelevant, too, though I find I still figure how many hours a given activity will take, just as I still often tell Carath to wait a fifth, or that I'll be back in a ten-tenth. I'll never be able to escape reckoning time, perhaps, but I can alter my dependence on it somewhat by changing the terms of it.

Carath and I watch the heavens together, and he's now so knowledgeable as I about the order of our star system that it seems he often spies a rising planet before I do. At least, there have been times when, by his remarking chirrup, I have noted a planet already risen. I've even learned from him how to distinguish the tinier companions to the planets. The major companions are clear enough on clear nights, but the minor ones require a special way of looking at them.

At first, when I wanted to point out the companions, I stared and strained to glimpse the minors, but without success. But Carath would tilt his head slightly and squeak as though everything were quite plain to him. At last, when I imitated what he did, I saw them too. In order to see such small bodies you must look slightly away from them—catch them, as it were, in the corner of your eye. Not that I really believe, I suppose, that he has the slightest idea what we're doing. What could any of this have to do with a cat? Actually, I merely thought to mimic him in fun, but when I did so, the attitude worked. Thus, Carath "taught" me.

At first, also, I shied away from watching Pleistar, which wasn't hard to do. That planet is up chiefly at times when, as in Spring, I'm still asleep, or as in Fall, when the air is chill and I'm too tired from harvesting to have much interest. Of course, I avoided Pleistar for the obvious reason. But now that I watch it, the sight pains me equally for just the opposite reason.

Where is the Starship?

The most unhappy object I can view is Pleistar's companion, and not because it's a solitary satellite, while the four outer planets have each more than one. Were I to indulge in that sort of sad symbolism, then Ath, having no companions whatever, should be the "loneliest" of our six worlds. No, Pleistar's companion is unhappy, to me, because it reflects—it literally reflects—the work of man, and because, although it was originally alone, it is once again alone, and I don't know why.

The companion shines nearly as brightly as Pleistar itself. Its surface is almost entirely covered by the enclosures of the Starship Base. Its sparkle is unnatural, the work of man, and when I see it, I know I'm not looking at a mere chunk of rock, but at an actual habitation, a place where men once were and could still be, or where there is what once were men and women, now all dead. Or are they gone?

The companion once had a twin that also circled Pleistar: the Starship, which amounted to a man-made planetoid in orbit about an adopted parent. Once everyone could point it out Spring mornings and Fall evenings. It glittered as it swung around one side of the planet, a false companion chasing after the equally glittering natural one. But it's no longer there. Was it destroyed?

It was scheduled to be launched on a trial in '04 or '05. There'd been a delay finishing several sections of it due to disturbances here in '02. It was habitable, if not entirely navigable. It was to begin its voyage to find another world for us in 9510—this year. But it's no longer to be seen. What happened to it? And if it was destroyed, did people survive on the companion? Or did a few survive on the planet's surface in the Base there? I don't know. Surely I would have discovered someone left, that time I tried my father's multiple carrier, if there were someone left. And I didn't. But could it have been launched, however lamely? I don't know that, either. And I don't know why it would have been. If there were survivors, they could have returned here. There's no one to threaten them. They should have come back. They must have had at least one shuttle operable. There must have been someone. They've left me.

That's silly. How do I know what happened? Unless I could see the surface of Pleistar, unless I could be there, it's all possibilities and no proof. And if indeed there were no shuttles to use, they could hardly have used the Starship itself to return to Ath, since it would have caused massive tidal disturbances that might well have destroyed the very place they were trying to reach.

I cannot reason what actually happened. I can only look up at the bright reflections of the companion and wonder. Pleistar must be a lonelier place than here, for here I have Carath, at least. Pleistar is left now to those organisms native to it that haven't the inklings of even a plant.

But what of systems other than mine? A hundred million of them visible in each of the Eyes, hundreds of millions of them when you consider that the Eyes of the One are just the same galaxy seen extending in opposite directions from this place in the midst of it. And the hundreds of millions more in the Swarm, that galaxy beyond us that glistens in the southern sky in Summer. And the many more than that in galaxies scattered so far distant in the void that they appear to be just stars.

To think that half could have planets, and half of those planets like this one, and half of those with life on them, and half of those bearing men, or beings like men, or beings with intelligence equal to man's, if not greater than man's. At least a full sixteenth of the whole Starry Sheath can be populated. I wonder what they're like, those populations.

Do they have star travel? There's speculation that many must. Would they come here? Another intelligence might pass by, it was thought, but seeing Ath populated, it might well refrain from stopping. Star travel can have only two purposes: to develop an unpopulated planet, or to contact beings of equivalent or greater sophistication. Ath, being both populated and possessed of a relatively young intelligence, would most likely be avoided. It would be left up to us to find *them*, and not in their interest to bother with *us*.

But there is no one left here but me, and who would notice me? If any intelligence came here now, Ath would seem a great deal more suitable. Such beings, I read, could be expected to have come from farther in toward the center of our galaxy, where older intelligence would be most likely. I wonder what they'd be like, such older intelligent beings. I can only wait to see, if in fact there's anyone to wait for. And would I want to meet them, or they me? I would be irrelevant to them, a mere curiosity. They could well be terrifying, if indeed they were not like me.

There's so much speculation in the books on what sort of life might exist, and on what way of life each sort might pursue. Some of it is not especially pleasant, though perfectly rational in terms other than my own. None of it is especially pertinent now, or at least not until some alien being finds me, or I he. It doesn't seem too likely. I shouldn't waste effort thinking about it.

Still, I also wonder whether such a being would have a cat, as I have Carath. Or something like a cat. I wonder if Carath wonders that. I've spoken to him about all this, but his interest seems only polite. Perhaps he's wiser than I in all this. He may not know as much as I, but I often suspect that the knowledge he holds he holds surely. It is unquestionably the curse of intelligence to be able to know so much, but trust so little.

197

What a busy time this has been. I've had so much to do, it seems I've had no time in several years to report on it. But I must take the time, if only for the perspective. I've found I do look back among these entries for information. And from what else I discover in the process, I find I get a different point of view about myself, about how I live and have been living. It's encouraging, often, when I've seen myself to have been so discouraged. I've endured— I've even endured thoughts of suicide. That endurance itself is heartening, but especially when so much seems to be going so badly. So, for what else I may reveal to myself in the future, I should relate at least what I've accomplished these past years.

But when did I do what I've done recently? In which year did I start what project? When, for example, did I have to repair the solar plant? Last Summer, early in the season, it seems. Yes, several collectors went bad, and I had to replace them and some additional wiring with parts salvaged from the lodge's solar plant. And I found the problem with my old water pump as well: The filter at the intake was clogged solid. So that now works again, whenever I need it. And I'm alerted to cleaning the filter of the pump I've had in use. I've decided to keep that running for as long as it will, rather than replace it with the original one. There's no sense going to the trouble until I have to.

I've built myself a sturdy workshop on the site of the old summer-lounge section. It has in it my kiln, which I've enlarged to accommodate some smelting, and which also now has an oven for firing pottery. That last was necessary, as I've managed by now to break most of the tableware I had, except the service for ten of my mother's, which I resolutely refuse to use, though I don't know why. Sentimentality, I suppose, though I can't recall my being at table when she ever used it. Still, it's a good deal more delicate than what I need, a good deal more feminine.

I've also set up a forging block, which I found in the

old sap house. And I brought over all the equipment that was stored in that enclosure, since the sap house is now starting to fall to ruins. I haven't maintained it. It's too far afield for me to visit regularly, even if I had a use to which to put the enclosure. The equipment is good for its metal, at least. The various saws help me clear the woods nearby for firewood. I've had a blazing hearth, winter evenings, which Carath and I both enjoy, though it's not yet especially necessary. It's cheery. And I've wood stacked neatly in my workshop for the kiln arrangement and for the hotbed by the forging block.

I hadn't reclaimed wood enough to build the kind of workshop I had in mind, so much of it has been erected with raw logs and then finished with my salvage. It has large double doors on each side, so that, when all are open, a pleasant and necessary breezeway is made. There's a loft for additional storage. I have much of the equipment from the sap house up there presently. And I've used the exposed rough-hewn beams for hanging some vegetables—weepers strung together and the like. I had an extraordinary crop of weepers last year, all of which I still haven't used up, even though the crop this year looks to be over-sized also. And in one corner of the place I've installed a carefully laid stone floor for winnowing the grains I harvest. My workshop serves all sorts of purposes.

It looks, I fancy, somewhat like an establishment of Ranoas, basing my opinion on what little Nata told me about the ways and means of the Workers' Section. Perhaps my workshop doesn't look like that of Ranoas at all; still, I get such an impression from it, the same impression Nata's vague descriptions gave me. So why not assume it's so? It might as well be so, given the reasons for which it exists. And whether or not, it does look well made and well finished. I followed *The Practical Woman*'s advice and instructions in all matters she covered, so at least the work-shop looks like something built according to those ways, if not according to others.

My gardens flourish beyond my expectations. The vegetable plots have been consistently bountiful, Summer before last giving me more to eat than I had ways to store. I ate a great deal and often, that Fall and Winter, until I thought I'd burst from so much food. I gained no weight, of course, but my physique has developed from being merely pleasantly well balanced to somewhat resembling that of Lin—very muscular, very attractive. Certainly that aspect is of no account now but to my own admiring eye.

Except for the blond hair, I could be taken for being of Ranoas, something that strikes me now as a pleasant mistake and not the stupid blunder I would have construed it as years ago—ten years ago, in fact. Except for the blond hair and my beard—Ranoas no more went bearded than the rest of us. But I like the beard on me. I sometimes wonder who, of those I knew, could have worn a beard so well. Likely only Loren. Theras and Morin would have looked silly. Paras would have seemed malevolent. But Beskin could have worn one well—he had the slightly wild look in his eyes that I do now, which sets the beard off so well. Sculptors do, I suppose, and refugees. And, perhaps, writers.

Along with my vegetables, my trapping has flourished as well. I always have bounders to eat, to prepare a hundred different ways to avoid the boredom of their plenty. I even no longer set out so many traps. In a day or two a dozen are filled. Where there was dearth, now there's surfeit. But I shan't complain. Dearth may yet come back. Meanwhile, I speculate on catching a breathswift. I can use both the meat for variety and the leather for clothing. I have a cartageweight of cured bounder pelts: a bounder-pelt bed covering I sewed two Winters ago, a bounder-pelt throw rug for Carath to sleep on by the hearth, a bounder-pelt head covering for myself, Winter days when I don't want to go hooded but find it's too cold to go bareheaded. I have bounder-pelt mittens. I have double-faced bounder-pelt pants, which are heavy as Summer's humidity but equally warm and very sensuous to wear. I have yet to make bounder-pelt draperies, but I'll have to do something with the excess. I refuse to simply throw it away. But I'm overproducing, and with no Great Ocean on which to slough off the surplus.

My other garden, the flowers, is spectacular. I can't understand how that's become so successful, but it does—and I do know this—look just like the work of Ranoas in Athlan. I'd never have thought I had a knack for plantings, just as I was sure I had no knack for sculpture. But everything I've arranged has blossomed mightily. The plants keep to their assigned locations—just as the weed continues to be verdant and self-limiting by the vegetable plots. And each bloom comes true each year, even those I have to reseed. No hybrids among them, I guess. Even the wild flowers I've uprooted and transplanted have done exceptionally well.

It's pure pleasure summer evenings to sit in the pond house, as I call it, and gaze toward my house at the colorful terrain in the twilight, to smell the fragrances and to hear birds calling the locations of their roosts to one another before they sleep. And it's more the pleasure to wake up to the sight and the smell, and to the sounds of the birds rousting each other out for the day. Nowadays I fall asleep satisfied at my day's work and wake energetic to begin again. They're often euphoric, these feelings. I'd have been concerned about myself years ago, but now euphoria seems only right.

Perhaps my greatest achievement among the flowers has been my success with the endurance-of-man. I decided to have some of it here around my pond, even though I knew I couldn't expect it to flower in Spring for many years after I moved it. But apparently I was wrong. I planted it year before last, and yet this Spring it blossomed as though it had been in place forever. That means, I guess, that it's found my garden safe and comfortable. I also find the garden so, but I'm pleased that the world agrees with me.

As for my reading and studying, I've done little over the past couple of years. I reread much of chemistry and metallurgy in connection with building my workshop, and I also reread some material on architecture for that project, in those areas not dealt with by *The Practical Woman*. She can't be expected to know everything. Other than that, I've read nothing. I've given myself free time from my studies.

But now, wait—

There. I never noticed that before: *The Practical Woman* has an error. In speaking of the endurance-of-man, she claims: "So it is also with women in the progress toward the Last Forming: They will always be fewer than men until all the world follow the way of the One together." That's wrong. We produce more females than males. How odd.

But maybe that reflects some old Dark thinking. It's a pre-Confederation book, and Darks at that time thought a good many erroneous things, just as I often do here and now.

But that is the only error I've come across in the book, and it's not an obvious one either. Perhaps it was just mis-written and never noticed in the printing because the mind tends to read the passage "correctly," even though it's blatantly the opposite of the fact. I know I misread it until just now, when I thought of it as I wrote about it and looked it up for amusement.

Well, that makes *The Practical Woman* all the more human as far as I'm concerned. She ranks next to Carath in my affections, but just one error only serves to enhance her standing.

I wonder if there are more. It wouldn't do to find she's made too many mistakes. But all her advice I've followed has proven sound so far, though there's much I haven't tried and haven't had to try.

We'll see in the future. But I doubt she'll mislead me.

Spring, 2: 2, 9517

The sound of the water pump is deafening me.

It happened at last. I should have known. I was finishing the planting and Carath was asleep under the great stay-alive. I finished and he was dead.

When I came around to the front of the house, it seemed unnaturally quiet. It seems so still that I cannot help no-ticing the pump now.

Now, having planted, I wonder that I've done too much. I'll have a larger crop than usual because there is only me to eat it. Not that Carath ever ate much of my food; but some, enough to make me aware I was sharing it.

I placed him at the foot of the garden. Near the weed. He'd like being there, as it had become recently the best place to catch vermin in Summer. They always come out to feast on my grain. And Winters he'd stare at the spot from the dining room, wistfully remembering and expect-ing another season, I suppose.

He's dead, and I'm alive. I'm alive and will maintain

myself. I'm twenty-eight. I'll always be twenty-eight. And no one will have to worry about missing me, for I'll always be around and about. Not Carath, certainly. Not now.

And the water pump continues its racket. It always did, but I notice it again. I have nothing to distract me. I'm alone. I hate the noise, and I hate this sudden, unnatural quiet.

Summer, 5: 3, 9528

At last I know who Heller was. And what he was. One of his reports was folded in the last pages of a *Starship Planning* volume. The report was on me.

My first reaction to this treachery was the expected one: I rushed to these pages to write about it here. But even as I start, I think, what's the point? What is there even to relate? My father had in his employ a man—apparently someone considerably older than any of us, my father included—whose chief duty was to ingratiate himself among my friends and watch me, and report on my activities. Heller was a regenerative and, it would seem, an associate of Heremis of long standing. Heller also had an eye for detail and a writing style that's rather effective. The report itself is filled with the banalities of my life in Spring, 9501, but banalities interestingly put. Did he report only by season? I wonder.

Heller was introduced to me by . . . No, I was talking to Theras. Loren and I were. I got into a discussion with Loren, and, when I turned back to Theras, he was talking to Heller.

But he'd never met Heller before. In fact, I believe he was turning Heller down. But Heller automatically introduced himself to us, to Loren and myself. And then we started seeing him around and about. That was sometime in Fall, 9500. And I think Heller later took up with an acquaintance of Theras's, and, as a consequence, he was sometimes with us after that Fall, often enough that he eventually became a sometime associate of ours.

Spring, 9501—Heller notes that *Tales of the Forty-Five*

was given out the first change, and that I was "almost insufferably euphoric" for a change and a half after that. As who wouldn't have been! He also notes that I had a disagreement with Loren. Thus, my father knew I was a second son. What joy that must have brought him. Well, it's as I always told Loren: If you don't want to hear the answer, don't ask the question.

At least Heller saw the correct reason for the disagreement I had with Loren: "A.'s obstinate curiosity presents considerable problems to his companion, L. Akaror. Obviously, creativity, as they claim, demands its own set of values be recognized, or else the creative person must face being considered aberrant by the practical-minded." Exactly. I only wish Heller could have told us that then, as neither Loren nor I really knew why we were having the problem we had and would continue to have. But I don't suppose Heller was employed to tell *us* what we were doing.

Heller also displays an excruciating perception of me: "A. tends to be somewhat pompous at times, particularly when he's in a good mood. Then he lapses into a rather emphatic drawl that his associates either accept or ignore, but which makes the stranger feel that A. considers himself somewhat withdrawn from his surroundings. A. is a distant sort of person, to be sure, a person who never seems to be fully engaged in whatever is happening around himself, nor to fully enjoy anything. Rather, he always seems to stand apart to watch—observing seems to be more a compulsion with him than a pastime. Yet his pompousness and his emphatic speech are actually indications to those who know him well that he is at that moment participating in whatever event is ongoing, participating as much as he will, and perhaps, in the only way he can."

Subsequently, Heller evinces extraordinary generosity: "For all the problems A. has dealing with others, I think compensation, if not also explanation, can be found in his increasingly creative point of view. He has a marked ability to compare two seemingly unrelated things and arrive at an often wholly unexpected but generally reasonable new conclusion. This, in combination with his innate intelligence, since he is also regenerative, will make him most valuable to us in the future.

"His problems with others seem to be chiefly, if not exclusively, derived from this creative point of view. On the one hand, people often take offense at A. because either they don't understand what he's saying or they do and find it uncomfortable to be in the company of someone who has a habit of making sententious remarks. On the other hand, because people so often take offense at A., and because he does not recognize why they do, A. often deliberately becomes obscure, more than occasionally so cryptic that not even those closest to him understand him, and they themselves have a great penchant for obscurantism."

Heller also mentions that he "rather liked" *Tales of the Forty-Five*. And that "for someone who is so distant and who so often remains on the periphery of events, A. has a quite decent knack for relating an event in writing. This will also have its value to us, and a rather more specific value."

Of what sort, I wonder. I sound as though I were an experiment. Of course, no one ever told me what was in mind for my future. I'm rather miffed at that, though it hardly matters what they had in mind.

As for "they," I wonder who the "they" were to whom Heller refers several times:

". . . creativity, as they claim, demands its own set of values . . ."

". . . in instances like this, they inform us, the best course is not to enforce an adjustment . . ."

". . . with regard to A.'s development, they say that moments of instability can only be adjusted by himself . . ."

". . . intellect, like creativity, they say, is also a control mechanism . . ."

Well, "they" must be others like themselves, I suppose: Heremis and whoever else took such an interest in my personal life.

As usual, my father has checked the margins of the report, items that most interested him. I can't understand why the ones he checked would. Among them are the various remarks on my distance from people and things around me. He was distant to me. What did he expect?

For some reason I feel myself beginning to miss all those things I never enjoyed doing and all those people I kept myself from. I feel regret, and I've never regretted much of anything before. What a silly regret! What a silly feeling. It's because of this report, I know. It makes me feel the more alone.

And, of course, I'm not alone. Now there's Enrath. And he looks a bit like Morin. Or else Morin has developed a feline resemblance in my mind. Whichever: Enrath is pudgy. He's gotten very pudgy very quickly, in fact. He appeared last Spring. Before that was Shefan, and he looked like a history lecturer of mine when I attended the School. And before that was old Carath, who looked like Lin.

I'm hardly alone, though I still cannot understand why that should be. I see no other cats. These appear and live with me a while and die and get "replaced." They're very much the same, for all their differences: with five digits on each forepaw, instead of six; all of them a bit clumsy as though preoccupied—and with Enrath's weight that's an especial problem; all immensely talkative, demanding, inquisitive; all of them with a propensity for sitting still and staring at me sometimes, until I can actually feel the weight of their gaze. They're all like cats, but not exactly catlike; or catlike, but not exactly cats—I can't decide which.

But I'm definitely not alone, so there's no reason that this summary of my activities in Spring, 9501, should make me feel alone. Probably I'm just piqued that there was such a report provided on me. I know I'd have been furious then, if I'd only known what Heller was actually about. But I can't fault Heller. At least he never tried to ingratiate himself with me—he did anything but, as a matter of fact. When I asked him back to my rooms once—a place in my life he never saw for as long as I knew him—he declined politely. He never pushed himself on me, but kept his distance. But my father saw my rooms—so, I suppose, why should Heller have bothered?

No, at best, I think, this discovery has merely made me start to consider myself and my past again. I haven't much since Carath died. Most of Shefan's life I spent trying to explain just the principles of our system of naming, and how a person could be both polite and insulting at the same time by the way he addressed someone. That took so much time because, like any of the ways people dealt with one another, naming and the use of names makes no sense whatever.

But now that I begin thinking on it all again, I must be careful of becoming too introspective. I've watched myself the few times that I have gotten that way since Carath, and all the different lines of thought I've taken I've developed in exactly the same way to exactly the same conclusions. This suggests either that I'm discovering a basic sameness in everything, or that I've begun to stagnate. The first makes everything pointless around me, and the second makes me pointless to everything else. I don't like either alternative, and if I wanted to take the time here and now, I would, typically, try to reconcile the two into one.

No, it's merely interesting now, that my father was having me watched. Quite honestly, I suppose, in his position I would have done the same. There's no telling what I'd be capable of, left on my own. Just look at what I'm capable of.

Fall, 3: 20, 9530

I'll have to begin replacing the outside walls of the house next year. The wood siding is beginning to split and splinter in places, a curious thing to happen. It's as though the house were much older than it is. It's no doubt due to lower-grade materials used, though why my father would have permitted that I don't know. I do know I'd only be able to repair it piecemeal for so long, before I found myself repairing repairs. Further, I've only a little wood left with ridge-and-slotted edges, and that's a detailing I haven't the means to duplicate, assuming I could produce planking of any sort. So I'm going to do it differently, and to this end I've already begun unearthing rocks from around and about again. This time they'll have to be fitted together mortarless, because I have nothing left for mortar. I can't quite envision success at it, but I know of no alternative just yet. A solution will probably come to me, however, as a solution always does, given time.

The inside walls remain sound, though there are developing fine cracks at the junctions of the walls with each other and with the ceiling. When the interiors start to disintegrate, I don't know what I'll do. I'll have to use planking then, unless I can find a natural source for alkalines somewhere nearby. This house wasn't meant to last so long without proper upkeep. Eventually I will have built a totally new dwelling by my successive haphazard repairs.

Remarkably, the solar plant continues to function well, so I can only assume it's constructed of materials the same as or similar to those used for the Starship. It would make sense. The water pump also keeps working, even though I've had to replace the housing once already. As a consequence I haven't made total use of my pond yet, but the time will come, I'm sure. I've become resigned to making do with less and less, and, amusingly, I find myself a little impatient because so much continues to function so well. I envision everything ceasing suddenly, and—let's face it—when the solar plant deteriorates beyond repair, that's just, in effect, what will happen.

If I don't use the pond fully yet, however, Enrath certainly does, or tries to. He sits atop the dam and bats furiously at the water as it flows along the trough. Carath used to do that, though Shefan displayed a great terror of water that was not absolutely still. But Enrath goes further: he leans over the edge of the dam, first on the valley side, then on the pond side, attacking the water that flows through the sluices. He'll kill himself. If not on solid ground, falling that way, then in the pond—he is so fat he'll sink. And, to be blunt, I sometimes wish that would happen. I do so miss Carath. He was so well behaved in comparison.

Shefan seemed to have no distinct personality, or none that I can recall. Enrath, however, is a total nuisance. He feels he must be everywhere all at once and must touch everything, move everything about, and he has a habit of taking small things of all sorts and hiding them in corners or under rugs, and by type, no less! I can't keep writing equipment in the open or else it all disappears under one corner of the small rug by my desk. All paper fasteners are secreted together behind one of the bookcases. Nails of one size have been stashed together behind a door upstairs, while nails of another size are piled in the space between two cupboards in the kitchen. I've never seen anything so deliberate from an animal—hardly ever from a person—or anything so nonsensical. But I must qualify that, as I have recently seen evidence of apparently equal deliberateness, but evidence I truly do not understand.

Enrath's activities are amusing, I suppose, but more an annoyance, for when I can't find something I always know that I must go search out one of his caches. And when my mind is on something else entirely, which it has been often recently, I always seem to come across yet another little hoard, which I must take time to pick up and put away where I want things. Enrath, for that, disturbs my order far too much. Carath never did this; he was a part of my order. Shefan, at least, never got in my way.

I imagine I would rather have done without another cat. There is developing a certain relationship between myself and the wild animals around and about me—a relationship that I cannot help but find a little upsetting, but one which does also eliminate some of the sense of isolation I've felt for so long. This new relationship doesn't, of course, alleviate my feeling of aloneness—in fact, if anything, it heightens it somewhat—but then, no cat could, either. At least, no cat since Carath. But as usual, Enrath descended upon me two and a half years ago, squalling out of the underbrush, a tiny ball of squirming fur. I searched after his source, as usual to no avail.

I've given up trying to figure out where all these cats come from. Obviously, there is a family of them hiding nearby, which wishes only the worst on me, which is determined to foist on me its mutants, its aberrant offspring. It's incredible, given Carath, Shefan, Enrath, and my penchant for self-indulgent speculation, that I haven't seriously tried to determine whether cats have their own concept of Imitators. Certainly, I seem to be sheltering "imitator" cats.

Perhaps, if there is an order to all things, then my being bestowed with these cats is a part of that order. I notice without even trying to that there is a near-sentiency about the world: a sort of logic or thought to events, which seems to pattern them into an apparently rational sequence. Matters are starting to seem to succeed one another with "good reason." I've seen this since I've become more familiar with the animals in the area, and now it seems so regular that I've virtually come to expect it. Yet it makes me rather apprehensive as well. I find it intimidating, though I can't figure out why I should.

First, the breathswifts, which have since proven to be very gregarious, started appearing nearby, watching me, whenever I went out to collect marshpillars or brainnuts. As I became accustomed to seeing them stand about, I started considering how I might get one or two every so often for meat. Bounders have become a very tiresome diet. But the breathswift's great branching horns are a very effective deterrent to my attacking one outright. And I have no guns, no hard-light equipment I could use as a gun, not even the sort of crystals necessary to make light coherent enough, and certainly no gas tubes. But I considered how to kill one, anyway. There are more crude methods I could use.

Then one of them one day made a great noise, snorting and stamping about in the underbrush, as though it knew what I was thinking: I had been thinking at that moment that a well-thrown rock might stun one sufficiently so I could then slit its throat. Though I was frightened at the breathswift's activity at first, I shortly seemed to get the idea that the beast was not coming after me, but that I was supposed to follow it. What nonsense, I thought. But I started toward it and, sure enough, it did begin leading me up the hillside—going on a distance, stopping briefly to look back for me, going on another distance, stopping momentarily again.

A half hour away it suddenly bounded out of sight, and when I got to where it had been, I found another breathswift, one of its back legs broken irreparably, just at the point of death. I took advantage of the situation and enjoyed meat for a little over two changes. But at the time I thought it all serendipitous. Since then, however, the same thing has happened repeatedly, two or three times a year, for the past two years.

I simply cannot attribute to a breathswift this kind of compassion, let alone any strong powers of reasoning. Yet it does seem as though I am being provided with this kind of food by being consciously offered those animals which, for one reason or another, are no longer able to survive by themselves. Moreover, there have been two occasions when I've come upon a breathswift dying of some sort of disease, rather than from severe physical injuries, and another breathswift has appeared to ward me away, as though it thought I might be affected by the fatal disease. I don't know whether I actually would be, but it's completely irrational to suppose that a breathswift might think I would be. It's irrational to suppose that a breathswift might think. But it's evident, nevertheless.

Besides this, groundscurries have taken to alerting me to places where I can find ripe nuts and edible roots for which I don't even have a name. Initially I thought they were getting upset that I was getting too near hoards of their own, but when I tried to go off another way, they quite plainly became upset that I wasn't doing what they wanted me to.

Birds and vermin have established a balance around and about my garden, so that each frightens off the other before either can destroy too much. And I find myself now cooperating in this association by setting aside a small amount of excess for each—useless roots of my leafy plants and useless leaves of my tubers for the vermin, stalks of grain for the birds. And each eats what I offer and rarely any more than that.

Even manlikes, which have never been known for their sense of propriety, now circumvent my house, rather than storming around and past it, as though out of consideration for my nerves. Even if it means they must use a more circuitous route, they apparently do so, and certainly not quietly—they seem to love to make a great deal of noise in groups. It cannot be that they're afraid of me. Why should they be? They're both larger and stronger than I. But, though it's a great deal more difficult for them, they now pass by way of the lodge's hill, rather than mine, on their forays up and down the slope.

It seems that all the world has accepted the place I have in it and, more, has begun to incorporate me into itself as an acceptable, functioning part. It cannot be so, yet it appears so. I could want nothing better, to tell the truth, but, having what I could want, I find it very unsettling indeed. It is so deliberate. But only I am capable of being that deliberate, or so I would have thought. Only I can truly think. Only I can tell time passing. Unless intelligence amounts to something altogether different from what people have always believed.

I suppose it's possible that as the only man I am no longer subject to a blindness to life caused by the presence of other men. The old notion that only man has "being" seems now irrelevant, if not rather ludicrous. And it may be that what I construe as conscious actions, motives, thought, is merely the natural expression of "being" in all

211

things. Man is, after all, an animal; is it when he ceases to recognize this that he ceases to recognize the ways of life other than his and that of his kind? I don't know.

I do know, however, that all this apparent kindness, all this generosity on the part of breathswifts and ground-scurries, all this thoughtfulness of the birds and vermin and manlikes—even these regularly appearing cats—the whole matter is a little frightening. It's strange. It's unexpected. It is, at least to my previous way of thinking, unnatural. I seem to find it somehow sinister, though that has to be one of the most ridiculous conclusions I've ever come to in my long history of ridiculous conclusions. Everything seems to be working for my benefit. But resolutely I must ask why. If this is nothing but the normal way of the world, I yet cannot accept it without knowing the reason for it.

The only thing I can think of that in any way resembles my present dilemma over my peculiar good fortune is the reaction of our First Fathers to the presence of the Imitators. Certainly, on the surface, it would seem stupid of man, if not actually against his best interests, to slaughter a whole population of creatures who, whatever else they might have been, were at least useful, knowledgeable, and, apparently, quite generous to us. And yet we did so, simply because they were "not like men."

That's not the interpretation history gave the event, of course, but I've long since recognized the fallacy of our perception of history. And I've long since also known that at the root of the conflict was not the issue of the One against Chaos. As it was conceived then, that matter was not real at all, though as a scientific tenet it is unquestionably valid.

No, it just seemed to man that only one group of intelligent creatures deserved to be recognized as such, and that man was that group, and that only men deserved to live on Ath. As blatantly foolish as that sounds, however, I find myself now thinking something of the same sort of thing as I perceive all this order and consideration around and about myself. It intimidates me, all this "thoughtfulness." It makes me feel the less. But why should that be so? And, in fact, why ought I feel so much greater than the world? There is far more of the world than of me. My contribution as the last of my kind is so minimal, I hardly deserve as much as I'm getting. But my saying that rankles me. Why?

Having just now looked over "The Destruction of the Lower City" from *The Generation of Athel,* I see I was wrong once more. The question of intelligence was not actually at issue at all. I've always thought that, but we seem to have been far baser than that. The First Fathers may have believed their ideals, but they were obviously willing to sink to any level to achieve their goals.

Having established the city of Athel, the First Fathers discovered "there was unhappiness among the men and women." For some reason people stopped working, and every man decided he wanted to get married. But, first of all, "there were not enough women, one for every man," which strikes me as strange, since we produce more women than men. This may be, however, where *The Practical Woman* got her erroneous notion. Then, secondly, "the women wanted many men who could also give them of the things of the Imitators." Perhaps there weren't "enough" women because they were holding out for gifts. At this point "the fathers spoke among themselves concerning the Imitators," and then designated Laniris of Galien to exhort the people against the Imitators.

Obviously, the First Fathers found the Imitators at fault for the disruption in the cities, and Laniris, after several false starts, managed to put the matter quite succinctly: " 'They would be better than we. They have now more than we.' " And, he adds: " 'You seek after their baubles and jewelry, but they keep the better part for themselves and give you only the trash, the leftovers, the poorly made.' "

Then, with hardly a moment's hesitation: "The women of the One bundled reeds from the delta lands together and used them to fire the southern parts of the lower city. The men of the One encircled the city from the east and from the west. Together they and the fire caused the Imitators to flee north into the waters of Atheril and into the waters of the Central Sea. Those that hesitated on the banks were slain by the men and women of the One, and those slain were hurled into the waters after their drowning fellows.

"Twenty-five full times of day were required—five mornings, five Middays, five afternoons, five evenings, five nights

—in the burning of the city of the flowers, and the flames changed their colors twenty-five times, and it was taken as a sign of the One in victory over Chaos. After the five full days, three more were required that all the Imitators there were dead. Then the women of the One brought water from the Central Sea and poured it over the lower city so that there should be no more flowers growing, so that nothing could live there for a great time. For the things of Chaos can only be obliterated by fire and by drowning them in seawater. And then the women gathered up all the foolish, strayed cats and took them to the city of the jewel as tokens and as useful hunters of vermin.

"The men of the One afterward set out for the Great Sea and came back after a change, all saying that the city there and the Imitators in it were all obliterated as well. It was said by them that the other city, which was called Bar in the tongue of the Imitators, was even larger than En Marabi-i-Bar and therefore more corrupt. They said also that the Imitators there were slain even more easily than the others because of their greater indolence. But it was also said how wonderful that never did any Imitator raise himself against a man or woman of the One, but accepted death when it came, quietly. This was taken as a sign that Chaos recognized the power of the One and the rightness of the deed."

The "deed" was an act of pure jealousy, I can see now. We eradicated them because they had more than we did. Our civilization was just beginning, and we must have thought ourselves splendid. In the face of the Imitators, though, we obviously weren't. We were intimidated, just as I have come to feel these past couple of years. Well, that, I suppose, is my answer to my dilemma. The world is not "better" than I, nor I "better" than it. If everything including myself exists together at all, then it's only reasonable that we exist together cooperatively.

I still feel no less apprehensive about the things that have been happening around and about me, to me. But as it all continues, I'll probably get used to it. The animals are obviously already used to me. I'm at fault for my feelings, not everything else for its actions in my behalf. I'm proud, too proud.

I'm also blind to opportunity: I have a source for mortar

sitting just outside by my workshop. The bones of the breathswifts I've slaughtered contain calcium. There must be a way to convert them to the alkalines I need as a base for mortar. I'll check *The Practical Woman*. If it can be done, she surely has a method.

Spring, 3: 9, 9553

Another cat.

And another cat!

Where do they all come from? I don't know. Enrath, Polech, now this one, and I haven't even given it a name. I'm running out of names. I even forget what to call some of the things I eat, some of the things for which I did have names. But everything has to have a name, I suppose.

I've been somewhat dizzy lately. I cut myself deeply while gathering wood, but instead of healing thoroughly, the cut became infected. Animalcules. It stays open and somewhat sore. I should have washed it out, I suppose, but I was away from the pond, up by the remnants of the sap house. I thought I was virtually indestructible. I never seriously considered an infection like this.

Since the solar plant stopped a few years ago, things have become less and less neat around and about me. Unsanitary, I suppose, but I've not given it much thought. Things seem to stay the same, with or without electricity. It wasn't at all hard to manage—it was easy to get used to. But didn't the makeshift water pump keep working right up to the end of it all! The last thing I expected. It would still work now, I'm sure, but that the power's gone. I can't imagine why I needed all those unnecessary things. Life is so much easier without the worry now.

But the dizziness is a bother to me. It's difficult to get up, mornings, and I tire easily. I often get giddy. Sometimes I forget things I've planned to do and sometimes get discouraged by simple tasks. I've got to get back to writing out my plans and to planning things thoroughly.

Occasionally my arm becomes quite warm, too. Often it itches, as that burn did when it healed, that time that happened. And twice I've had a general fever. It feels strange, since I've never been sick in my life. I can appreciate how bad Morin used to feel whenever he suffered a particle infection. But I don't get particle infections, Heremis says. I've got an animalcule infection and the body has no complete defense against that. It's odd, too, how, if I look very closely, I can almost see the animalcules and my body at work against one another, one destroying and the other healing. It's somehow fascinating.

And that makes me feel a little ill, too.

I found my tattered copy of *The Practical Woman* finally. For some reason I'd mislaid it several years ago and never thought once to look for it, though I knew it wasn't where it was supposed to be. There are some remedies in it I think I can concoct. I don't know if they'll work. She might have made further errors than the one I once found. And remedies for nonregeneratives mightn't work on me. But she's never disappointed me before.

I find, if I strain too hard doing something, the wound is liable to tear open a bit more. Thank the One, I finished the façade on the house several years ago, so that's secure for at least as long as my mortar holds. I can still plant, and I imagine I'll be able to harvest, although it might take longer than usual. Anything requiring both hands is difficult, but my right is fortunately unhurt.

I believe I shall name the animal Gresech, "seeing," as he seems to be able to view things through blank walls, the way Carath could. The demonstration was something like Carath's, seeing snow through a solid door and trying to chase it. "The cat sees into nothing." At least this one does, too. Yes: Gresech. And about time. It's been a year we've been together already.

I've still a good deal of paper left, surprisingly. I'd anticipated using much more by now than I seem to have. There are some sheets which have odd sketches of things on them: buildings and machinery, facilities of a sort, and other equipment, and calculations. It's nothing that makes much sense to me now, though I can recognize what the buildings, the equipment—what these things are or are supposed to be. I don't recall doing any of the sketches, and certainly not the calculations, which in fact make no sense to me whatever. But they look like conversions of some

216

sort or another. I suppose I must have done all this, since there's nobody else, and cats can't write.

I suppose I must have thought at one time to build a model of the Starship Project facilities, for that is indeed what the buildings and machinery are for. It must have been at the time I was making the model of Athlan for Carath. That's long gone: My glue dried out and disintegrated. Or perhaps it was the time I was going to do the other model, of whatever I was going to do a model of— En Marab-i-Bar. And maybe then I thought for a moment to do this. I suppose that's what all these sketches were for, though I don't remember. And the calculations must be for scaling down the size of the elements in the model, though they really don't look like those kinds of calculations. But what can I tell at the moment? What can I tell about mathematics clearheaded?

It's a wonder, among these slow waves of dizziness, I can think as much as I have. These waves are often like some similar unsettled feelings I had some years ago, with the same problem of vision, as though I were looking through water, and with the same sense of distraction. In fact, in a certain way, this dizziness is not unlike the effects of dreamweed, but unpleasant, as those effects could be once in a while. I haven't seen any of that growing around and about up here. I've never thought to look. Perhaps I should. If I can make the drink you make from it, it might help alleviate some of this discomfort, if only by making me disregard it.

I can tell one thing about all this paperwork, though: its age. My ink lasts well, but glancing back through all these entries I can tell where I ran out of the prepared stock and began using my own dyebark. Over the years, dyebark brown becomes black or black-like, and the red turns brownish. The prepared stock was always black.

The sketches and calculations I did in red, as though they were quotations—I wonder why that? And they're now brown, so they must be fairly old. But they're later than the time I ran out of prepared stock.

Unless they're recent and I did them with new dyebark. But that's not true, since I can't remember doing them, and, therefore, I didn't do them recently.

It's absurd the way I look after the things around and about me without bothering enough for myself. I contracted this infection from an old axe, and I think at that moment I cared more for the blade than my arm. Was it damaged? My arm will always heal. Did I chip the edge? And now I've a bothersome infection from it.

It's not fatal, but I should get rid of it soon. The prolonged incidents of dizziness could keep me from my work at the wrong time. And I do intend this year to visit the Broadcast tower. I have put it off so long. Perhaps there's a way I can get some of the equipment here back in working order, courtesy of new supplies. I don't need most of the things here, as I've found out, but hot water without work would be nice.

I wish I had a flier. That would make things so much easier. But I wouldn't know how to control it. Like Loren, I'd wish for something I wouldn't know what to do with.

No, I don't care enough about myself. This "disease" is a deceptive thing: Regeneration doesn't keep you functioning; it just keeps you from stopping entirely.

But I haven't willfully relaxed in years. I have been so driven to keep myself busy. Perhaps I can use this infection as an excuse, if I can manage to organize things sufficiently that my absence won't be catastrophic. That should be no trouble. And if I can manage to find something to keep my mind peacefully occupied, which is why I've kept myself so busy for so long.

And then maybe I will take the time to go visit the Broadcast tower, get some of the equipment there, get some of the electricity back on here. Then I can listen to the sound ribbons again. I haven't listened to them in years, really not since Carath, I think. It would be nice to hear them, hot water or no hot water.

Summer, 9559

I can see most clearly today.

Even the smallest leaf, even the mountains across from me, are sharp without my having to make an effort to focus.

I can almost see within things. I can certainly see the intentions of things, and today all is at rest. Not even the

218

wind stirs. It is the fifth day, of course. Only I act just now, and it is always to me to set motion going. Always me.

Yet it is hard, for I always feel so languid. The One has set this disability upon me as a test, I know, and I must overcome it in order that all around and about me not stop. It is a test of my will over things, they say. So I cannot fail.

I am confident, because it is in the way of the world around and about me. The way of the One. A way I at last recognize as the purpose of all events.

This wound festers. I cannot seem to move. It increases. It drains me and makes me oblivious of my surroundings, but it also brings me this awareness. When the pain is greatest, my head clears remarkably, so that all the world becomes apparent to me in strong relief: the world here, and the world before, and what the world will one day become. I can see these at times, if only briefly. Otherwise, I am in darkness and confusion. I sleep half awake, never resting, but never fully awake, either.

Days I have sought and found plants she has patiently described to me. I have prepared them and applied the preparations. The pain increases, or it does not, or it diminishes. Yet the wound does not heal, for I have not found the proper combination.

On her advice I vary the ingredients. Things change and they do not change: The sense of them mutates while the substance does not, they say. And nights he comes by me when the pain is great. His fur brushes my face. I hear and feel the soft rumbling in his throat. I have my friends. They try to help, and they always try to comfort when they cannot help.

Another darkness is coming, though. I can feel it before I see it. Night, or just darkness. I have some moments in the daylight and then am attacked by watery blindness again, and then blackness.

I could have used this time for my own help, but instead I have wasted the moment drawing letters with my pen. And what silly words! I could at least have set forth what I've seen, what I see, what I will see.

I must eat. I must find something to eat.

The garden is ready. Things are being brought to me for my meal. By the world. By the One.

This horrid thing disgusts me. It never heals, never worsens. It festers. I seem to have had it my whole life. I will have it forever.

At times, ugly though it be, it doesn't agonize me as much, and I can accomplish some things. But my garden is a ruin. It's only near the end of Summer and already what there is to be gathered is rotting, and there's not much to be gathered. For the most part there's only what reseeded itself from last year.

A great deal has been choked by the weed, which has spread right up to the house now, as though it would force its way indoors and choke me, too. The irrigation channels have many of them overflowed, washing away the topsoil and leaving only deep gouges that run right over and down the edge of the depression. It's as though that's a track I myself should follow. I must go out and rummage as an animal.

I've thought it might be better to cut off the whole arm and let it grow back whole, but that frightens me. What if I only spread the infection?

And would the arm actually grow back? I know what Heremis claimed. But does that apply to me? I heal, but can any man heal so much? Could I trust what Heremis said?

I've had terrible dreams: Creatures like manlikes seem to come around me. I feel invaded by a host of horrors bent on destroying me. Awakening, I find I've hurled furniture about. Often I'm in another place in the room than I remember having been when I fell asleep. At least ten times I've found myself huddled in a corner or crouched in a cupboard. These creatures seem to drive me there.

Manlikes have never attempted to enter the house before. But I've violated every rule of life by now. There is life all around me, but I feed on it ravenously, strangling animals caught in the few traps I still have and eating them raw. I uproot plants and simply devour them as I find them. I no longer recognize any order to things, nor do I care about any order. And life around me will have its vengeance for this. I interrupt the way of the world. I'm in the way.

Life seems not to know that it takes an unusual act to kill me. They don't know I am greater than they. I am above life. I'm outside it.

They're clever, though, and only come at me when I'm most ill. They take advantage of my weakness. There is a pact among them and I am no longer included; a pact, and it is against me. Was I ever included?

They have delegated manlikes to best me, to destroy me —creatures most like me to eliminate me. But the cowards do not come when I'm well enough to face them. They wait for me to be weak, and then they stand about gloating and growling to themselves, poking me, chasing me about. But even in my weakness I can fend them off. "He resists us," they roar to each other. "He can resist us."

Weather conspires as well as the rest of the world. Last Winter was worse than I ever remember, leaving me starving many days, because I couldn't get through the snow to find food.

And this Summer has been dry, dry. But the weather cannot reach me in my house, for I've built walls against it, stone walls.

And the pond is low, but the pond is there: I created it. I'm creative, they say. Even Heller said that. So, let the snow come, let the wind batter, let the cold eat at the stonework and the heat and the dryness shrivel everything around and about. I may hunger, but I am safe from all of it, all of them.

Only these visions of creatures can reach me. But they cannot harm me. I'm too creative, they say.

I look like death. I do not recognize my face. I'm gaunt, so gaunt, and am I that young, nevertheless? I don't feel a part of this body. I'm old, old, and yet I look like a child, so thin a child! I'm like two people side by side, one that thinks and thinks, and the other simply a shuffling shell. And death will not come to me, to either one of me. I ward it off, too, though I wish for it often now.

Was it so wrong, then, letting others die? Aren and the others, and all those others? Should I have helped him and died, too, then and there? And now I've let the garden die, all the plants, the vegetables, the flowers.

But death shuns me. The Second Son to life, death offers the guise of freedom until the Last Forming, when life and death, First Son and Second Son, necessity and fulfillment —when these distinctions themselves no longer exist. I am forbidden the natural end of all things. I am thus forbidden the ultimate end of all things as well. And even now I am forbidden the distinctions among things, for I am no longer myself distinct. Already a part of my mind has entered that of an animal, and I can no longer tell when that happens, nor can I stop it, though I fight against it. Nor can I tell my self from that part of me overtaken by the animal. Thus, I cannot make any choice. I have no choices. And the heavens watch with the Eyes and gloat, for among them are my own kind, they say, and I know I am forever cut off from them. They call to me. They want me to find them. And they laugh. What can I do?

Is this why I was left? Did I survive, and so well at first, just so I might be more easily reduced? Am I the victim because my own kind chose to destroy itself and upset the order of things? Am I the victim because I, too, had my victims?

I didn't want them to die! But twice I did the same thing, and twice there were deaths because of it. And before the second time I left I said I wouldn't leave them, and I did, and then I didn't come back, though I could have. I was only a short distance away watching. Both times.

Aren's father hated me. He wanted me killed when he found out about me. He would have killed me himself. That was the first time I left: Aren sent me out to the grove to keep me away from his father. I went because I knew I had to. Aren thought he could talk to his father, but his father also knew then about Aren and me, not just that I was Mekthedden's son and regenerative. I was someone with the Disease, who might infect his whole family. I could bring upon them all the destruction that we could see on the Broadcast being brought upon all Athlan. But I'd already taken his son away, his First Son. It was my fault Aren was now a second son. I had to leave.

Then the flier came. Other fliers had passed by during the afternoon, careening off in one direction or another, but bypassing us. Now this one came and set down by the house. I could see enough of it from the grove to know it was a Starship flier, and at first I thought it was from the Starship Project. But then I remembered the other fliers; many of them were also Starship fliers. I hesitated. I saw a figure come out of the house and motion at the vehicle. I saw a second, smaller figure come out of the house, aim a gun and fire it. The hard light happened to strike the flier's power source, and in a ten-tenth the whole thing shimmered blue and destroyed both itself and the first figure.

I ran back from the grove then. Aren had by now come out and was holding Elenie, who was holding the gun. Their father had tried to use the private carrier to have someone come to kill me. The gun was only for birds, and Elenie had only wanted to stop her father and the men in the flier, not kill them. She stood staring at me and repeating, "I wanted to help you, Lecturer Mekthedden. I wanted to help you." And that was how far beyond life I was even then, that I could cause her to kill her own father for me.

We went back into the house. Their mother was sitting by the shattered private carrier, pieces of glass all about her, like some fine Lady in the midst of fine crystalware, looking just tired, as though she had returned from some great and important and wearying gathering of the First Family. A polite smile came to her face as she saw me, and the smile stayed, frozen, for as long as I saw her after that.

Aren asked me what we ought to do. He asked me! I thought; and I thought we couldn't get help without the private carrier, and with it we might have only attracted the wrong attention. The Information Broadcast was still on, and the visual was one unchanging view of people being killed and people killing, of fires being set and fires burning. It was all so indistinct that it took me a long moment to realize that we were seeing the City Center from some vantage.

I said, "That's from the House of Judgments. From the top of it." I didn't know why this should be so, though, and I didn't try to explain why. The voice over the visual was calmly reciting events, instructions, warnings, as though it were describing a mountainside or giving shipping reports. And Elenie replied to me, "That's Ketis,

Ketis Barenillen. You lectured him last year. He's from The Land. I went around with him a bit last year. He works with the Westland Entertainment Broadcast now. Why are we hearing him and seeing Athlan?"

I didn't know that, either, so I turned to Aren and told him we ought to shut off all the house's power in order to make it appear no one was there. We did that and then took Elenie and their mother into a small room off the kitchen, the most unobtrusive room in the house, just in case. We waited: Elenie sitting on the floor, wondering out loud how this Barenillen could be so composed; their mother sitting in one corner, smiling at nothing in particular; Aren beside me touching my wrist, but not holding it, as though keeping contact without committing himself.

It was, perhaps, hours later, or, perhaps, just a fifth—there was no way of knowing, for the sky was black and would stay black for a long while, so the air was filled with the shrill voices of birds at their evening songs. The birds seemed to be singing continuously, just to make sure they didn't miss the right time for their performance. Then Aren remembered that without power there was no water. Elenie was thirsty. I volunteered to go out to the grove to fetch water from the stream there. I went, although I'd promised I wouldn't leave them.

Before I left, Aren leaned against me, put his forehead against my shoulder, reached up to touch my face. "The stream," he said, "is muddy. Reach out with the containers and get water from as near the middle as you can. Try not to disturb the bottom of the stream. Be careful."

It was difficult to do as he said, and I took a great deal of time getting each of the containers full. I had to cling to a branch to be able to get far enough out. I nearly fell in twice. I worried about doing it as he told me to.

I heard the throbbing hiss of a flier just as I'd finished with the second container. I turned about and saw a Starship service vehicle land by the house, by the ruins of the first flier. A Starship service vehicle is very large. It was unmistakable. All its safety lights were ablaze, as though there were no trouble anywhere and no reason to be cautious. I grabbed the two containers and started back, because I knew these had to be Starship personnel, though why they should be there never entered my mind. I only got several paces by the time figures had clambered out and begun firing at the house those silent, pale white beams that left neat smoking circles in the walls. I stopped then, concealed at the edge of the grove.

The men broke into the house and shortly dragged out a silent mother, a screaming Elenie, a struggling Aren. One of the men took something like a bar or a piece of wood and beat Aren unconscious, while another held him. That may have been the best thing. They weren't so kind to Elenie and her mother.

The two women and Aren's body were hauled over to a fencepost and bound together to it. Then the men went back inside the house and began bringing out furniture and broken pieces of furniture—drawers and table legs, and cushions and rugs, chairs, lamps, everything they could carry. All this they piled up around the three tied to the post. When the pile was satisfactory to them, they poured some sort of liquid all over it—alcohol, I don't know what. There was no wind then, and I couldn't smell anything. One of them aimed his gun squarely at the pile and fired. The whole pile erupted.

The men began chanting, "Burn! Kill them! Burn them! Kill them!" They began gyrating to their song. One tripped out a Herald's step, and they all fell in together prancing back and forth, singing their few words to a lively tune, a family song.

I found myself swaying slightly in time, as though I were an animal myself.

They went on with this until the blaze had subsided enough that it could be seen there was no longer any fencepost or furniture. I waited until I was quite sure I could see what they saw, or could no longer see what was no longer to be seen. Then, as they went back to their flier, I set down the two containers I no longer had any reason to be holding, turned, and walked away through the grove, away from the house, across the stream. I was confident the men had not seen me.

But I was seen, I know that now, though not by men. I am seen, and now I'm known, and I cannot walk away again. I cannot escape. There is no place to go. I am no longer hidden alive. I'm no longer truly alive.

How much the Imitator I am! Like they, I am driven out. Unlike them, the world will never have done with me.

I will not die for all of it, if I would not die for the one I cared for. There'll be no victory now, not even the hollow victory of complete extinction. This will all just go on and on, I fear, and things will happen and happen and happen.

Winter, 9614

I'm uncertain of the date, in fact, but many years must have passed since my last entry. How aberrant I'd become!

Things are not the best now, but better than they seem to have been. Yet I cannot really remember what the actual matter was then. I can't really remember things clearly before then. My mind seems a blank about the whole time I've been here. I feel as though I've been born into this situation now, with all the necessary instincts and general information by which to survive, but with only vague recollections of the way I've gotten to where I find myself now.

I have no infection. My left arm is whole. There are no scars or other signs of that terrible, ephemeral passion. My house is in order. My garden thrives. I have meat and the skill to hunt a breathswift. My cat sleeps on the couch. My stores are plentiful.

What could have possessed me to write those things I read?

I do tire rather easily sometimes, or rather I might say I still do. But I'm quite sure that's nothing more than a result of thoughtless, boring, routine work. There is a good deal of that involved in gardening and general maintenance. For that I'm glad the season's now passed, though Winter with its complete lack of activity is hardly inviting.

If I did have some sort of illness—and I cannot seem to reconcile the idea of that—then I must have found some cure. I was obviously trying to find one. Otherwise, it was a delusion, which is a more acceptable idea, as I know I cannot be permanently harmed. The things around and about me show the damage of age, but I do not. My book bindings are in tatters; fabrics begin to shred easily; many of my cooking utensils have worn thin—others have broken completely; the top of my dam is starting to crumble in places along the water trough—that will need repair next Spring. But I am regenerative and will stay exactly as I am. I can see that's so: I look a bit wan, but my color is gone for the year; I look rather tired around the eyes, or old, but that's the only evidence.

Whatever happened must have been purely illusory, brought on by loneliness. I am terribly lonely sometimes. I have my cat, though—Brach, "the comfort"—and while he's not like me, he's a good enough companion. He follows me everywhere, listens to my ramblings diligently; he even alerts me when I've caught a bounder in one of my traps, though he doesn't care for that animal himself. Apparently he considers the meat too tough and stringy. Yet he eats vermin. Well, each kind is due its own preferences, I suppose.

After harvesting, this year, I thought to go over to the lodge. There's only the foundation left, a pit filled with barely recognizable pieces of wall and roof, scraps of furniture, bits of glass. You'd never think there was once an enormous wedge-shaped building there looking out over the whole valley. The foundation seems so small.

And the grounds, or what had been the grounds, are nothing but dense overgrowth. Still, I felt compelled to push my way through to get down by the landing area. Of course there's no sign of that burned spot any longer, nor had I really expected there would be. But it seems I had to check. It was as though, by assuring myself there was no trace left of that incident, I could now guarantee my continued safety here. But that's already a given, isn't it? The visit was a needless exercise.

Across the valley the Broadcast tower no longer stands, its fate most likely the same as the lodge's.

I cannot distinguish the valley stream. The vegetation in the valley is so dense now, aided no doubt by the contribution from my pond's overflow, that even with the leaves gone, the stark thickets seem an impenetrable wall.

Even the sap house is so obliterated that I would never be able to find its old location, were there not an obviously artificial pile of stones on the spot—the remains of the once-great hearth it contained. In another hundred years, even that evidence will be gone. Sooner, I expect, as I plan to put those stones to use repairing my dam. There is really nothing left now but my own house.

The house itself remains sound enough, though I'll have to start refinishing the inside walls at last. I don't know if I have bones enough to make a finishing compound. Perhaps I'll have to rough out planking again. That's arduous work, but it interests me. At least, it's not routine—it breaks routine.

I'll start, I think, with the dining room. It's the smallest, and the downstairs room I use least, so what mistakes I make in the process won't matter much. I want to be able to do the work properly when I come to doing the winter lounge's walls. That is the chief room in my life—the room containing all that matters most about the Aten and about me—so I want it to be refurbished most soundly. With no electricity any longer, the winter lounge must be able to hold in as much heat Winters as possible. Winters now, it's the only room I use, or can use.

Among my crazed scribblings—or despite them—I seem to have been right about a number of things. The quality of life around and about me is remarkable. There does seem to be a sentiency to it, a planning, an order, and a mutual respect for individual territories and interests. But it's not so "conscious" as I seem to have believed, and certainly not malevolent. The order to it often startles me, even now. Before, it must have come as a shock.

But men, I suppose, assume a certain pride because they can think, which then requires them to feel as though they're better than their surroundings. No groundscurry can build a house, for example. Yet there are things about a groundscurry's activities that do have knowledge of a sort behind them, and a knowledge man wouldn't necessarily possess or be expected to possess. I imagine that, when I first discovered the existence of this animal knowledge, I was taken aback—"intimidated" as I put it then, it seems. For all the liberality of my outlook on things, apparently it was emotionally safer for me to have my generous assumptions about life and the ways of life, than to be confronted with the proof of my assumptions. Perhaps there are things man wants to believe are true, but which he cannot bear to have proven true. Perhaps it's just me.

Then, apparently, in the process of trying to accommodate what I'd discovered, I went too far. Starting by trying to make people out of cats, I seem to have gone on to find sentiency in everything, instead of recognizing simply that there is an overall balance in the world into which man can easily fit himself if he wishes to. But man never did before. He made use of the balance for his own purposes, but otherwise ignored it. To be brought up ignoring this balance, only then to be thrust into the midst of it—to have to live in it and, sooner or later, by it—man will obviously at first view it as an opponent. I did. And the balance of life is an opponent to anyone who would try to work against it or in spite of it. But a stone wall is injurious only to those who would run headlong into it.

All the skewed notions of mine from that time might well be due to the illness I suffered. But if I had an illness, I cannot say now what cured it. I've reread *The Practical Woman*, but it gives no indication which, if any, of the concoctions might have worked. I have only found what I should always have found in the book: the basic principle that everything has some use for something else, whether I know it or not—whether I need it or not. If there can be said to be an "order" to life, then that's what the order amounts to.

As I look back over all this writing, however, I am struck by how little I recall of what I wrote so much about. There are brief fragments of events that come to me— events from the time of my last entry, or so I seem to think. But after that, until a year or two ago, it's all dreamlike at best. At times during the past year I have sensed bits of what may have happened during the subsequent blankness, but they lurk in the corners of my mind, much in the same way the companions of the planets are visible, but only by looking away from them.

Those bits seem involved with creatures other than myself, though somewhat like me—"manlikes," as I referred to them—entities of some intelligence, or something. I feel an old chill and want to write "Imitators," however foolish I know that to be. It's as though I'd believed my father's tales. And I feel a fresher chill and want to write "men," knowing that to be foolish now, also. It's as though I still hoped that there were men. I suppose I do, even now.

My mind must simply have gone wild out of loneliness and produced hallucinations of all my fears and all my hopes, hallucinations I interpret in retrospect as reality. I know I am alone after all these years, or someone would have found me, or I him. There would be some indication, even if only a flier passing overhead. There would be some sign. But there isn't.

And I have the irrepressible feeling that it's really unnecessary to determine exactly what happened to me, as though I could indeed learn it, but as a result discover that the knowledge is irrelevant. I think that is the case: A person can know too much and, in the knowing, find it was altogether too little.

And, then, what is the use of knowing everything and all at once, right now? If I did know everything, then I should have to endure a hundred million tomorrows nevertheless. That last is indeed a fact. Better, if I am eternal, that I make eternity worthwhile, leaving something to discover even on the day of the Last Forming, if it ever come. Even if that something left is only what exactly I did on a fine morning one Summer, millennia before. But I really have no fear: There will aways be something new to discover, I'm sure.

Summer, 9615

I am trapped absolutely, and there's no escape.

I know now what's happened to me all these years, what's been done to me.

This is monstrous, this discovery. I wanted something new to discover—"always something new to discover"—and now I have it, the last thing I'll ever discover. After this, what's left for me? What's left of me?

There are Imitators. They exist, and they always existed. We never killed a one of them. Their city is just a day or two away, north of here, in the wasteland, which isn't a wasteland at all.

They obviously know I exist here. They were the ones around and about me when I was so ill. Perhaps they're the reason that I was ill. They may even have brought about the destruction of my kind. They probably did. I don't know, but it wouldn't surprise me. Nothing would now. I am numb to all feeling, and helpless, utterly helpless.

I don't know how much time I have left before they come for me, which they surely will now. They must know that I've found them out. They know things like this—they have that ability, their "thinking." I've fought them off before, but before I didn't realize what I was fighting against. Now that I know—now that I'm so overwhelmed —I don't know that I'll be able to continue to fight. I will not work for them, though I may not be able to work against them. But to begin with, I've killed that cursed cat —Brach, "the comfort"! The very name makes me gag. At least they cannot reach me that way any longer.

I knew the moment I discovered the journal that something was terribly wrong. I'd started to tear out the old walls of the dining room, and it was there, hidden between the studs of the wall, Heremis's journal in his isolation. He built this house, just after the start of the Confederation, when he was already thirty-eight. He knew there was something wrong with himself, but he didn't know what, so he provided himself an escape. He had this house built as his escape. And this is where he first met the Imitators, and this is where he agreed to cooperate with them. The Imitators are the "they" of Heller's report on me. My father knew of them—he must have known them. He cooperated with them. What am I going to do?

I can't panic. I must keep a clear head. The less doubt and fear I have, perhaps the less they can do to me. The one thing that stands out in my memory—virtually the only thing from those lost years I spent fighting them that I can remember—is that it was my determination that kept them at a distance, my will to remain independent of them. I haven't regained my strength since that battle, I know. I'm still mentally weary enough that they might finally overcome me. But I must do everything I can to prevent that. They can now have this planet all to themselves, for all I care. But they will not have me with it. They will not have the last man, or at least they will not have him sane.

I've also destroyed that wretched book, *Ganrach Thekh* —*The Practical Woman*. I should have known when I found that error that it wasn't a human book. And how much else is there as false as that? All of *The Generation of Athel*—it has the selfsame error in it. I should destroy Heremis's journal, too. That would be fitting for the likes of him. He left a note with it that says in part: "Besides being proof of my continued existence, this journal, when it is one day recovered, will, I hope, serve as a form of thanks to those who have agreed to this undertaking we will shortly begin." I'll give him thanks myself. There—it burns quite nicely, and I don't mind the heat. It's relatively cool today.

I should burn all the *Starship Planning* volumes and everything else my father worked on. I'll burn that report of Heller's. I should burn everything, and let them find me in ashes.

The One! I wish I could find just one thing good in all this. The only even slightly amusing thing is that Osir Heremis began life as a Second Son. His brother died in his twenties—he died in a fire, so Heremis never knew whether he, too, was regenerative. And Heremis, as was the way, took over his brother's position and wife and became a First Son by default. What made everything easy for him after that was that he and his brother's wife never liked one another a bit. So Heremis never fathered any children by her, and she had borne none by her original husband. Heremis could remain aloof from her, and she remained so from him. He had his own way and he went his own way, and when he began to suspect there was something wrong with himself, he had ample opportunity and the funds from the facility in Westland his brother bequeathed him to arrange for this house, to arrange for his continued future, and to arrange his own "death." He remarked that his wife must not have been in the least saddened by his demise. I can't blame her.

But what can I do? I can't burn everything, much as I'd like to. It galls me that I've had all this through Heremis's courtesy. It galls me that I am in any way beholden to him. But if I hadn't this refuge, where would I go? Where would I live? And how? I'd become subservient to the Imitators then for certain. At least here I have doors to bolt, windows to barricade, and stone walls to keep me from them for as long as I can keep myself from them.

What could they want of me? I'm a man, a regenerative—I'm physically stronger than any one of them, and I'll last forever wtih proper care. I'm a good piece of equipment. For that I'd be handy. But what else could there be of me for them?

Oh, Chaos! Those drawings, those calculations—the

Starship Complex, the Starship. They want to find the rest of us. That's what they wanted out of me before. As if I knew. But isn't it possible I might know? Mightn't I have heard something from either Heremis or my father, or read something in one of the *Planning* volumes, come across something somewhere, somehow, that might give a clue to where the Starship is? I don't know. I don't consciously know.

But I don't have to consciously know it. Where does Heremis say . . . I burned the journal. He said something like, "If there is a memory, however deeply buried, they have the ability to find it. If there is a fear, however deeply ingrained, they have the ability to remove it. Their powers of mind are immeasurable. They can control a mind, utilize it, do with it what no man could ever achieve alone." Not with me they won't. I'd be better dead than forced to reveal anything I know about the Starship and its whereabouts.

But: If they want to know where the Starship *went*, then it did go somewhere. They must know that. Then there were people saved. Some did escape. There are men, and they did leave me behind.

I can't, I can't go on like this. I must do something before they come after me. Should I burn all this, my house —Heremis's? The cat's dead. At least they can't get to me that way.

I can't burn everything. I can't bring myself to. Heremis may have built this place, but what I've done since then has made it mine. I can't just destroy it. I can't destroy myself.

The animals around and about me—did the Imitators make them do all that they did, all that apparent order? All that nonsense!

What are those creatures not capable of?

My only escape is madness. Then they can use me as much as they want, but they'll get nothing from me, nothing coherent. And I'll never know that they're using me. But how do you make yourself become completely aberrant?

The valley looks peaceful enough, as though nothing were wrong or could ever go wrong. It looks just the same as always: dense, green thickets with a group of manlikes lumbering their way through, off to forage.

They're not manlikes. They never were.

They've taken my library. They say I won't need it.
They've left me these pages and plenty of ink and paper.
They told me to write. They seemed very nice. I don't
think they believed me mad, though. They patronized me.
They think I'll write what they want, sooner or later, without my even realizing it. I know what they want, though
they told me simply to write whatever pleased me.

Well, I've thought about what to write. I've come upon
something. It doesn't matter that they come upon it here,
since, by the time they do, I'll have done what I plan. If
it works, there is likely no undoing it. And if it doesn't,
I'll find another way. There must be another way.

Simply put, I'll give them something to consider. I'll
write it out here just once, in basic form, a set-piece, if
they want writing. Then I'll memorize it, and memorize
it so well that it not only becomes a part of my thinking,
but becomes virtually all my thinking. I know how to do
this—they taught me, in the old writings of theirs I read
years ago. It's part of their process of being calm, of becoming calm. I can use their own methods on them. Like
Ranoas, I can have a "process" of my own, and an equally
debilitating one. It may not make me truly insane, but it
will make me as good as insane.

So, the piece that will consume the rest of my life:

I STILL SEE sometimes the fires of Athlan, the burning,
twisted metal, the crumbling blocks—just as I still see
Aren tied and in flames with his sister, his mother. I can
imagine much of what must have happened to those I
never saw again, if only because I know what I witnessed
happening—and not just to Aren, but to total strangers,
to hundreds at a time.

Those pits, those dreadful holes into which people were
pushed and then set afire, the blackened shells of houses,
the burned fields, pathetic machinery sitting silent in a
wasteland. I remember bodies writhing as though they

234

were Heralds; panes of glass bursting out with heat, like crystalline snapkernals; trees and bushes on the distant Embankment withering like so many pieces of fine paper. Everything solid seemed ephemeral in the heat. Thus, unreality takes place:

The air around the city is filled with black specks like an invasion of pesters swarming in Summer's heat. At a distance the landscape seems dark as night, while close up everything can be seen as clearly as if all the Middays the world had ever witnessed were occurring at once. Larger portions of gauzy, charred debris float gently down through the cloud of fine ash, disturbing it and making the cloud undulate as though annoyed. And the whole atmosphere moves outward and forward, a solid-looking wall that simply flows over more tangible objects, the negative image of an oncoming snowstorm.

Metal cables slacken by the sides of the spires they guy in place, and one by one the spires pitch and shatter on the ground. Stone walls char—amalgam walls dry out too suddenly and crumble. Cautious, gentle Old Style curves crack and bend sharply. Geometrically aligned railings bend and twist into unique, shapeless lines. Windows pop out, doors fall inward, steps heave up as roofs collapse. Each part of each building responds after its own nature, as though it had always been prepared to do this.

The unremoved scaffolding around unfinished buildings rattles harshly against the shuddering roars of descending masonry. The hisses of ruptured heating systems compete with the whistling that comes from newborn winds rushing past shards of glass and around fractured partitions. There are rappings of minor explosions, and the duller blows of large ones. It seems the sounds of a festival: hootings and chimings, the plucked sounds of rupturing wire, the heavy percussion—a macabre celebration for the participants.

People pile out openings or pile up in slumped heaps between fallen beams. Others make a frantic attempt to get inside in the hope of saving valued articles, muchlabored work, or their companions. Some even push their way against those escaping in order to escape the mob that's calmly prepared to divide survivors among themselves equitably.

This sudden, inexplicable disturbance began in fearful

235

confusion. People streamed wildly from one place to another, swinging and striking blindly. But when the Hall of Judgment was at last invaded, the Assembly decimated, the speaking Representative beaten shapeless before the passive lenses of Broadcast cameras, then the crowd came to a deadly calm like that momentary brightness at the center of an ocean storm. And after that their every action was casually careful, sure and certain, automatic, thoughtlessly planned and delegated according to some bloodthirsty order they all seemed to acknowledge. Then their actions were much more specific, much more accurate, and ever more devastating. The first yelling became organized into chants, songs that had never been, sung by the world's most incredible assembly.

Pitched at one another, these songs agree or disagree in tone and volume, rise and fall in cadence or in syncopation with the movements of the crowd. The people join together loudly against a large structure, and fall back quietly to allow few the honor of a particular slaughter, the pleasure of a special burning, an exceptional act of annihilation.

Theras would be hurrying to Morin's rooms, if the fire wasn't up to that section yet. Knowing Morin well, he'd assume his friend was still deciding what outfit to wear for the occasion. But there might be an odd silence when he knocked.

No movement is heard, no expected declamation, no response whatsoever. Theras opens the door to be confronted by a shambles: priceless earthenware and exotic wooden furniture shattered everywhere, scripts strewn about and clothing piled at random. He picks his way through the rubble, calling out gently. He stops midway as two figures appear in the bedroom door.

"Another," says one of them.

"A dainty one, too," says the second. They advance together, forcing Theras back toward the hall.

But a third appears in the entry, remarking, "I never saw yet a regenerative try his regeneration. Any of you?"

The other two vow that they haven't, that out of everyone so far they haven't managed to hit on one.

"I'm not," Theras says shakily. "I'm not a regenerative. I couldn't be."

"Why not?" asks the man in the hall doorway with genuine curiosity.

236

"I . . . I get fat. I do. They don't. They're not supposed to. I do. I'm pudgy now. See!" He pokes his stomach testily.

"How long do you suppose it takes him to grow back a finger?" speculates the man in the hall doorway.

"Never!" yelps Theras. "I can't."

"Let's experiment," suggests one of the other two.

"Yes," agrees the second.

"No!" Theras begs.

"Yes," the second repeats thoughtfully. "The Families always experiment, don't they?"

"Yes," concurs the first.

"Please!" Theras screams.

"We could try a finger on one hand," hypothesizes the man in the hall doorway, "and the whole hand on the other arm, and time them."

Theras stands and whimpers, "For the sake of the One, have some kind of pity. I'll die. You'll kill me." Then he moves suddenly, trying to force his way past the man at the entrance.

"Don't worry," soothes the man as he holds Theras firmly. "You'll do that anyway. Finally. They say we can find ways of killing even you. I don't remember what to do just now, though, so we'll just have to try everything. I speak rightly, don't I?"

A long blade flicks out in the hand of one of the other men. A clumsy procedure is begun, joint by joint, as Ranoas continues its first science experiments.

"Of course," one of the inquisitive men remarks, "if you don't have the Disease, this will keep you from getting it and giving it to your children."

As he begins to faint from pain, Theras glimpses a hand lying on a chair, grasping what looks like a page of dialogue. It is just a hand alone. "Morin," he whispers finally.

"A bad subject," a voice says quietly. "A failure."

There is some laughter at a great distance.

Athlan is now like a giant hearth, the whole city beginning to glow from its center, the glow spreading slowly around and about. Fiery fingers begin stretching along the avenues, gently distributing sooty dust in gestures a fine Lady might make during the course of light conversation by a fireside.

Whichever way people run, the very design of the city traps them. They are caught at the juncture of an avenue and a radial, or forced by fire or by marauding groups around the great half-circle like vine-seeds rolling back and forth on one side of a tilted bowl. They are trapped at Shopping and South, or in the rail stops, or on the Embankment, from which their only escape is the river, assuming they can also evade the guns. Or they're driven out onto the Peripheral Road, where others in cars wait for the next moving target to shoot at or run down, whichever might seem more enjoyable.

But it's also possible some might survive a moment or two more than could be expected. They would merge into the storming crowds, spread wet ash on themselves to avoid being recognized as anything but a gray figure. They might even join in some of the pastimes if they thought it pragmatic to do so.

"Heller," hisses a voice. "Is that you?"

Heller peers cautiously sideways as he is carried forward by the mob. "Do you speak to me?" he hisses back as though he were of Ranoas.

"It's me, Salis," comes the simpering.

"Salis?" Heller scrutinizes the grimy face and slowly, reluctantly, recognizes it.

"Isn't this remarkable?" Now a gleeful smile leers from the blackened visage.

"Shut up! We can't speak!"

"But it's so remarkable!"

"You fool! You'll have us killed!"

"We'll get out of this. The School is close, one more block, I think. Then we can break away down Seventh South."

"You know what that building was we just passed?" Heller growls. "Maronnen's, or what's left of it. This is Shopping."

"Shopping?" Salis tries to turn to get his bearings, but Heller pushes him away into the throng.

"You little vermin! Just keep on! Leave me!"

"But I . . ." The crowd parts as he speaks, and Salis finds himself standing separate, encircled, facing a battered figure crouching low to the ground.

"Deviant!" the crowd intones. "Imitator! Kill him!"

238

Without a moment's hesitation, Salis reaches out, is given a club, and hoists it high above his head.

Heller, a few paces distant, tries to avert his eyes without being noticed, but his gaze fixes on the crouching form and he plainly recognizes Loren Akaror. "Oh!" Heller moans. "Oh, the One! No!"

The club comes down swiftly to crush Loren's head. On the instant, Heller leaps at Salis, who is grinning broadly. The blow is averted; the two sprawl to the ground beside Loren.

It would make no difference to save him. All three would be killed now without further ceremony. Many tried to save their fellows only to be destroyed with them.

It was everywhere the same, in all the cities—that was said on the Information Broadcast I saw at Aren's father's house. And it was the same in all the outliers, in all the countryside I passed through. Anywhere that there had been people was nothing but a smoking, dead ruin. Anywhere there were still people, they were formed into small groups, coldly organized, determined, premeditated, and thorough. Their sole purpose was to seek out and obliterate all other such groups. The number of victims became fewer and fewer, but the sense of accomplishment for those few remaining must have grown greater and greater until, at last, the last man would kill his last victim with the finest joy any man had ever felt, only then to discover there was no longer any point in his living on, either.

But, then, there would still be I, the greatest mockery of that greatest of joys, and the deepest disappointment of all. For I am now reduced to sitting by my hearth, alone, and gazing at the coals in which I still see sometimes the fires of Athlan . . .

*   *   *

Hundreds of years have gone by, perhaps—centuries and centuries, I suppose. I've fairly abandoned my perpetual song by now, though I keep it in reserve. This generation of Imitators has scarcely any notion why I'm here. They just assume I should be, or seem to.

Of course, I trust nothing about them. This disregard of theirs for a reason for me could be a ruse. But they have been quite willing to keep me well supplied. My house is

239

quite tidy and quite well furnished, my grounds so well kept up that they're no longer quite natural.

I suppose it does now begin to appear I live where I do —in the midst of one of their developments. But there's virtually no real way to know that: The illusion they've constructed around my territory is so perfect that I am essentially convinced of what I see. The mountain rises behind me, before me is the valley with its dense green overgrowth. The lodge's hill is across the pond from me. The seasons change as they always have, with some regularity, with some exceptions in timing. Only the Broadcast tower across the valley from me disturbs the illusion. I know it had ceased to exist already. But they don't know that. And, of course, they can't get into my mind to discover it.

I seem to have developed a defense against their mental intrusions, a barrier to them, or so the Imitators say. I don't know that I trust that, either, but by the evidence it would seem to be true—they've certainly not entered my mind in years. But they may not have tried to, especially if they neither know nor care why I take up space among them.

But this defense seems to have come out of my repeating my old set-piece, or out of the procedure I was following as I did it, or from some source of that sort. At least they think so. But they've never known it to happen before among men. It makes me no more "telepathic," as they put it, however—just not susceptible to telepathy— so I still haven't a hope of checking up on them as they might on me. And conversation of any length with them remains too great an effort to manage. I can't imagine how our First Fathers did it.

So I live quietly in the midst of an illusion. Everything seems perfect to me—too perfect, I think—even to the animals. I continue to obtain breathswifts with some regularity in the way breathswifts and I have long since agreed upon. I grow my vegetable garden, I bathe in my pond, Summers. In good weather I go without clothes as I was accustomed, assuming—right or not—that the wall of illusion is perfect enough to show something equally distracting and equally convincing on the other side. And anyway, if not, my nakedness can be of no consequence to a pre-bearing animal. I live as I like, and they let me.

Still, I remain on my guard. The illusion around me is just that, after all. And I have read much of their literature by now. They willingly supply it. They seem quite proud of it.

From that, I can deduce that their concepts of appearance and reality, in combination with their mental and mechanical means for altering the appearance of reality, make it impossible for the likes of me to ever fully figure out what's "real," "true," or even just valid about what Imitators say and do and are. I suspect it's impossible for them to figure those things out about themselves, too. But there's nothing about them that can be trusted, just literally and neutrally speaking. So I don't trust them. I can't imagine how Heremis could have been so stupid as to do so. My father, perhaps, I can understand in this.

I hesitate to write here, as the past will crop up—it has just a few lines ago. I try to keep my thoughts in the present exclusively. The past is just what they want, or what they originally wanted. I must be careful writing, but I must write something. It's been so long since I've done anything that was exclusively of my own kind. Not that writing is something that mattered to my own kind, but the language is Aten. There's that much that's exclusively mine to exercise.

Their weed, I must add here, proves to have a use. Eating it, they say, protects against many ill effects of emissions. Of course, the emissions of the wastelands were merely part of an illusion to conceal their cities. But they've had technical experience with emissions in the past. Thus, they developed the weed as a source of protection.

There's something handy to know. It makes the weed taste no less appalling, however, and no less a nuisance, where it grows in my garden. I hate the sight of it. That and cats.

*　　*　　*

Illusion or no illusion, I've seen a flier. It looked just like a flier—oblong and domed—and it changed color with its speed, as fliers do. It could go much faster than I remember fliers traveling, and it made some maneuvers fliers were never capable of making. It also seemed to make no noise.

But, as I reason it out, what purpose would the Imitators have for including an element like that in this illusion of theirs?

Perhaps they think it will stimulate me to talk or write here about the Starship. But it won't. I just note here the event.

And the impossible conclusion that, if the flier was not a part of the illusion, then there are men on this planet, and the Imitators have not told me.

And why would they?

And who are the men?

If they're from the Starship, then the Imitators have what they want already. So why do they still hold me?

These men can't be from the Starship, so who could they possibly be?

Perhaps they're some alien life form.

I think I can dismiss the possibility that they're survivors like myself. Otherwise, the Imitators would have them, too.

I wonder who or what they are. I wonder, too, if I really want to find out. Imitators will never be my boon companions, but they may be preferable company.

In any event, the flier noticed me. The craft came down for quite a searching look, but I couldn't see through the haze of its field to make out what sort of figures stood at the windows. It had a remarkably dirty field around its base, as though it needed repair. Perhaps they are aliens and haven't got the system right yet.

Well, whether or not, I expect I'll either find out more or I won't. If the flier was real, I was plainly seen. If the occupants are interested, they'll be back. If the Imitators don't stop them by throwing up another illusion. If the flier wasn't itself another illusion.

I'm not going to be concerned. As long as I can't separate the real from the imaginary around and about me, then there's nothing substantial to become concerned about. I will only debate in circles, and my mind will shortly begin to resemble a typical city plan, one of our typical city plans. I have no idea even yet by what sort of plan Imitators build their cities, if indeed they have a plan. I have not yet seen the city which I'm supposed to be in the middle of.

Stes promises to get me out of this cubicle and into a real house as quickly as possible, but I hold out no great hope for the "quickly." So much depends on the Head of History, though he claims to favor me—I am a "survivor." For a man who does not have the burden of higher position, he certainly can wield a great deal of influence. But someone ought to, I suppose. The other dolts on the Council lack either the ability or the will.

But it's up to the Head of History to approve of the house being built. And even if he does favor me, these regeneratives have no sense of urgency. It is, however, becoming urgent that I escape this horrible room in this horrible tower of rooms. It makes me feel claustrophobic and vertiginous. How these other fellows do it I don't know. They've never known anything else, I guess. Well, that can be dealt with, if the Head of History is serious.

This is all so peculiar. It's as though I'd just been born, full grown and with all the proper instincts, but without the proper knowledge to correctly stimulate those instincts. Everything seems at first glance to be totally unfamiliar, yet at second glance it seems somehow reminiscent of something—of what, however, I'm reluctant to say. It appears coherent enough—for that, it might as well be real—yet the coherency is made up of the oddest parts, things together that have no business being together. For that, it's ludicrous. And, more, there are things I see that I should not be seeing among men, and things I think I should not be seeing at all. There are some aspects to this city that appear totally unrelated to anything I've ever known. It's difficult to know where to begin to sort all this out, never mind how to do it.

The only solution I've come upon is to escape the city itself, to see it from a distance, both physically and conceptually. Hence my house—at least, this seems to be a very valid reason for having a house, though in truth it's the malaise this city has brought me that made me think of having a house in the first place. But I don't suppose I've fooled anyone: a person would have to be completely insensitive not to realize that, after having been in total isolation for what I understand to have been roughly eight thousand years, I could hardly readjust to the society of men at once, or even after merely five centuries, the length of time, they tell me, it took them to restore my sanity. Assuming, that is, that all this is real.

That is a problem that I don't know whether I dare solve. As little as I recall of the eight thousand years, I do seem to be impressed with the inherent untrustworthiness of the whole time. In the first place, I can scarcely believe the length of it, but I know I'm prone to thinking within the confines of mortality because I was raised to do so. None of these men ever were. So perhaps the vast amount of time I spent alone seems outrageous simply because I can't conceive myself having lived so long. People die in their nineties, as a rule. I know that's impossible for me, but eight thousand years? Yet there are men here who claim to be just over half that old, and they think nothing of it. And who am I to doubt them, particularly since many of them are Workers? They would have no reason to dissemble.

But then, I doubt what little I do recall. I remember having a cat, but it seems I had this cat for many more years than cats can possibly live. And in the end I killed it —or I seem to recollect that I did. That doesn't sound like me at all. I never had a cat before the final disturbance, but even if I had somehow acquired one—and how in the mountains, alone, would I acquire one? Even if I had one, and even if it did live so long, why should I have killed it? Moreover, why does it seem that that cat was so important? That's a very perplexing question. And, in fact, I recall the cat's name was "question," *Carath,* to use the Imitator word. A question, indeed.

Then there's the matter of science and technology: I recall having read an immense amount of it. But Stes tells me there were no books with me when I was found, outside of the ones I'd written as a youth, and some sort of record I'd kept for the first few years I was alone. Apparently, the Head of History had my books copied and distributed around the city at once—a most unlikely thing for a man to do—but this record of mine, Stes tells me, the

Head of History intends to keep a while longer, to "analyze." I can't imagine what's in it to analyze. But Stes knows his companion better than I do, certainly. They've been together nearly forty-five hundred years. I've met the Head of History only twice, to my recollection, and both times he was quite formal and aloof. It would be impossible for me to determine his predilections on the basis of those meetings. But as for the science and technology, I remember a good many of the facts now, and I know I never concerned myself with those subjects when I was young. I was a historian in those days. I'm absolutely no good in mathematics. But I seem to have learned a lot somehow. I wonder how.

Next, I seem to remember building certain things: a forge, a sap house and, of all things, a pond! Can a person build a pond? Stes tells me that all they found was a one-room stone structure on a mountainside with a small, badly cultivated garden beside it. Apparently the guest-house had burned to the ground at some point. There was no evidence of the lodge at all. And further, during the five hundred years I was totally aberrant here, I often raved about having built the city of Athlan. It's too absurd. I can't separate fact from fantasy.

The most telling item, however, is my memory of Imitators. There are, of course, no such creatures. Man killed every one of them eighteen thousand years ago. Yet I seem to recall that they were around and about me, that they had built a city around me. I recall that they were holding me captive for some reason. I recall that they told me there was a purpose for me. No doubt it was all my imagination trying to give myself a reason for continuing. I must have thought myself the last remaining man alive—I know I thought that early on—so I must have needed a motive for remaining functionally alive. I could never commit suicide, nor would I naturally want to. The motives I seem to have tried to give myself, however, apparently didn't work. Stes tells me that when they first found me I was indistinguishable in actions and outlook from an animal.

So it seems that, if I can't trust my memory of what has already happened to me, I'm reluctant to trust my perception of what's happening around and about me now. I know that makes little sense. I know that what's around

245

and about me now is perfectly tangible, perfectly demonstrable, and thus must be perfectly real. Yet it sticks in my mind that reality can be changed to look like anything but itself. And that is simply foolishness. Yet I cannot rid myself of the notion, nor can I rid myself of the uncomfortable feeling that Imitators have something to do with that notion. I wish I knew why. Perhaps the explanation is in that record I kept, which the Head of History has currently. I must ask him for it back one day soon.

Nevertheless, accepting that this world in which I find myself is real, I cannot understand the source of much of it, and some of it I cannot justify as being of man. The city itself is a veritable jumble of gargantuan buildings, which look as though they could be familiar, except that somebody has taken great pains to disguise them. This one I'm currently housed in is an excellent example:

It's forty-five floors high—all four hundred of its sort are. A few by themselves might somewhat resemble the new section of Athlan—ancient Athlan—though the architecture is too banal to be called New Style. New Style did have variety of design and detailing to it—surface texture, coloration. But these are such undistinguished structures, all the same—the same size, shape, and color, which is flat grey. Yet set in concentric circles nevertheless! I shouldn't even attempt to describe what's to be found in the center of those circles, except to call it the City Center, which, as a term, is not quite meaningless enough. Only a term in an alien language could do the spot justice.

But further, the first five floors of this—and each—residential building contain various facilities which, altogether, make each building completely self-sustaining. There is a variety of individual food and sundries shops assembled as a market, but a market assembled as if it were Maronnen's. Each shop is in a space of its own off a central hallway, and you must browse to find the shop you want. And then, there are places to have meals, and places to have small meals, and places for entertainment. But they're all essentially the same place: with the same appearance, the same Workers, the same meals, prepared in a central kitchen. These five floors have such a uniformity to them that I often get lost in them and end up not going anywhere for an evening.

The upper forty floors contain rooms like mine: a

lounge that doubles as a bedroom, in which is a Great Ocean–like screen sort of partition that hides a kitchen. This "kitchen" is rudimentary—a quick oven, a counter with two spots to one side of it for pot-cooking, a small sink with waste grinder, a dishwasher, a cold box—everything in line against the wall. It takes up just a tenth the long way and provides only a five ten-tenth-wide walkway. And also there's a bath. I'm lucky that there's only me—as a "survivor," not to mention an ex-aberrant, I have the privilege of living alone. The others are not so fortunate: They live two to a cubicle, eight cubicles on a floor. Everyone has a companion but me. All quarter of a million of them. Every last man.

There are no women!

More than that, no one I've spoken to remembers women. I haven't asked the Head of History if he does, but that fool, the Head of Ath Services, wasn't even aware that a man is only half his sort. He said it had never occurred to him to wonder. I don't wonder about him any longer, either. Aren would have called him "rock-bottom stupid."

But perhaps I'm being a bit unfair. If these fellows can't remember women, then no wonder their city looks like it does. Apparently they've tried to recreate a typical Aten city, but without any information on what such a city looked like. As I think about it, this might have been the best arrangement anyway, whether, as I gather, they were trying to recreate a city or not. The life here is absolutely boring because there's no texture to it, no coloration, no depth. But these people don't know what those qualities are for themselves. Though why that's so is something else I don't understand. It's not for lack of example. But these people don't know that they're being bored. They're materially satisfied; they can have what they want. They just don't know how much there is that a man can want. This worries me a little.

The Head of History has declared that, now that they've recovered me, they will be able to return to the old ways. His intention, it would seem, is to have me add the density his city lacks by having me recreate the things of life I can remember. I'll be a one-man Choice Program. I'm not sure I can do that. But already people are expecting me to provide them all sorts of new ideas. My books have been read, and widely. I find these men have no clear idea what

247

my books are about—there are women in them, of course, besides the more obvious problems—but they read that there used to be several kinds of Broadcast: Information, Entertainment, Household, Family. And, ignoring everything else, they ask me when they will be able to see different Broadcasts.

The Broadcast they already have is quite adequate for their needs. It provides them any information they want from the Library; there are hardly any events at all to report on. And otherwise they have no family stories—they don't know what a family is. They have no variety of goods, so there's no necessity for a Household. And they have nothing on which to base an Entertainment. The places below should, I think, be entertainment enough, all things considered.

Yet now I'm committed. There seems to be no rush, since it's been two years since the Head of History made his declaration, and he has yet to pursue the matter with me in detail. But there is the general sense and confidence that I am, in fact, going to do this for them. They haven't the slightest idea what it amounts to, yet . . . but why am I being so concerned? That's it: They haven't the slightest idea what it amounts to.

I can do anything, suggest anything, describe anything any way I please. Who's to know? And I was worrying about my obviously faulty memory. Well, I have my books to rely on for a general scheme. They adequately cover our general history, looked at that way. And when I run out of ideas, I can use the Library myself. Who ever would know?

They have about a million Explorers throughout the galaxy assiduously gathering information on alien intelligences. They have more people off the planet than on it. But all this information goes into the Library: Storage, as they call it. Technically, the Library amounts to the Historians who spend each day processing the information for Storage. And they do nothing with it. I haven't asked the Head of History why everyone is so intent on this project, but the Historians I've spoken with have said generally that they view the work as the duty of our kind, since only we can live to the end of the universe. It's up to us to record the universe.

That's all well and good, I suppose. It certainly seems

like a reasonable thing for a regenerative to do. But wouldn't you have thought they'd take a look at what they're doing? I already have. The information is fascinating. And it's useful. I've already located something from another planet that I might have wished to have when I was young—though of course, man would never think of it: a private boat. Unlike the circumstance of a private car, there are always rivers. And unlike fliers, private boats are very easy to control. In one alien Broadcast transmission I saw them being used purely for pleasure. I'd have much rather sailed along a beach than walked along one.

So I needn't worry, after all, that I might not have the ability to stimulate these men to want things because I lack the memory to recall the necessary details. An alien idea is still an idea, and since most aliens are proving to be relatively like us, at least in general appearance, I have a lot of feasible alien ideas to draw upon. I can generate a suitably exciting life for these people, even if it isn't exactly like what man once had. After all this time, even the life of my youth would have changed, and, outside of Athlan, I'd thought that was static. We might have had pleasure boats by now. And we might even have had the kind of house that I'm hoping to have built. Who could say what we might have done?

I'm still a little embarrassed about my house, should its construction ever come to pass. Knowing, the moment I took over this room, that I'd never be able to tolerate it, I casually said to Stes that I only wished I could have my old house back.

He said, at first astonished, "The one in the mountains on North? What ever for?"

But I said no, not that one, but the one I had long ago in Paragathi. This perked his interest.

When we're together, he constantly asks me about the past, rather like a child might ask his father to explain how plantings happen in the city. He's always done this, and always with the same exuberant questioning. So I thought, why not? I cannot bear to live in this building. How will he know that I'm lying?

He didn't know. I've since all but drawn up the plans myself. It's to be located just a brief walk from the rail that goes east to the farmlands. That's a half hour from the city, on a slight rise overlooking the city. They'd have to put in a rail stop for me, and perhaps that's why the Head of History is taking so long deciding. He's had all these details a year now. But regeneratives seem to have lost all concept of time. It must be the boredom that they notice no other way. Or, as an Imitator might put it: "a surrogate reaction."

But, in fact, I lied. And it was easy. I hadn't had to lie about this writing machine, I merely had to design it— or, more likely, redesign it. They offered me a carrel and even a printer, if I wanted it. But that would all take up a quarter of my room. The carrel alone would be unsatisfactory, even though I could have my writing printed through the Library, because I've never before written onto a carrier, and I do not wish to begin doing so now. So I asked for a simple machine. And I had one in Athlan. If it didn't look like this one, well, in the future there will likely be a good many things that won't look like they used to. I'm going to have to lie.

I wish the Library at least had information on the history of this settlement. There seems to be none before the official founding of this city 4459 years ago. Thus, I have no idea how things got to be the way they are. There's not even a partial progression of events. Things just suddenly start, as though it were the founding of ancient Athel.

What's odder is that I've met no one yet who is older than the founding of this city. Stes and his companion date very nearly from the founding, as, I think, do most companions, at least all the ones I've met so far. Perhaps the older ones are now Explorers. Certainly I'd rather be an Explorer, most often bound to his starship, than a resident of this tower, if I'd been here long enough. But that means there's no one to ask for personal reminiscence. These people seem as negligent about their own history as I used to be about myself when I was young. But then, there must be other "survivors" among the Explorers. I wonder if one of them couldn't be at least as old as I? And whether I might know him?

But perhaps not. Stes, or the Head of History, would surely have said something. When my mind had finally righted itself, I found myself being treated as cordially as though I were my father. Apparently everyone knew of the discovery of me. Someone would have said something— there are only half a million men on the whole planet.

Perhaps any "survivors" among the Explorers would have come after the final disturbance. That would make more sense.

Another strange thing is that there are no cats, none at all. It's not that I'd want one. One, it seems, was enough, since the thought of a cat just now has sent something of a shudder through me. I must have become frightened of them, courtesy of this Carath I had. I never was before. But perhaps this Carath had gone wild, or been born wild. Morin, I think, once told me: "Cats that are wild, they say, are the ones that will talk to you. If we domesticated the human, do you think we could get him to be equally docile with us?" Dear Morin. How he'd love my situation. But I don't suppose I mind that there are no cats. I just note it here, along with everything else.

I wanted this writing machine most, I suppose, because I thought I would never be able to do without one. It was virtually the very first thing I asked Stes for, certainly the first nonessential thing. Yet it's been four years or more that I've had it, and today is the day I finally make use of it. How strange my inclinations must have been then. How strange my perceptions of things. The one thing I wrote then—clumsily and briefly the moment I got it—was: "I cannot encompass what I've seen unless I write it!" True enough, I suppose. Didn't someone once tell me I was distant and detached, never seeming to take part in anything, always observing? Whoever that was—Heller, I think—never knew that this is where whatever happens to me finally comes alive. This is where I participate in events. It's my own way. Everybody has his own way.

Now that I've finally started using the machine, though, I believe I'll make these pages a way of planning the elimination of this boredom. That is in essence what Barenillen wants, and I'll need all the help I can get. It should be fun, though. I think I really do look forward to it. And however I've acquired the technical knowledge I've got, thank the One I've got it. It's already made explaining things a great deal easier. I just foolishly left the design of the case of this machine up to them. It's a squat, grey metal box that looks very much like an air pack for a void-suit. But it works. That's the main thing, and it'll always be the main thing.

Yet another curiosity—and this is what does unsettle me

251

—is that these people know nothing of the thinking of the One. They also know nothing of Imitators, or First Fathers, or any of it. When I asked Stes after the Imitators and their city, he was prepared to return me for further rest. He told me they have equipment capable of registering life forms—equipment the Explorers use regularly, since they rarely land on a planet they're investigating. And this equipment would surely have found the Imitators, if they existed. First, of course, I had to explain to him what Imitators were, and when I did so, I felt like a fool. Imitators do sound so unlikely to someone who doesn't know them as I do. But I convinced Stes that they had indeed once been real, even if I'd really never seen one but just dreamed them out of my knowledge of them.

But there are so many oddities about this city and the way these people live. And, each by itself, an oddity is meaningless. I'll have to trace out the way these elements connect here and now, at least. It looks a hopeless task, but, I suppose, I'd do better starting with what's here than just by adding density and detail to these people's lives by the cartageweight.

But then: Perhaps I can speed up the procedure of getting my house if I suggest to Stes that it's an essential part of what I plan to do under his companion's auspices. That will probably work. That's the main thing.

And if I unravel the oddities of this settlement sufficiently, perhaps I can garner some idea of the way they got to be where and what they are. But some of these oddities are so peculiar. The City Center looks unfinished, to be blunt. It's not, and I can only assume that it was *meant* to look unfinished. But one whole side of the Library is a blank wall, and a wall on such a scale as the Library's is overwhelming.

And then, there are no flowers, no plantings of any sort. Everything is neatly trimmed grass, but without even the smallest shrub to break it up.

Still stranger: These people seem to prefer what Paras preferred. And yet, they cannot envision women. How remarkable.

And the strangest thing of all: These people dance! This is unheard-of. I remember one evening in a place, long ago, that Morin gave me a very disparaging glance because I was simply tapping my hand inaudibly to the music. "Only Imitators dance, my dear," he advised me. Well, apparently that's no longer true. I can't imagine why.

Yet, despite all this, they call this city New Athlan.

Well, we'll see.